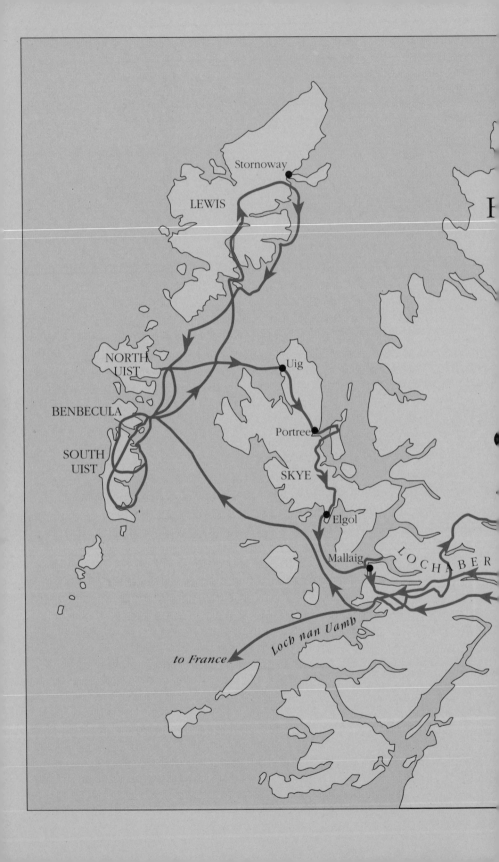

Stornoway

LEWIS

NORTH
UIST

Uig

BENBECULA

Portree

SOUTH
UIST

SKYE

Elgol

Mallaig

L O C H A B E R

to France

Loch nan Uamh

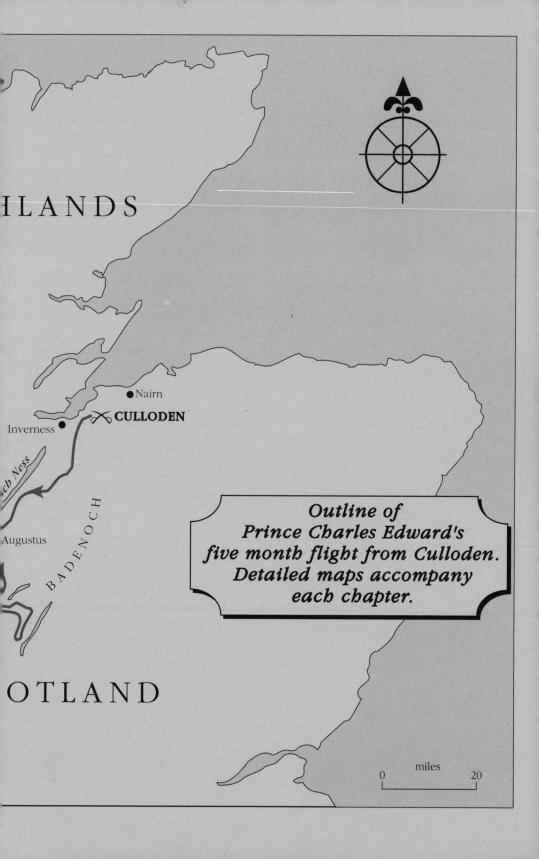

HLANDS

●Nairn

Inverness● ╳**CULLODEN**

ch Ness

Augustus

BADENOCH

OTLAND

> *Outline of*
> ***Prince Charles Edward's***
> ***five month flight from Culloden.***
> *Detailed maps accompany*
> *each chapter.*

miles

0   20

A BIRD ON THE WING

A BIRD

ON THE WING

Bonnie Prince Charlie's flight

from Culloden retraced

*

JOHN URE

CONSTABLE · LONDON

First published in Great Britain 1992
by Constable and Company Limited
3 The Lanchesters, 162 Fulham Palace Road
London W6 9ER
Copyright © 1992 John Ure

The right of John Ure to be identified
as the author of this work has been
asserted by him in accordance with the
Copyright, Designs and Patents Act 1988
ISBN 0 09 469890 2
Set in Linotron Caledonia 11pt by
Servis Filmsetting Limited, Manchester
Printed in Great Britain by
St Edmundsbury Press Ltd
Bury St Edmunds, Suffolk

A CIP catalogue record for this book
is available from the British Library

This book is dedicated to
the memory of
MY FATHER
who passed on his love of
the Scottish hills and Scotland's history

CONTENTS

ILLUSTRATIONS

Except where otherwise stated, all photographs are by Caroline Ure or the author.

Endpapers illustrate the whole route of the Prince's flight from Culloden. Separate maps at the start of chapters illustrate sections of the route.

FOREWORD

THE bicentenary in 1988 of Prince Charles Edward Stuart's death was the occasion of a number of new studies of Bonnie Prince Charlie, some of them making a major contribution to our knowledge and understanding of him. There have also been a number of books over the years about the Prince's five months as a fugitive after Culloden, most notably Eric Linklater's *The Prince in the Heather* in 1965; there has even been a lively television series featuring Jimmie MacGregor on the subject. To those who might therefore wonder why one should embark on another book on this theme I would offer two answers.

The first is that no one so far as I know has ever attempted to walk the whole route undertaken by the Prince. Most of those who have embarked on the project have been content to visit the scenes of the highspots of the story, but to eschew the long and rigorous slogs in between. Linklater, for instance, looked at the hills of Lochaber and declared 'that country, from Lock Arkaig to the head of Loch Hourn, can be traversed only by those habituated to hill-walking; but a useful impression of it can be acquired from a boat . . .'. I have become almost excessively habituated to hill-walking while trying faithfully to cover every pace of the Prince's route. Without such fidelity, much is lost.

The second reason is that it has seemed to me that previous accounts of the Prince's travels have not put them sufficiently into the context of Scottish legend and tradition as a whole. Those who travel through the Highlands – whether themselves on foot or vicariously from the comfort of an armchair – may reasonably be expected to be interested in all aspects of the region: the wild life, the fascination of deer stalking, the vagaries of highland dress, the manufacture of Harris tweed, the stirring story of the highland regiments, and the feuds and fights of the local clans. I therefore make no apology for digressing to enlarge on these subjects as and when the occasion arises.

It could also be objected, to one who has usually written about travel in remote and wild parts of the world, that there is little point in retracing a highland journey when Scotland has become the preserve of tourists. But the fact is that, once one is away from the roads which tend to follow those glens which always carried tracks and were for that reason shunned by the fugitive Prince, the Highlands are less populated today than in Prince Charles Edward's day; the nineteenth-century Clearances, when landowners chased their tenants away in favour of sheep, have been responsible for this. Much of the Prince's route lies through one of the last wildernesses in Europe. The traveller who is prepared to bury himself in the folds of the hills in Lochaber or Badenoch will see today almost exactly the same scene as Prince Charles Edward saw in 1746.

Although therefore most of the journey was as off the beaten track now as it had been two and a half centuries ago, there are inevitably some stretches that follow the road. A secondary road, for instance, now follows the route the Prince rode for the first few hours of his flight, from Culloden Moor to Fort Augustus; another more substantial road runs through Glen Shiel, down which the Prince passed between more arduous stages of his journey. It seemed to me perverse to walk the route where this is now tarmac, and when – in any case – the Prince had ridden some of these stages rather than walked them himself. There was more than enough footwork to do in the fastnesses around Loch Hourn, in the hills of South Uist or on the slopes of Ben Alder. So for those few parts of the journey where a road now exists I drove in a hired car or – more frequently – in my Landrover Discovery which also, on

occasions such as in Glen Moriston, could take us off the road
by rough tracks for the first stage of some marathon hill walk.
Similarly, I felt no obligation to charter a separate boat for those
crossings of the Minch or the Sea of the Hebrides which are now
served by regular ferry boats; there were to be more than enough
stages where I had to make my own nautical arrangements. Nor
did I feel it necessary to sleep in the caves, woods or hollows
in the heather which had so often been the only shelter available to the Prince. To walk the course was one thing: to have
gratuitously shared every avoidable discomfort would have
been quite another, and probably only have ended by emulating
the Prince in one respect I did not need to do – in taking to the
bottle.

Anyone writing about the Prince's flight is indebted to Bishop
Forbes of Inverness who, in the years after the Forty Five, was
assiduous about interviewing anyone involved in his rescue, or
at least obtaining statements from them. Some were illiterate;
some were forgetful; some were vain-glorious. The resulting
annals are therefore frequently confusing and self-contradictory.
But a generally consistent overall picture emerges, helped by
the fact that everyone involved in assisting the Prince was aware
that he or she was stepping – however briefly and improbably –
onto the stage of history: whatever the Prince did, said or even
ate seemed worthy of note. The bishop's record is remarkably
comprehensive. I have of course also studied other contemporary
accounts, notably O'Sullivan's narrative and Lord James Stewart-
Murray's anonymous manuscript edited by Henrietta Tayler for
the Roxburghe Club, and have tried to piece together a coherent
story.

It has sometimes been propounded by cynical readers that the
English commanders after the Battle of Culloden were not really
trying very hard to capture the Prince, and that his escape owed
as much to his pursuers' half-heartedness as to his own ingenuity
and endurance. After all, it is argued, it would have been a considerable embarrassment for the House of Hanover to have
brought to trial for treason the legitimate heir to the English and
Scottish thrones. Public sentiment would have been repelled by

an execution, and the precedents for a long state imprisonment were not promising for those who remembered Mary Queen of Scots. But any such argument can, I think, be refuted by examining the number of warships and troops committed to the search, and by the words of their own commander – Lord Albemarle – who wrote to the Duke of Newcastle on 15 October 1746 announcing the Prince's final escape to France in the following terms:

'nothing is to me more convincing proof of the disaffection of that part of the country [the Highlands] than that of His lying so long concealed amongst these people, and that he should be able to elude our narrowest and most exact searches, and at last make his escape notwithstanding the great award offered to apprehend him'.

One of the problems of retracing and recording such a trip is that highland place names are remarkably repetitious. There are two hills both called Sgurr nan Coireachan within six miles of each other on the Prince's route out of Moidart; and there are two other hills both called Meallan Odhar which feature importantly in the story but which are 40 miles apart. Numerous burns have identical or very similar names. I have tried to steer the reader through these hazards with fewer problems than I experienced myself.

In writing any book of this sort one becomes indebted to many people. Some – but only a very few – of these who helped me along the way are mentioned in the text; my gratitude is none the less to those who are not. My publisher – Ben Glazebrook – provided consistent moral support and latitude on the timescale for completing the task. My wife took most of the better photographs and drove our Landrover Discovery down many a long glen to essential rendezvous after long walks. And lastly I am grateful to my thirteen-year-old son Alasdair not only for accompanying me on much of the journey but also for enduring with patience and apparent interest rather more

information about Scottish history than he may have sometimes
desired.

JOHN URE

Netters Hall, Kent, 1992

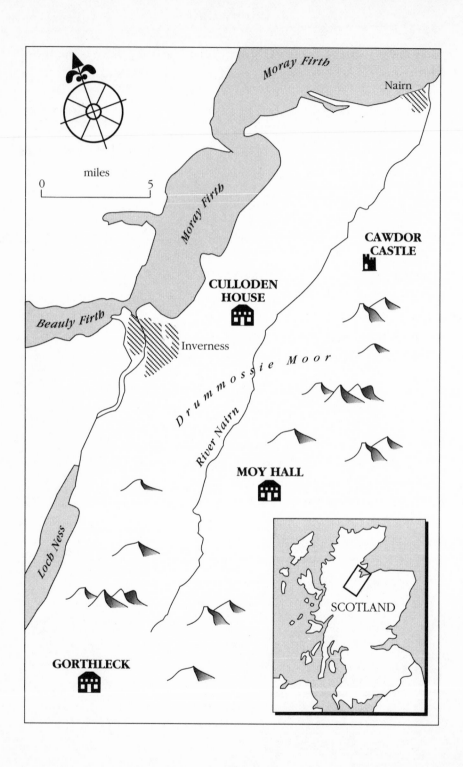

CULLODEN:

'IN MY END IS MY BEGINNING'

EVEN for the north of Scotland, the night of 15 April 1746 was one of exceptionally dirty weather. It had been raining earlier, and the rain was to turn to sleet. The four thousand rebel highlanders who set out at 8 p.m. – soon after the last daylight had faded – were already weary and hungry. They had good reason to be both.

They had been marching on and off for six months, and the last few days had been a crescendo of activity. The Camerons had covered the fifty miles from Fort William in two days; and other clansmen, many of whom had gone home to their native glens after the battle of Falkirk, had been hastily reassembled by their chiefs to rally to Prince Charles Edward's standard at Culloden House. For it was clear to one and all that the decisive battle of the Forty Five Rebellion was about to take place. The Duke of Cumberland's English army, reinforced by the Campbells and other 'loyal' clans, was encamped at Nairn some ten miles away, within sight of its fleet of provision ships anchored off-shore.

No such provisions were standing by for Prince Charles Edward's highlanders. Indeed, according to Lord George Murray – the lieutenant-general of the Prince's army – 'the men had only got that day a biscuit each, and some not that'. Hunger had reached such a pitch in the highland camp that at about 7 p.m. that evening, just when the night march was about to begin, 'an incident happened which had like to have stopt their designed attempt'. Lord George Murray goes on:

'The thing was this. Numbers of men went off to all sides, especially towards Inverness, and when the officers who were sent on horse back to bring them back came up with them, they could by no persuasion be induced to return again, giving for answer – they were starving . . . the officers might shoot them if they pleased, but they could not go back till they got meat.'

But despite weariness and hunger the gruelling night march began. It was a desperate last throw. The Duke of Cumberland's regular army was twice the numerical strength of the Prince's motley mixture of Scottish clansmen, Irish volunteers and French mercenaries. And numbers were not all. The Duke had a cavalry of some three regiments of dragoons, while the Prince's cavalry was – in effect – reduced to his own half squadron of Life Guards under Lord Elcho. The Duke had an effective artillery (as was to be amply demonstrated the next day) while the Prince's guns were few and manned by untrained gunners. By any reckoning, a formal pitched battle was a bleak outlook for the rebels.

So it was that the idea of a sudden surprise night attack on the Duke's camp at Nairn had taken shape. That very day – 15 April – was thought to have been the Duke's twenty-fifth birthday; there were those in the rebel ranks who argued that in consequence the English army would be not only dazed but hungover if surprised in the small hours of the morning of the 16th. Once the idea of such a scheme had been mooted, Prince Charles Edward himself 'was vastly bent for the night-attack'. He maintained that Cumberland's men 'would never stand a bold and brisk attack' and that it was best to press on without waiting for the expected reinforcements from those clans – Frasers, Mackenzies and others – which had not yet come up. The march was set in motion.

The Clan Mackintosh was given the task of providing the scouts and guides in front of the main column. This was a natural choice: they were in Mackintosh country. Indeed, it was while sleeping at the house of the laird of Mackintosh – Moy Hall – that Prince Charles Edward had nearly been captured by government forces a week or two before. On that occasion some of Lady Mackintosh's house servants had been scouting around the policies of Moy Hall, further from the house than the Prince's personal guards, when they 'spied betwixt them and the sky a great body of men moving towards them'. Lady Mackintosh's men fired a few shots at the intruders and (according to Captain Malcolm Macleod who recorded the story for Bishop Forbes) one of them called 'Advance my lads, advance!' naming some particular regiments so that the government troops thought they were being set upon by a large body of highlanders – and promptly withdrew. The Mackintoshes had proved themselves sharp-eyed and loyal in the service of their Prince; none disputed their claim to lead the way through the bogs and peat hags that beset the path to Nairn.

Also with them in the vanguard of the marching column of high-landers was Lord George Murray himself. He was feeling dis-gruntled on a number of counts. He considered that, on all grounds, he was the most distinguished soldier in the Prince's service, and it irked him that his views did not always prevail. A brother of the Duke of Atholl, he was described* as not only 'tall, robust and brave' but also as 'fierce, haughty, blunt and proud'. Lord George's military skills had been largely responsible for Prince Charles Edward's suc-cesses, but he had been disillusioned by the Prince's misleading assertions that a French army was on the way to help him and that he had promises of support from the English Jacobites. He had, in consequence, been one of those who had urged withdrawal and who was therefore in some measure responsible for the rebel army meet-ing its adversaries in the north of Scotland rather than further south. For this the Prince had never forgiven him. Now Lord George had somewhat reluctantly assented to the proposed night march and attack, largely because his advice had not been heeded regarding the choice of terrain on which the highlanders had been drawn up earlier in the day for a pitched battle on Drummossie Moor in front of Culloden House. In the event, they had not been challenged by the Duke of Cumberland's army that day; so now Lord George grasped at the chance of avoiding a pitched daytime battle by making

---

* By the Chevalier de Johnstone, a lowland Scottish gentleman (the 'de' was some-thing of an affectation) who had joined Prince Charles Edward at Perth and who had been successively aide-de-camp to both Lord George Murray and the Prince.

this desperate night assault. As events progressed throughout the night, his temper did not improve.

One of the problems of a night march, as any soldier knows, is that it is difficult for those at the back not to get left behind. The difficulties are compounded if the going is rough, and the going over the moors between Culloden and Nairn was very rough indeed – particularly since they had determined to keep well clear of all tracks and to 'shun houses' for fear of sounding the alarm. Lord George subsequently recorded that:

> 'Before the van had gone a mile, which was as slow as could be to give time to the line to follow, there was express [messenger] after express sent to stop them, for that the rear was far behind . . . which retarded them to a degree that the night was far spent.'

This last point was what was worrying Lord George Murray and his companions in the vanguard. Because of the numbers of highlanders who had slipped away to forage for food in the earlier part of the evening, the departure had been delayed. Now the endless requests to pause or go slower meant that the whole column was badly behind schedule. By one in the morning they had only reached Culraick, a point some six miles from where they had started and still a good four miles from Cumberland's camp.

It was here that Lord John Drummond came up from the centre of the column to speak with Lord George Murray. They were soon joined by the Duke of Perth* who had been marching at the rear of the column. Perth was Murray's fellow lieutenant-general in the Prince's army; at 34 he was an easier-going and less prickly figure than Lord George Murray although (according to John Murray of Broughton who knew him well) 'no man knew better when anyone failed in the respect due to his birth'. Lord George did not get on well with his fellow lieutenant-general: for one thing he considered the young Duke to be 'Frenchified', and it was a fact that after being brought up until the age of nineteen in France, the Duke of Perth

---

* The title of Duke (as opposed to Earl) of Perth was always a Jacobite one and never recognised by the Hanoverian court. It became extinct in 1760 and is now possibly best remembered as the name of a well-known Scottish reel.

had never really learnt to speak English properly, in part because of 'his overfondness to speak broad Scots'. It was the arrival of these two officers which caused Lord George to halt and take stock of the situation.

The hard fact was that if the vanguard did not slow its present pace it would become separated from the main body of the column; and if it did not increase its pace it would not arrive at Nairn until after dawn. A night surprise attack by the highlanders was one thing: an assault in broad daylight on a regular army twice their size was quite another.

While Murray, Drummond and Perth were debating the pros and cons in muffled voices in the pitch darkness, they were joined by another martial but less popular figure – Colonel O'Sullivan, one of the Prince's closest Irish companions and advisers who had fought with the French army and who had been one of the original 'Seven Men of Moidart' to have come across with the Prince from France. O'Sullivan (according to his own subsequent account*) had been a strong advocate of the night attack when it had been first mooted. He had argued that Cumberland's cavalry, in particular, would be easily destroyed when dismounted and surprised:

> 'A regiment should be named . . . that would attack the horse, to cut the horses Collars, while the rest wou'd fall sword in hand upon the Tents, that troopers a foot were no dengerous enemys.'

So it was only to be expected that O'Sullivan would be for pressing on.

As frequently in the past, O'Sullivan presented himself to Murray as the mouthpiece of the Prince, with whom he had been marching near the rear of the column. His message was, in fact, somewhat equivocal:

> 'The Prince was very desirous the attack should be made; but as Lord George Murray was in the van, and could judge the time, he left it to him whether to do it or not.'

* Edited by A. & H. Tayler and published under the title *1745 and After* (Thomas Nelson & Sons, Edinburgh 1938).

Murray invited the opinions of his fellow chiefs and found them to be
'much difficulted what to resolve upon'. A number of the younger
gentlemen volunteers were all for pressing on regardless, reassuring
themselves with the thought that 'the red-coats would all be drunk'
after their commander's birthday celebrations (in fact, they were not:
the rum ration had been a very modest – almost token – one).
O'Sullivan later claimed that he had been hotly for pressing forward
and had told Murray:

> 'If yu retire yu discourage your men who suffer badly enough
> already, you loose all yr advantages, and give all over to yr enemy
> . . . If Lord George will permit me, I offer to march in the front
> rank of his vanguarde and will give my head off my shoulders, wch
> is all I have to loose, if he does not succeed'.

But some of the cannier old Scottish campaigners declared that it
would be 'perfect madness' to proceed. Possibly the decisive voice
was that of Cameron of Lochiel, the most respected as well as the
most gallant of all the clan chiefs (and of whom much more will be
heard in this story), who was with Murray at the head of his clansmen in the van, but who also declared that although he 'had been as
much for the night attack as anybody could be' the laggardliness of
those in the rear made it necessary to turn about and retrace their
steps to Culloden. The council of war had only taken a quarter of an
hour: the march back to Culloden House took most of the rest of the
night.

There can have been few of the highland host who did not have
their own poignant memories and sad reflections as they tramped
back over the rough moorland. Some of them had been with the
Prince since that first euphoric day in August of the previous year
when he had unfurled his standard at Glenfinnan, at the head of
Loch Shiel, and 'the Forty Five' had begun. All who were there that
day recalled the joyous moment when the skirl of the Cameron
pipers had been heard as 'Gentle' Lochiel led his 700 clansmen
down the slope of the glen to the Prince's side. The contingent had
been the largest and most vital ingredient of the embryonic rebel
army, and its appearance could by no means have been taken for

granted. A few days previously, Lochiel had come alone to visit the newly-landed Prince, and to explain why he could not 'come out' on the Prince's behalf; he advised the Young Chevalier to return to France. But the Prince had told him that he was not returning and that

> 'Charles Stuart is come over to claim the crown of his ancestors, to win it, or to perish in the attempt: Lochiel, who, my father often told me, was our firmest friend, may stay at home, and learn from the newspapers the fate of his Prince.'

These well-chosen words, delivered with that curious mixture of courage and charm which was to become the Prince's hallmark in history, had won over Lochiel – hence the 700 clansmen.

From Glenfinnan the road had led to Perth, with little resistance offered. It was here that Lord George Murray and the Duke of Perth had rallied to his standard. The way was then open to Edinburgh itself. The Provost and his magistrates, after a half-hearted attempt to persuade a volunteer corps to defend the city, decided that a fighting resistance was – in all the circumstances – perhaps asking too much. While they parleyed with the highlanders, the latter – taking advantage of an opened city gate – rushed in and took possession of the city for the Prince.

Many of the weary highlanders marching back from Nairn after the aborted night attack, even if they had not been present at Glenfinnan, could at least recall with nostalgia the glamour of the weeks spent in Edinburgh. The officers remembered the balls at Holyrood. The clansmen remembered the Prince's appearances in highland dress in the park, in a 'light-coloured periwig . . . a blue bonnet . . . the star of the order of St. Andrew . . . and looking graceful on horseback' (according to John Home who witnessed the scene). All remembered how recruits had flocked in, how the highlanders had routed General Cope's army at the nearby battle of Prestonpans, and how eventually the fateful decision to march into England had been taken. Most of those now stumbling through the heather on their way back from Nairn had been among the 5,000 foot-soldiers and 500 cavalry who had crossed the border into England on 3 November 1745.

For many of the rank and file, memories of England would have been mostly happy ones. Carlisle had surrendered to them – despite its fortress – without a fight. In Manchester the local regiment had come over to the rebels. No Hanoverian army had appeared to bar their progress south. They had finally arrived unopposed at Derby. But the clan chiefs, as they led their foot-sore followers back towards Culloden in the pre-dawn mist and drizzle of that April morning, would have had less happy recollections of the march south into England. They had been waiting for news of a supporting French army landing on the south coast, and no such news had come. They had been expecting English and Welsh Jacobites to rally to their cause, and no such expectations had been realised. At Derby, Lord George Murray had led the faction urging retreat. The Prince had been incredulous, furious and churlish in turns; but he had had no option but to comply with the advice of all the clan chiefs. The clansmen themselves had shared the Prince's chagrin at turning about when within 127 miles of London. So unpopular was the order to march north again, that the officers had been obliged to start the retreat before dawn so that the rank and file should not realise in what direction they were marching; when they did wake up to the fact that they were going in the direction of Scotland rather than of London, there was much muttering in the ranks.

Now, as the same army – more hungry, weary and disillusioned than five months earlier at Derby – tramped back once again from another avoided confrontation, there would have been many in the ranks who still regretted the decision to retreat from Derby. They must have speculated in their minds about what might have been. Had they pressed on to London, they might have reached the capital before the various Hanoverian armies had managed to combine against them. In that case they would have found the city defended only by the militia and a few Guards regiments formed into a make-shift army at Finchley – a force which would, in all probability, have crumbled before the impact of a highland charge. And had they pressed on, the two elements they lacked might have been forth-coming: Prince Charles' brother – Henry – was on the point of persuading a French army to embark for England in support of the Jacobite cause; and the Welsh Jacobites were on the point of coming to the assistance of the Scottish invaders. No wonder that there were some rueful thoughts in the minds of the highlanders as they retraced their heavy steps to Culloden.

The last four months – since the rebel army's return to Scotland – would have been fresher in the minds of the trudging highlanders. The high-spot of that period had been 17 January; on that date Lord George Murray had proved that his highlanders could not only withstand an English cavalry charge, but could give chase

'pursuing them vigorously with sabre strokes, running after them as quick as their horses, and leaving them not a moment's respite to be able to recover from their flight'

(according to Alexander Macdonald – the poet who gave an account of the Rising). The Battle of Falkirk had been a cheering victory to the rebels; the English general – Hawley – hanged a number of his own men for cowardice on the gallows he had thoughtfully erected in advance for hanging captured rebels. But after that there had been a steady withdrawal further into the highlands as Cumberland's army had made its inexorable way north in pursuit – first to Perth, then to Aberdeen and now almost to Inverness, which had been the last stronghold of the Prince in Scotland.

At Falkirk, the victory of the highlanders had been at least in part because the terrain had favoured them and the Hanoverian artillery had got bogged down. Broken terrain was always to be important to the highlanders, and this was just what they had not got on the bleak open moor of Drummossie in front of Culloden House to which the highlanders were now withdrawing to fight their final battle.

It was already full daylight by the time the highlanders had regained their camp in the policies of Culloden House. The men lay down to sleep in the open, wet and hungry as they were, only to be roused two hours later by the bagpipes summoning them back to their battle stations on Drummossie Moor. Many were too exhausted to be roused and slept on through the ensuing battle – only to have a rude awakening from Cumberland's cavalry later in the day. The Chevalier de Johnstone, who had also taken part in the march, rode on into Inverness to get some sleep,

'But (he recounted) when I had already got one leg in the bed and was on the point of stretching myself between the sheets what was my surprize to hear the drum beat to arms and the trumpets . . . sounding the call to boot and saddle.'

He returned to Culloden as weary as the rest.

On the moor itself there was friction among the re-formed rebel army. The Macdonalds were particularly affronted. The right of the line of battle had been their traditional and honoured position ever since they had distinguished themselves there at Bannockburn in 1314. And the Macdonalds had always had a reputation for being sensitive about questions of *placement* whether on the battlefield or at the banqueting table. There had long been a tale* of the chief of the clan being invited by King Henry VIII's Lord Mayor of London to a banquet and placed 'rather too near the wrong side of the salt, as if he were a simple squire'; when someone told his host – halfway through the meal – that Macdonald was in fact a great prince in his own country, the embarrassed Lord Mayor sent a message down the table inviting him to move up higher and sit at his right hand, to which the clan chief replied: 'Tell the Lord Mayor not to be fashing himself. Wherever Macdonald is sitting, that is the head of the table.' Now Prince Charles Edward – for whom the battle was to be his first in effective command – had given the Macdonalds' cherished position to Lord George Murray's Athollmen.

But Lord George – far from being gratified – was still disgruntled for more substantial reasons. He had reconnoitred the field of Drummossie Moor several days before and had – rightly – concluded that it was too flat and firm to suit the highlanders: Cumberland would be able to deploy his artillery and cavalry here; while on the south side of the Nairn Water lay terrain which was 'steep and uneven, consequently much properer for Highlanders'. But not for the first time Lord George had been over-ruled by the Prince who thought that moving to the other side of the Nairn Water smacked of withdrawing. So now it was on the broad open expanse of Drummossie Moor that the clansmen formed up.

* Recounted elegantly by Sir Iain Moncreiffe of that Ilk in *The Highland Clans* (Barrie and Jenkins, London 1982).

Many of the clans were led not by their chiefs but by an eldest son or the head of some cadet branch of the family, since the canny clan chiefs did not believe in putting all their eggs – titles, castles and land – in one basket, even at the behest of so persuasive a Pretender as Prince Charles Edward; their own lives and those of their kinsmen they might willingly hazard, but the total extinction of their family fortunes were less readily jeopardized. Depleted and tired as they were, the clansmen must have made a brave sight as they formed up – yet again – on the moor. Almost the entire army was kilted, although some chiefs and officers (including from necessity all those mounted) would have been wearing the tight tartan trews. On their left arms they carried the round highland targe – a shield made of wood, covered with leather, studded with iron and often completed with a central spike. Some of the highlanders carried muskets, pikes or even battle-axes, but most would have carried in their right hands the basket-hilted broadsword; this was a derivation of the ancient highland claymore and was considerably longer, broader-bladed and heavier than the ordinary infantry sword which would have been carried by the officers in Cumberland's army. (The swords of officers in Highland Regiments of the British Army still follow this pattern.) As well as their broadswords, the better off and better-armed highlanders would have worn a dirk on their right side; this short dagger was an emergency weapon for a quick thrust in a hand-to-hand mêlée; it was often ornamented with a bye-knife (for eating) and even a fork in its scabbard. Over one shoulder would have been the broad-belted tartan plaid; this was protection from the elements by day and night – mantle and blanket in one – but could be cast off in battle to give greater flexibility of movement. The tartans of the clans would not have reached the refinement of pattern and colouration that was to characterize the romantic revival – post Sir Walter Scott – of the nineteenth century; but some were already both established and recognizable even in a battle – like the tabards of medieval knights. To top it all would have been the universal blue bonnet with its white Jacobite cockade. As the uniformed ranks of Cumberland's red-coats looked across the moor they would therefore have seen a horde as distinctively colourful as themselves.

Indeed, the sharper-eyed and more knowledgeable of the Duke of

Cumberland's men might well have been able to distinguish the
line-up of the clans facing them. In the front rank, in the coveted
position at the right of the line, were the Athollmen under Lord
George Murray, flanked by the Camerons under Lochiel – who was
to be shot through both ankles in the course of the ensuing battle;
next to them came the Stewarts of Appin – the Prince's own clan – in
their bright scarlet tartan; then came the Frasers, commanded by
Charles Fraser the Younger of Inverallochie – a twenty-year-old
kinsman of the 'old fox' Lord Lovat who was too old and obese to lead
his clansmen into battle, but not too old to pay for this day's
involvement on the scaffold later; beside them came the hybrid ranks
of the Clan Chattan, including elements of the Mackintoshes, the
McBains, the Macphersons and the MacGillivrays – whose giant of a
chief commanded this whole confederation of clans on behalf of Lady
Mackintosh (the hostess whose vigilance had saved Prince Charles
Edward from capture at Moy) – and others; beyond them and some
inadequate guns lay the Farquharson clan in their sombre green kilts;
then those MacLeods who had not stayed at home with their chief in
Skye; then the Maclachlans whose chief commanded 115 of his own
men in their distinctive red and blue checked tartan and 182
Macleans, who was accompanied on the field by a kinsman who was
the sword-bearing Chaplain General to all the Jacobite clans; next
came the hundred-odd men of the Clan Chisholm who stemmed from
the central highlands due west of Culloden – a region to which not a
few of them had slipped home already; and lastly, the three regiments
of disgruntled Macdonalds – Clanranald's, Keppoch's and Glengarry's
– amounting to some thousand warriors under the command of the
Duke of Perth, and all of them as fierce in their hatred of the
Campbells (now fighting in the King's army opposite them) as in their
loyalty to the Prince. Never had the clans of Scotland known such a
line-up before: never would they know it again.

Behind the front line was a second rank of somewhat less ferocious
demeanour. There were some lowlanders and some dismounted
cavalry, whose horses had not survived to this late point in the
campaign. There was the ancient and rheumaticky figure of John
Gordon of Glenbucket – 'old Glenbucket' as he was universally
known – at the head of a hastily press-ganged regiment of Gordons

from his farming Deeside estates. There were some deserters from the English army (still in their red-coats – which would bode ill for them if captured) and rather more men from the Scots Royals, a regiment of the French army which was not to be confused with the Royal Scots, a lowland regiment fighting beside the English opposite them. Here too were to be found recruits from the Irish regiments of the French army.

Further back still were what passed for the highland cavalry, including Pitsligo's Horse – under command of the saintly old Lord Pitsligo whom even the Hanoverians respected as a romantic figure of misguided honour rather than a rebel (remarkably little effort was made to capture him after the battle) – and Lord Elcho's Life Guards protecting Prince Charles Edward's person.

The Prince was mounted on a grey gelding and rode confidently among his followers, accompanied by his standard bearer. Here and there he asked to feel the sharpened edge of a clansman's sword and remarked on how many limbs it would dismember in the ensuing fray. He had seen the ranks of the red-coats broken by a highland charge at Prestonpans and at Falkirk and he still believed he had an invincible weapon in his hands. The earnest entreaty of the Count d'Eguilles – the King of France's personal envoy to him – to avoid a confrontation so heavily loaded against him, and Lord George Murray's similar cautions made no impression on the head-strong and self-confident Prince. All would be well when the pipes skirled out their pibrochs and the magic word of command for the charge – 'Claymore!' – rang out.

One of the Prince's greatest errors was that he waited too long to give that word, and when he did he sent the order to the front line by a runner who was promptly killed by a cannon ball. The highland army – like many non-professional armies – was an impatient army: it was bad at waiting for the action to begin, and particularly bad at waiting while already under fire and sustaining substantial casualties. And this was exactly what the Prince was about to subject it to. Cumberland's cannons fired solid shot into the massed phalanx of the highlanders for almost an hour and a half before the Prince gave the order to charge. During all this time the ranks were being thinned as men fell – decapitated, severed in half, deprived of limbs – as the cannon balls cleared a path through them, often felling three or four members of a single family as they stood close behind each other in the ranks. After a lengthy bombardment of the highlanders' front line, Cumberland's master of artillery raised his trajectory and landed some cannon balls so close to the Prince that the latter – despite his position at the rear of the army – had his groom killed and was himself splashed with mud and blood.

While the Prince had been delaying giving the order to charge, presumably in the hope that Cumberland would advance his front line and thus shorten the distance across the heather that had to be covered by the charging highland infantry, an equally serious error was being made by Colonel O'Sullivan who – as usual – had fallen out with Lord George Murray. On the right of the rebels' line was the walled park of Culwhiniac, and Murray had been uneasy about this ever since he had had to concede that the battle would be fought on Drummossie Moor. But O'Sullivan had argued that the dry-stone wall of the park would protect the highlanders' flank, particularly from cavalry. What he had overlooked was that Cumberland's men could advance under cover of the wall to a position from which they could fire into the flank of the highland army while remaining behind cover themselves; even more serious was the fact that they could quickly dismantle the wall and thus allow Cumberland's dragoons to harry the flank and rear of the rebel army. It was an oversight that was to cost the highlanders dear.

Although it was a shot from the antiquated rebel guns – aimed at an English lord provocatively prancing between the two armies – that formally opened the engagement, it was the sustained barrage of Cumberland's artillery (already described) that constituted the first phase of the battle*. Some while before Prince Charles Edward gave the order to charge, Cameron of Lochiel – at the head of his clan on the right flank – had informed Lord George Murray that he could hold back his highlanders no longer. But it was not the Camerons who first drew their broadswords and surged forward over the

---

* There have been many notable accounts of the Battle of Culloden but John Prebble's in his *Culloden* (Secker & Warburg, London 1961) will surely remain the finest and fullest, based as it is on his deep understanding of the clan system and his extensive use of contemporary sources.

heather, but the men of Clan Chattan. As soon as Cumberland's master of artillery saw the tartan horde bearing down on the line of English red-coats he ordered his gunners to exchange their round-shot for grape-shot (small leaden balls, old nails and scraps of iron); at short range this thinned out the attackers even more effectively than the longer-range cannon balls had done; soon the clansmen were stumbling over the fallen figures of their mutilated and maimed comrades.

Clan Chattan was soon joined in the charge by the rest of the centre and right of the highland line. Gathering up their kilts, casting off their plaids, screaming their war-cries, slashing with their broadswords, on and on they came. But rush forward as they might, relatively few were to get to hand-to-hand combat. Eighteen of the twenty-one officers of Clan Chattan alone fell in the charge. Those who survived the grape-shot often fell to the sustained volleys of musket fire coming from the three-deep line of Cumberland's infantry; and those who survived the musket fire often perished on the long bayonets* of the same infantry – a thrust under the arm-pit felling the wielder of the broadsword.

Now the other clans were as heavily engaged as Clan Chattan: the Camerons and the Stewarts penetrated but did not break the ranks of Munro's and Barrell's regiments. John Prebble vividly describes how Lieutenant Colonel Rich of the latter regiment

'held out his slender sword to parry the swing of a broadsword, and both hand and sword were cut from his wrist'.

* The bayonet was a relatively new-fangled device. In the previous century, the pike had been the decisive infantry weapon, but as artillery and musket fire improved in accuracy, pikemen became increasingly vulnerable. Yet they could not be dispensed with because the one defence the infantry had against the final stages of a cavalry charge was a fence of tall pikes; so pikemen continued to mingle with the musketeers. Then, in the early years of the eighteenth century, Marlborough, Charles XII of Sweden and other imaginative commanders started equipping their musketeers with bayonets – knives which could be rammed into the barrel of a musket at the last moment to convert the latter into a pike. Soon the ring-held bayonet was developed, which enabled the musketeer to fire while having a bayonet attached to, but not thrust down, the barrel of his weapon. This provided him with pike and musket in one. And it was this weapon which was to be the mainstay of Cumberland's infantry, and used with devastating effect.

Another officer in the same regiment later wrote to a London newspaper describing how

> 'I had eighteen men killed and wounded in my platoon . . . my coat had six balls [from highland pistols] through it'.

The casualties were not all on the one side, but predominently it was the highlanders who were massacred. Some clans were stopped dead in their tracks by the withering fire: too numbed to go forward and too brave to retire, they stood at bay, thrashing at the heather with their broadswords or hurling rocks at the red impenetrable ranks. Still the carnage went on.

The left wing of the highland line – the various Macdonald septs – were slower off the mark. They had further to go – some 800 yards – than the other clans as the highland line sloped away from Cumberland's ranks on the left, and the ground was steeper and marshier. Thus they presented a target for grape-shot and musket ball for even longer than their comrades further to the right. At one moment, Macdonald of Keppoch found that his kinsmen and tenants were not keeping up with him and had to urge them forward; soon he was hit himself and brought to his knees, being carried to the rear where he was hit again; he died in the arms of his clansmen as the battle still raged. The final *coup de grace* for the Macdonalds was the arrival on their flank of one of Cumberland's dragoon regiments. Although at Falkirk the highlanders had savaged Hawley's cavalry, they had a long-standing dread of a form of attack to which they were unused: the appearance of Kingston's Horse was too much for them and despite the Duke of Perth's ever more urgent cries of 'Claymore!', they broke and ran.

There was running on the right too by now; and as the Athollmen, the Camerons, the Stewarts and Clan Chattan streamed back across the moor, their opponents and old enemies the Campbells of Argyll – who had outflanked them behind the stone wall of Culwhiniac park – first fired into them, then threw down part of the wall for Cobham's dragoons to pass through, and finally scrambled over what was left of the wall to make their own charge to the battle cry of 'Cruachan!'. It was a thrust from the side that the retreating rebels could have done without.

If the rank and file of the clansmen were in disarray, their leaders were no less so. Macdonald of Keppoch was dead. So was Lord Strathallan, who had received the last rites on the battlefield in oatmeal and whisky. Cameron of Lochiel had been carried from the field. The Duke of Perth had abandoned his attempt to rally the left wing. Lord George Murray, hatless, wigless, and with a broken sword, was swept back with the retreating right. Colonel O'Sullivan declared roundly to Colonel O'Shea that

> 'yu see all is going to pot. Yu can be a great succor, so before a general deroute wch will soon be, seize upon the Prince and take him off'.

The Prince, although still accompanied by Lord Elcho and his Life Guards, was now in some danger from the English dragoons who had swept around to the rear of the original Jacobite position.

Accounts of the Prince's behaviour at this desperate moment vary. Captain Felix O'Neil reported:

> 'The Prince gallop'd to the right, and endeavouring to rally them had his horse shot under him.'

But James Gib, who was a member of the Prince's household, told Bishop Forbes three years later in reply to a direct question about the incident:

> 'he himself was near the Prince all the time of the action, viz, in the Prince's rear, and that it was not true that the Prince had a horse shot under him'

and this was confirmed to the bishop by two other attendants on the Prince – Goodwillie and Stewart – who also claimed to have been only a few paces from him throughout. Both of them confirmed however that

> 'the bullets continued flying very thick about their ears upon the spot where the Prince was, and that they saw Thomas Ca's head blown off with a cannon ball very near the Prince's person'.

Most accounts – notably O'Sullivan's – speak of the Prince's inclination to join the mêlée and reluctance to leave the field; indeed some
witnesses claimed that O'Sullivan had taken hold of his bridle and
led him away. Prince Charles Edward himself later wrote of being
led off the field by those about him. The only dissenting note was
struck by a nephew of Lord Elcho who claimed that his uncle's
unpublished memoirs included an account of how Elcho had begged
the Prince to lead a last charge, and that when the Prince had
refused, Elcho had rounded on him with the words 'Run, you cowardly Italian!' But Elcho's *published* memoirs did not include this
exchange and if Elcho later in life spoke or wrote privately in this
way it may only have reflected his – by then – bitterness towards the
Prince, a bitterness largely related to an allegedly unrepaid financial
debt. What appears to have been generally resented about the
Prince's leaving the field was not so much its timing as that he left
accompanied by a group of his Irish cronies rather than by his
remaining loyal Scottish chieftains.

All accounts agree that the Prince was very distraught at the rout
of his invincible highlanders, at the extent of the carnage and at the
magnitude of the defeat. Most accounts describe him as weeping (it
was a lachrymose age) while he heard his enemies cheering the
victory of his cousin and exact contemporary, the Duke of Cumberland. And certainly he had much with which to chide himself. Had
he heeded the French ambassador and others among his gallant
supporters and avoided a pitched battle, he might have withdrawn
into the highland glens and waged a successful war of attrition. Had
he listened to Lord George Murray, he might have fought the battle
on the hilly, swampy ground beyond Nairn Water, where Cumberland could not have deployed his artillery and cavalry nearly so
effectively. Had he not left his front line to face an hour and a half's
bombardment before allowing them to charge the enemy, he might
have had many more live highlanders to take part in that charge, and
those extra numbers might have tipped the balance and broken the
faltering front of Munro's, Barrell's or other English regiments. It
had been his one battle as commander in the field: he would have no
second chance as a General.

But he was to have a second chance as a man. The long flight that lay ahead, the hardships, the narrow escapes, the constant dangers, the tests of loyalty, the need for resilience and cheerfulness . . . all these were to be challenges to which he would stand up much better than he had stood up to the demands of military command. The legend of Bonnie Prince Charlie was about to enter its most exciting, most moving and most memorable phase. From the ashes of defeat he did not pluck victory; but he did pluck a reputation for courage and manliness that had not been his before and was to be his afterwards, and which was to inspire his countrymen as long as tales of romance endure. Like his ancestor Mary Queen of Scots, he could truly have said as he left the field of Culloden in tears 'In my end is my beginning'.

CAIRNS AND CASTLES

WHEN William Howitt visited the field of Culloden in 1836 he walked from Inverness, enquiring for the Moor along the way from those whom he encountered; he could find no one who could speak sufficient English to help him. Things could hardly be more different today. The visitor is confronted by tourist signs pointing to 'the battlefield of Culloden' from whatever direction he approaches. On the moor itself, there is an information centre with a permanent display explaining the lay-out of the battle and the circumstances that led up to it and ensued from it. There is a video film every fifteen minutes relating in simple terms the story of the Forty Five and making good use of contemporary portraits and material. Postcards are available depicting the tartans and crests of all the clans involved in the battle. Two wax-work figures greet the visitors at the entrance to the exhibition: one represents the Duke of Cumberland in tricorn hat, scarlet coat, high boots and a face like a pork butcher; the other represents Prince Charles Edward in a bonnet, a pinkish tartan coat (which bears a suspicious resemblance to the nineteenth-century Balmoral tartan devised by Prince Albert), a highland broadsword and a face like a slightly chinless deb's delight.

But when one emerges from all this mild razzmatazz into the open air and onto the battlefield itself it is easier to sense the special nature of the place. To start with, the moor seems very big and wide and shelter-less; the position where the different clans and regiments on both sides took up their stance before the battle are clearly marked; the distance between the two opposing lines – in reality only some 400 metres – seems formidably far to charge; the height of the heather – probably no greater now than in 1746 – seems daunting. There can be few battlefields where it is easier to trace on the ground what happened; not only are the original positions of the units marked, but rocks inscribed with the names of the different clans indicate where they may have fallen and been buried. Although the old wall of Culwhiniac Park no longer stands where it did, to give false comfort to the highland army and a safe line of advance for Cobham's dragoons, there is a dry stone wall close to the line where the Campbell Militia made the breach for the dragoons and it is easy to see how it happened. Even walking through the high heather is tiring (there are wide paths to make it easy for the visitors) and the thought of charging that quarter mile – broadsword and targe in hand – raked by grapeshot and musket fire towards the solid phalanxes of redcoat bayonets makes one wonder how so many clansmen managed to reach the Hanoverian lines at all. Even on the highland flank, although there is less deep heather there, it must have been heavy going for the dragoons. But looking over that flat 400 metres, one could see exactly why Lord George Murray was apprehensive about Cumberland's artillery: the highlanders must have felt like sitting ducks as they were pounded for that hour and a half.

I was accompanied round the battlefield, as I was to be accompanied on much of the journey that lay ahead of me, by my thirteen-year-old son Alasdair. Indeed it was his persistent questioning of me about all aspects of the battle that led me to collect most of the material in the preceding chapter. He was interested in all practical aspects of the battle, but disinclined to give credence to the more sentimental myths surrounding it. Climbing to the top of a fence he declared roundly that he saw no sign of those grassy patches among the heather that are said to be evidence that the heather will not grow over the ground where highland warriors are buried.

Earlier in the day we had been watching sheep dogs working their sheep on the hillsides as we approached Culloden. Now we were almost bowled over as an enormous Alsatian puppy sprung out of the

heather ahead of us and set off in pursuit of a hare. An Alsatian of this
sort would almost certainly have been hailed, at the time of the
Forty Five as a wolf. There had been a recorded killing of a wolf by a
certain Macqueen in Mackintosh territory – not far from Culloden –
just two years earlier. Instances of wolves attacking living humans
seem to have been rare in Scotland, but wolves had a disconcerting
habit of digging up and devouring corpses. Of these there were
always plenty resulting from the warlike nature of life in the glens,
and for this reason many clans buried their dead on wolf-free islands
such as Inishail on Loch Awe or Eilean Munde on Loch Leven. The
fear of wolves and the desire to eliminate them had also been one of
the reasons for burning down some of the old highland forests in the
previous century: this regrettable policy also had the attraction that
it destroyed the haunts of brigands – usually a more numerous and
active menace than the wolves.

From the battlefield we went on to Culloden House, the home of
Duncan Forbes, Lord President of the Court of Sessions at the time
of the Forty Five and a prominent supporter of the government –
where the Prince had spent the night before the battle and where
Cumberland had spent the night after. Now a very superior hotel, it
remains one of the finest houses in the north of Scotland, and Ian
McKenzie who runs it keeps a small library of books about the battle.
In one of these I came across some examples of the Prince's own
letters and drew them to Alasdair's attention.

One characteristic of Prince Charles Edward which endeared him
disproportionately to Alasdair was his total inability to spell. Alasdair
had stumbled on references* to some choice blunders in the Prince's
letters: 'God nose' for God knows, 'Gems' for James, and many lesser
aberrations such as 'country hows' for country house and 'the rite
man' for the right man. Alasdair had also noted with envy that very
few of the Prince's letters were written in his own hand: his tutors –
such as Sir Thomas Sheridan – wrote letters for him well into his
adult life and most of his companions had to turn their hand –
literally – to this from time to time.

'Spelling mattered less in those days', I told Alasdair with as much

* In Susan Maclean Kybett's *Bonnie Prince Charlie* (see bibliography).

conviction as possible. 'And the fact that other people wrote his letters for him was just like secretaries typing letters now; it didn't mean he couldn't do it himself'. I found myself rallying to the defence of the Prince – or possibly to the defence of literacy.

But in reality it was not only written language that defeated the Prince. At a time when most European aristocrats in Paris or Rome were at least bilingual, Prince Charles Edward never totally mastered the command of any European language. As a child he spoke a mixture of English, French and Italian; and although English was his natural tongue he was never comfortable in conversation with the highly articulate even in this, while his Italian remained rudimentary. Possibly one reason why the Prince was so relaxed and popular with his companions on his flight was because they did not strain his linguistic or intellectual attainments. It was to be very different on his return to France where he was to find the sophisticated conversation of the Paris *salons* altogether too demanding, and where his *mots* were seldom as memorable as they had been in the bothies of Lochaber or Badenoch.

After our short browse in the library, we went out on to the broad green lawn in front of the house. The present handsome facade dates from a renovation, some twenty-five years after the battle of Culloden, thought to have been carried out by Robert Adam. The earlier house – or 'castle' as it was sometimes known – standing on the site in 1746 was considerably larger than the present one, built round a square and solid enough to support a cannon on its crenellated roof. Ian MacKenzie maintains that the present front door gave onto the internal courtyard of the old house. As Alasdair looked up this imposing entrance, he said with a puzzled frown: 'It must have been very difficult to know which side to fight on. Forbes seems to have been a hero for remaining loyal to King George II, and Cameron of Lochiel seems to have been a hero for joining Bonnie Prince Charlie. But they were both Scots. How did they know what was right?'

How indeed. Alasdair had articulated a problem that was to perplex me throughout my journey. As a Campbell of Argyll, my own – and Alasdair's – ancestors had fought against the Prince at Culloden, and had fought with courage and conviction.

The answer I suppose (and it was not an easy one to rationalize to a thirteen-year-old boy) was that every clansman followed his chief and that the moral dilemma only applied to those in positions of authority and influence. For some such the dilemma was easily resolved; for others it was acute. Duncan Forbes had taken on the high office of Lord President of the Court of Session in Scotland – a position of trust and profit under the Hanoverian Crown; to have betrayed that trust would have seemed, to him, and to most others, a dishonourable act. But Lord George Murray had also accepted a position of trust – that of Sheriff-Depute – and this did not deter him from rallying to the Pretender's cause. He probably justified the change of allegiance by arguing that, while there was no challenge to the House of Hanover it was reasonable to serve the crown, but that when an older and more legitimate challenger came forward it was right to throw up everything to join him. It was not an argument that would have saved him from the direst retribution if he had fallen into Hanoverian hands: the officers of the Manchester regiment who had changed sides were to be hanged, drawn and quartered for their pains. Others, like Lord Lovat, were to follow their own calculation of their best interests in deciding their loyalties.

'There's no easy answer,' I said to Alasdair. 'When Talleyrand was asked how he justified having changed sides so often during the years following the French Revolution, he answered that he never betrayed anyone till they had betrayed themselves, and that he never conspired except when he had the people of France as his fellow conspirators. A nimble answer, but not one that saved him from being considered as slippery and self-interested. It was the same in Scotland: important people had to decide where their real patriotism and loyalty should lie. You and I would have fallen in behind the Duke of Argyll and that would have been the end of the matter.'

'Pity,' said Alasdair.

Having talked about the Clan Campbell and being anxious to see what the terrain was like between Culloden House and Nairn – the route over which the famous night march had taken place – I suggested that we should combine a journey to Nairn with a visit to another great Campbell stronghold – Cawdor Castle, the seat of the

Thanes of Cawdor and now of the Earls of the same name. It was here that Macbeth was reputed to have murdered King Duncan in 1040, giving rise to the story of Shakespeare's play.

The present Cawdor Castle dates from 1454 and is a model Scottish castle, with a formidable central keep, a working drawbridge (which collapsed into the moat when a particularly heavy fireplace was being carried across), and a splendid collection of clan portraits. It was this last which prompted Alasdair to ask me why the Campbells were so frequently referred to, by Jacobites and others, as 'black Campbells' and why their reputation in the highlands was such a controversial one. I tried to explain that this was a grave injustice on a number of counts.

The Campbells had been consistent in their loyalty to the Hanoverian Crown since the Treaty of Union in 1707 and had for some time before that tended to support Parliament, Protestantism and the Glorious Revolution in all its manifestations. Not for nothing were they the natural supporters of the 'Establishment' which – particularly since 1714 – had been increasingly synonymous with the Whig Supremacy in England: they were the largest land-owning clan; their possessions were founded on legal title as frequently as on forceful occupation; they had more to lose than any other clans – many of which had no fixed assets of any sort except disputed land.

The first Marquis of Argyll who headed the clan in the middle of the seventeenth century was not a martial* and romantic figure, like his protagonist the first Marquis of Montrose, but he was a scholar and intellectual of high calibre and one of the most formidable statesmen of seventeenth-century Scotland. That indelible stain on

* But the martial streak is as pronounced in the Campbells as in any clan in Scotland. The clan regiment – the 91st (Argyllshire) Highlanders which later amalgamated to become the Argyll and Sutherland Highlanders – has distinguished itself throughout the annals of recent British military history: it formed the rearguard during the retreat to Corunna. Sir Iain Moncreiffe of that Ilk – no Campbell himself by any measure – has calculated that the fifty male descendants of the Campbell thanes of Cawdor, who have been of military age in time of war over the past hundred years, have between them won forty-five gallantry awards – including sixteen DSOs and three Victoria Crosses. Campbell prowess has not been limited to the Court Room or the study.

the clan honour – the massacre of Glencoe – was not the work of
the leaders of the Campbell clan but of the duplicitous Master of
Stair – a lowland Dalrymple – and of a disreputable blackguard from
a cadet branch of the clan – Captain Robert Campbell of Glenlyon.
As the recognised champion of highland honour, John Prebble has
written:

> 'The use of Campbell soldiers [at Glencoe] had little to do with
> their ancient feuds, they were the only disciplined and reliable
> force in John Hill's district, but the selection of the bankrupt and
> drunkard Glenlyon was perhaps deliberate . . . he had particular
> reasons for hating the Glencoe men . . . they had burnt and looted
> his glen for the second time . . .'

Prebble also points out that, although Jacobite hacks and agents
made good use of the massacre in their propaganda against the
Campbells, the Glencoe men themselves put it in perspective by
fighting alongside the Campbells shortly afterwards. By the time of
the Forty Five, jealousy of the Campbells was a more potent sentiment than resentment or desire for vengeance. During the Forty
Five itself, the Campbells did not equivocate like so many other
smaller clans: they put their weight firmly and decisively behind the
government to whom they had consistently professed allegiance.
And when the fighting was over, it was General John Campbell of
Mamore who saved many a prisoner (including Flora Macdonald)
from torture and abuse. Nor did the Campbells who were not in
government service betray Prince Charles Edward when it was in
their power to do so: Donald Campbell of Scalpay was one who not
only protected him but chased off less honourable would-be fortune
seekers. The misfortune of the Campbells was that their reputation
(though not their fortunes) once again suffered from being on the
surviving and unromantic side – as they had been in the wars with
Montrose. To the losers, the victorious Campbells were 'black'
indeed.

By the time we had finished visiting Cawdor Castle and talking
about the history of the Campbell clan, it was time to find Ballagham

Farm where we were booked to spend the night. We had imagined there would be little difficulty in finding a farmhouse the address of which was simply 'Culloden Moor', but when we started to explore the byeways of the moor, on our return from Nairn, we found there was a positive labyrinth of small roads and tracks intersecting the whole area of Drummossie and Culloden Moors. Lots of signs pointed to the battlefield; very few seemed to point to anywhere else, and none to Ballagham Farm. The light rain began to get heavier. Alasdair remarked that if we didn't find our billet soon we should be too late for supper and – like the army returning from the night march to Nairn – we would be going hungry to bed.

Just when we were beginning to think we had been along every road, lane and track across the moor at least twice, we found a shepherd plodding home who pointed beyond a circle of ancient Druid-type stones to a trim farmhouse on rising ground. It was not a big farm: a hundred acres and one of several which the laird's widow continue to lease to tenant farmers.

The welcome we received from Mrs Alexander was worth all the hunt. She had never doubted we were coming. Of course there was time for a hot bath before dinner. By the time we reached our warm and cosy beds, even Alasdair had eaten himself to a standstill, and there was no more talk of knowing how the Prince's army felt as they dossed down on the moor for their fitful (and for many of them – their last) night's sleep.

Alasdair's mind was however still running on the events of the day. Our journey to Nairn had made him feel that the Jacobite's had missed a great opportunity by turning back ('It really wasn't very far', said Alasdair) before they had launched their attack on what might have been an English army recovering from their commander's birthday celebrations. Clearly thinking of that birthday still, Alasdair asked:

'How old was Bonnie Prince Charlie at the time of the Forty Five?'

When I told him the answer was twenty five, Alasdair asked if he was married. I told him he was not.

'Did he have a girl friend?' was the predictable next question. This was a harder one to answer.

Flora Macdonald, as will be amply demonstrated as this tale de-
velops, was certainly not a girl friend. Reluctant at first to get involved in his escape, she subsequently helped him with courage and
ingenuity – being rewarded with sincere but hasty thanks from the
Prince, a two-year prison spell from the English, and immortality
from a romantic-minded public.

But one lady did feature more emotionally in the Prince's time
in Scotland. Clementia Walkinshaw was the pretty niece of his
host at Bannockburn House when he spent a few days there in
January 1746 (before Culloden) recovering from a cold. She had
looked after him during this period solicitously. Whether or not
she became his mistress (as Hanoverian pamphleteers later maintained) she clearly made a deep impression on him and he on her
because, six years later and long after his return to the Continent,
he sent a message asking her to leave the religious institution
where she was living and join him in Paris, and she complied with
surprising alacrity. Whatever may have been the case in Scotland,
they indisputably became lovers in France and a daughter was
subsequently born to Clementia who was recognised by the
Prince as his natural and only child. This girl – Charlotte – was to
write him poignant letters when she grew up and eventually was
reunited with the Prince and succoured him in his drunken and
declining years. But Clementia Walkinshaw hardly qualified as
what Alasdair had in mind as a girl friend in the Forty Five:
Clementia had at best been the object of a one or two night affair at
that stage.

Nor did any of the well-born and starry-eyed maidens of Edinburgh, who attended the balls at Holyrood during the weeks when
the Prince held court there in 1745, become coupled with the Prince
either in fact or in popular report; though doubtless many would
have liked to have been. In fact when the Prince returned to France
it was to older and more experienced women that he seemed to be
attracted. Louise de Montbazon became his confidante and mistress.
And when he eventually married it was a dynastic and unhappy
match with a princess more than thirty years his junior – Louise de
Stolberg-Gedern. 'Bonnie' the Prince may have been, but sexually
romantic he seems not to have been.

'No', I said rather diffidently, 'I don't think he did really have a girl friend during the Forty Five.'

'How sensible' was Alasdair's only comment as he rolled over and went to sleep.

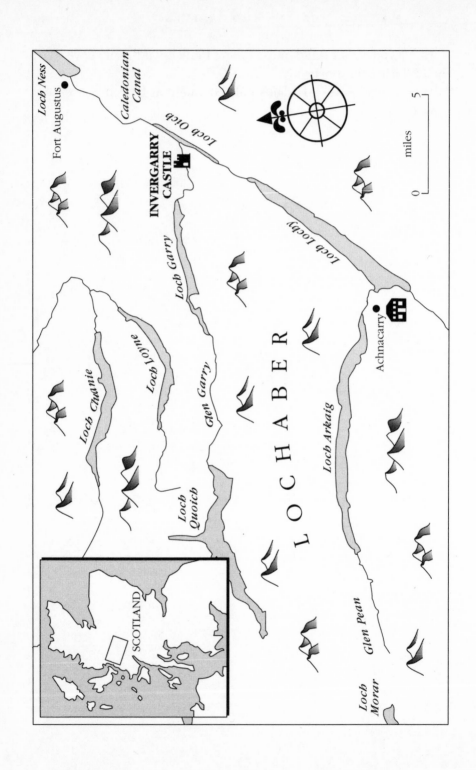

Loch Ness

Fort Augustus

Caledonian Canal

Loch Oich

INVERGARRY CASTLE

Loch Garry

Loch Lochy

Loch Chuanie

Loch Loyne

Glen Garry

Achnacarry

Loch Quoich

L O C H A B E R

Loch Arkaig

Glen Pean

Loch Morar

SCOTLAND

0   5

miles

— 3 —

THE ROAD TO THE ISLES

THE confusion which attended Prince Charles Edward's departure from the battlefield of Culloden was to continue to domi-
nate subsequent events. There had been no very clear plan as
to what was to be done in the case of defeat. The Prince had been
understandably reluctant either to contemplate or to discuss such an
eventuality. But he had – at different times and none too clearly –
proposed to the chiefs that in the event of a reverse the clans should
withdraw to Ruthven or to Fort Augustus.

The only Jacobite regiments to withdraw from the field in anything approaching good order were those of Lord George Murray
from the right flank. He led them to Ruthven in Badenoch where,
once he had secured the narrow glens leading in to the rallying
point, he sent messengers to find the Prince and invite him to come
and resume command of the remnants of his army. According to the
Chevalier de Johnstone, most of the surviving Jacobite leaders were
at Ruthven and thought that they could carry on the campaign, and
'every one beseeched the Prince most earnestly to come thither
quickly to put himself at their head'.

But the Prince was elsewhere and had other plans. He had left
the field of Culloden accompanied by a small group of Irishmen
(a fact – as we have seen – which was to rankle with his Scottish
supporters) and made his way not towards Ruthven but towards
the alternative rallying point of Fort Augustus. He had exchanged
his wounded horse for another, had crossed the River Nairn and
started his flight down the track running parallel to Loch Ness on its

eastern side; this took him in the late hours of 16 April – while
Cumberland's troops were beginning their butchery of the wounded
on the battlefield – past Tordarroch, Aberarder and Farraline to
Gortuleg where he found the house of Lord Lovat's 'doer' (or
factor).

Here he encountered the 79-year-old Lord Lovat himself, who
gave him supper and (according to Ned Burke – the Prince's body-
servant) several glasses of wine. The Prince must have been ravenous, having refused breakfast on that day because his troops were
unfed and having been in the midst of the battle at the hour of the
mid-day meal. Over supper, Lord Lovat gave the Prince his advice.
He was a curiously tainted source of advice, either about the Jacobite
cause or any other aspect of life, but – for the moment at least – he
appeared to be on the Prince's side.

Prince Charles Edward had met Simon Fraser, 11th Lord Lovat,
before and would – in any case – have known much of the quite
extraordinary career of this most slippery and rascally of all highland
chiefs. Simon Fraser had not been born to a title nor to clan chief-
dom. He had started life as an ardent Jacobite, being three times
imprisoned for his political convictions (if the word 'conviction' can
be applied to any of his tactical loyalties) before he reached the age
of sixteen. He had taken a degree at Aberdeen University in 1683
and remained a classical scholar throughout his otherwise lurid life.
Abandoning his intention to go into the law, he had travelled with
his cousin, the then Lord Lovat, to London and had persuaded that
somewhat simple-minded relative to make a will leaving his estates
to his (Simon Fraser's) father. When his cousin promptly died,
Simon Fraser's father assumed the title of Lord Lovat and Simon
that of Master of Lovat. But it was not to be so simple. The deceased
cousin had left a daughter and she claimed that the title passed to
her and assumed the style of Baroness Lovat. Simon Fraser saw his
plot frustrated and decided that he should square the circle by
marrying the baroness himself. She declined the offer, despite some
attendant threats. So he turned his attention to her mother, the
dowager Lady Lovat. He seized Castle Dounie where she was living
and proceeded to perpetuate a crime which, even by the robust
standards of the age, was so shocking that it resulted in his being

outlawed. The state papers relating to the trial give an account rich in circumstantial detail:

'He (Simon Fraser) and his accomplices made the lady close prisoner in her chamber under his armed guard, and there came upon
her with Mr Robert Munro, minister of Abertarff, and three or
four ruffians, in the night time, about two or three in the morning,
and having dragged out her maids . . . he proposes to the lady that
she should marry him, and when she fell lamenting and crying,
the great pipe was blow up to drown her cries, and the wicked
villains ordered the minister to proceed and declare them married
persons . . . though she often swarved (swooned) . . . the ruffians
rent off her clothes, cutting her stays with their dirks, and so
thrust her into her bed.'

Lady Lovat was then raped, as her cries were drowned by the screech of the pipes.

Simon Fraser took to the hills and organised an outlaw band. His father having fled to the isles and died, he adopted the title of 11th Lord Lovat, by which he was henceforth to be known. He managed to set the Dukes of Atholl and Argyll against each other and then persuaded the latter to intervene on his behalf with King William III who eventually granted him a pardon. Meanwhile he was also becoming simultaneously and treasonably involved with the Jacobite émigré faction in France. Sometimes he was received by the Old Pretender at his court at St Germain; at other times he was sus-pected of spying on the Jacobites and imprisoned in France. He escaped in time to participate in the 1715 uprising in Scotland. After a characteristically equivocal start, he threw in his lot with the government forces and captured Inverness on their behalf. So when the Fifteen ended ignominiously, Lovat was rewarded with estates and honours. He established himself at Castle Dounie as a laird of extraordinary power; those whose favour he valued, he entertained at magnificent feasts with French cuisine and French wine; those whom he mistrusted he strung up by the heels from trees in the castle policies. And all the while he continued to correspond, in letters full of well-turned Latin phrases, with the erudite and powerful in France, England and the lowlands of Scotland. He remarried – twice – largely for dynastic reasons and even prevailed on King George I of England to be godfather to one of his children.

This was the man who had come out for Prince Charles Edward after the latter's victory at Prestonpans, when it seemed to the wily old chieftain that the Jacobite cause was winning. He himself had been too aged, fat and lame to lead his men into battle; and the Master of Lovat (perhaps out of a canny instinct to preserve some part of the family from total commitment to the rebel cause) had failed to appear on the field of Culloden either. The Fraser clan had consequently been led by the young Charles Fraser of Inverallochie who had died on the field a few days before his twenty-first birthday.*

As Lord Lovat watched the fleeing highlanders passing Gortuleg on their way down the Great Glen he must have rued his decision after Prestonpans. But he had never been one to despair, and now he counselled the Prince to remember the story of his ancestor Robert the Bruce who had – Lord Lovat reminded him – lost eleven battles to the English before winning the battle of Bannockburn and consolidating the Scottish monarchy. The Prince left Gortuleg about midnight on the 16th (still the same day which had opened with the fateful and aborted march on Nairn) and – with Lord Lovat's words ringing in his ears and his dinner warming the inner man – pressed on down the Great Glen.

His route continued down the east side of Loch Ness to Fort Augustus. He reached this supposed rendezvous in the early hours of the following morning and sought shelter nearby at Invergarry Castle where Ned Burke with his sharp eyes spotted a fishing net in place and hauled it in to discover two salmon which he promptly cooked 'in the best manner he could'. Otherwise there was no

---

* Not killed in battle, but murdered in cold blood as he lay wounded after the battle, on the orders of General 'Hangman' Hawley. The order to shoot him had originally been given to Major James Wolfe (later of Quebec fame) who had roundly declared that he would resign his commission rather than execute such an order. Hawley had then found a more compliant executioner.

hospitality except a little wine to be had as the castle – though not yet burnt down, which was shortly to be its fate – was already deserted.

The Prince spent nearly twelve hours – precious time for a fugitive – hovering around Invergarry and Fort Augustus in the hope that some of his supporters would show up there. None did. So he left Captain O'Neil (one of his Irish companions) behind there 'to direct such as passed that way the road he took'; but O'Neil recorded later that no one paid any heed to him as all the fugitives were 'every one taking his own road'.

Indeed, there seems to have been good reason for their so doing, because at some point in these first days after the battle of Culloden the Prince had sent a message to Lord George Murray and the other chiefs who had gathered at Ruthven (again, according to the Chevalier de Johnstone who claimed to have been there) urging 'that every man should look out for the means of saving himself as best he could'. On receipt of this message, the remnant of the highland army had disbanded, and Murray himself had sent back a reproachful letter of resignation as the Prince's general.

Prince Charles Edward was, from now on, intent on following his own advice and concentrating on saving himself. For him, the best prospect of escape seemed to be being picked up by a French ship from the west coast of Scotland. He was further encouraged to go west by the belief that – while waiting for a ship – he would be safest among the Macdonalds in the Western Isles. At such a juncture, any man would have been likely to think first of his own survival; but in Prince Charles Edward's case, it was not a purely selfish instinct. He was convinced that the only long-term hope for the Jacobite cause in Scotland lay in his reaching France and persuading King Louis XV to send the army which he had so notably failed to do the previous year. Furthermore, he was convinced that he alone could persuade Louis to that action.

Six days later, Prince Charles Edward was to write to Sir Thomas Sheridan (another of the Irishmen who had accompanied him from the field of Culloden and who had subsequently been dropped in the interests of keeping the Prince's party small) enclosing a letter to the clan chiefs explaining why he was leaving for France. In this he said:

> 'When I came into this Country, it was my only view to do all in my power for your good and safety. This I will always do as long as life is in me. But alas! I see with grief, I can at present do little for you on this side of the water, for the only thing that can now be done, is to defend yourself till the French assist you . . . [if I go to France I shall] certainly engage the French Court either to assist us effectually and powerfully, or at least to procure you such terms as you would not obtain otherways.'*

The tone of the letter was sadly different from the spirit of the Prince's remarks to Cameron of Lochiel on that morning of bright hope and reckless courage at Glen Shiel in August the previous year; there was no talk now of winning or perishing in the attempt. The clan chiefs who received the letter blamed the urgings of the Irishmen around the Prince for this change of heart.

Having decided to head westwards – to take 'the road to the Isles' – it now seemed more prudent to travel in an even smaller party. For the next stage of the journey the Prince was to be accompanied only by O'Sullivan (whose account we have), Ned Burke (whose account we also have), and Captain Allan Macdonald of Clanranald. To further conceal the character of the party, the Prince changed outer clothes with Ned Burke; this was the first time he had resorted to any form of disguise.

Burke's clothes would have been of the simplest. Despite his Irish name he had been born in the highlands and had come to Edinburgh as 'a common chairman' – that is one who carried sedan chairs through the city for the more affluent citizens. Bishop Forbes, to whom he made a long disposition about his time with the Prince, reports that Burke 'though true as steel, was a rough man, and that

---

* The unusually accurate and consistent spelling of this letter is attributable to the fact that it was not written in the Prince's own hand, but in that of John Hay of Restalrig, one of those who had escaped from Culloden with him.

he used great freedoms [familiarities] with the Prince'. However, the Prince clearly liked him and would sit and play simple games with him to the amusement of the rest of the party.

All those involved agreed that the next few days of rough marches along the north shore of Loch Lochy and Loch Arkaig, through Glen Pean and on to Loch Morar were exceptionally tough going. O'Sullivan, who seemed to be still unused to highland scenery, describes his march along the shore of Loch Lochy as having 'terrible mountains on his right', and the route through Glen Pean as 'the crullest road that cou'd be seen', and the hills around Loch Morar as 'the highest and wildest mountains of the highlands'. But even the native-born highlander Burke tells how 'in this road we got ourselves all nastied'. The ponies had to go another way.

Arduous as this passage had been, Prince Charles Edward had at least got the first night's sleep he had had since before the battle. Donald Cameron of Glen Pean had a house at the Glen Pean end of Loch Arkaig, and there the Prince rested on his march. The next morning – 18 April – Donald Cameron escorted the Prince through Glen Pean to the eastern end of Loch Morar, where they waited four hours for a boat to take them down the loch, but as none came they set out just before nightfall again. At the foot of one of O'Sullivan's 'wildest mountains' the Prince was offered 'some milk, cruds (curds) and butter, at one McDonells, and was as satisfied and eat of it, as well as if he had the best cheer that ever he made'. Once more the ponies had to be abandoned as the going was too rough even for them.

On the next day – 19 April – he reached a croft at the western (coastal) end of Loch Morar belonging to another McDonell, and O'Sullivan records that 'he was pretty well here; he had a little meat, lamb, butter and straw to ly upon, he wanted it for he had not eat a bit of bread since he supt at Ld Lovat's the night of the battle'.

Now the Prince took stock of the situation: both his own situation and that of the Jacobite cause. John Hay of Restalrig arrived with news of Cumberland's troops having reached Fort Augustus and of a strong detachment being sent to Fort William. The Prince (again according to O'Sullivan) reacted sharply to this intelligence:

"'Ah!" says the Prince "there is all communication cut with Badenoch, by the troops that are at Forte Augustus, & since that
detachment is gone to Forte William without being attacked in a
Country where they cou'd be cut to pieces, there is nothing to be
expected." The next day or day after (O'Sullivan goes on) he had
accounts that Louden recd orders to quit the Isle of Sky, & go to
Forte William by Arisaig & Mouidiert & ravage all that country.'

This was bad news indeed for the Prince. Not only did the arrival of
Cumberland's troops at Fort William show that the highlanders'
resistance had totally collapsed, but the rumours that John Campbell, 4th Earl of Loudoun, was coming with government troops to
the very part of the mainland where the Prince was hiding up,
signalled clearly the immediate danger in which he stood. It was at
this juncture that the Prince sent the letter to Sheridan and the clan
chiefs – explaining why he was decamping for France – which has
already been quoted.

But decamping for France was not as easy as he had supposed.
The hoped-for French frigates or privateers were nowhere to be
found. (Ironically, a number of those whom the Prince had sent away
from his party when numbers had to be reduced – including Sir
Thomas Sheridan and John Hay of Restalrig – were themselves
picked up by the French privateer *Mars* on 3 May and sailed to
safety in France while the Prince still had months as a fugitive ahead
of him.) By 20 April the Prince felt he could wait around Arisaig no
longer: Lord Loudoun's troops were reputed to be only some seven
miles away. There was still no news of a French rescue vessel. So the
Prince decided he would be safer on one of the Hebridean islands
than on the mainland. The only question was how to get there. The
intervening waters of the Sea of the Hebrides were not only tricky
from a navigation point of view – being beset by currents, small
islands, rocks and sudden squawls – but were infested with English
warships, all of them on the lookout for Jacobite refugees.

One man who knew better than most how to navigate his way
through these hazards was Donald Macleod, who had been
employed as a pilot by Aeneas Macdonald when the latter – another
staunch Jacobite – had been over to the island of Barra to collect

some money that had been earlier dropped off by a French ship to aid the cause. Aeneas Macdonald now sent Donald Macleod to find the Prince and take him off to the outer islands.

Macleod's meeting with the Prince would sound altogether improbable had it not been described in such circumstantial detail by Donald Macleod himself (to Bishop Forbes some years later). As he approached Borrodale, in Arisaig

'the first man he met with was the Prince in a wood, all alone . . . The Prince making towards Donald, asked, "Are you Donald Macleod of Guatergill in Sky?" "Yes", said Donald, "I am the same man, may it please your Majesty, at your service. What is your pleasure wi' me?" "Then," said the Prince, "You see Donald, I am in distress. I therefore throw myself into your bosom, and let you do with me what you like. I hear you are an honest man, and fit to be trusted." . . . Donald made this return to the Prince. "Alas, may it please your excellency, what can I do for you? For I am but an auld man, and can do very little for mysell."'

The Prince then went on to ask Donald to do the one thing that he felt he could not do: take letters to Sir Alexander Macdonald and the Laird of Macleod. Donald Macleod was convinced that these two highland chiefs were not to be trusted and were indeed joining in the hunt for the Prince. In his own account Donald – while stressing that he spoke respectfully to the Prince and addressed him as 'Majesty' – says he declared roundly:

'These men have played the rogue to you altogether, and will you trust them for a' that? Na, you mauna do't.'

This must have been another blow to the Prince's hopes, and probably helped to convince him that there was no time to lose. He therefore changed his request to Donald to the expected one: would he pilot him over the sea to 'the islands where I may look for more safety than I can do here?'

This time there was no hesitation. Donald Macleod declared he would do 'anything in the world for him' and promptly procured 'a

stout eight-oar'd boat' from the same Macdonald family with whom
he had so recently sailed to Barra. The first stage of the Prince's
flight was over. A more perilous chapter still was about to begin.
Although he did not know it, the Hebrides were to prove even
more alive with red-coats and government supporters than the mainland; and the cover and scope for retreat was less. But first of all
there was the danger of the crossing itself, and that was to prove
nearly fatal.

In the twilight of the evening of 26 April, with five companions
and eight oarsmen, they pushed out from the shore of Loch nan
Uamh at Borrodale – the very spot where he had first landed with
such high hopes just nine months before.

* * *

We were up early at Ballagham Farm and, after a breakfast that
would have satisfied an eighteenth-century master of foxhounds, we
set off on the first leg of the Prince's flight – across the Nairn water
and down a track (now a 'passing places only' secondary road) towards Gorthleck House where the Prince had been entertained and
given fatherly advice by old Lord Lovat.

We found the old road had a line of high hills between it and Loch
Ness, so although we were driving parallel with the loch in a south-
westerly direction we saw nothing of it; instead we passed down a
gentle secluded glen with some minor lochs – such as Loch Mhor –
of its own. Gorthleck itself was a disappointment. What appeared to
be the old 'factor's house' (Gortuleg) looked like a crenellated shooting lodge and was undergoing extensive repairs: there was no sign of
life. We passed on down the glen, with even less delay than the
Prince, to Fort Augustus.

Here we saw the Caledonian Canal in action. Linking the North
Sea at Beauly Firth with the Atlantic at the Firth of Lorn, it is – in
effect – a series of short canals (stretching to 22 miles in all) between
those lochs that run east-west, the longest and greatest of which is of
course Loch Ness. The level of water between the lochs varies very
considerably, so there are a large number of locks which inevitably
delay the passage of small boats passing through. Alasdair leant over
the canal sides watching the yachts tying up and ropes and tempers

fraying; his interest had an intensity which the exploits of Prince Charles Edward could seldom command.

'Did you know', I asked him, 'that the first study for constructing a canal of this sort across Scotland was made only about 25 years after Bonnie Prince Charlie had passed this way? It was done by James Watt.'

'It must have held him up a bit, when he was trying to invent the steam engine', was Alasdair's only comment. It was truer than he knew.

Like the Prince, we pressed on from Fort Augustus to Invergarry down the line of General Wade's military road linking Loch Ness with Loch Oich. The General had constructed the road between the time of the 1715 uprising and the Forty Five, essentially to link Fort William (already a small highland fort and village named after William III) and the fort and village that was shortly to be named Fort Augustus (after William Augustus, Duke of Cumberland and victor of Culloden).

On our way, also like the Prince, we stopped at Invergarry Castle on the shores of Loch Oich and now in the grounds of the impressive Invergarry Castle Hotel. The castle was deserted when the Prince reached it; it was soon afterwards burnt down as part of the retribution inflicted on this part of the highlands, and it stands as a ruin – but a haunting and imposing one – to this day. This was where Ned Burke had spotted the salmon net that had provided their supper, and Alasdair insisted on clambering down to the steep edge of the loch on the pretext of finding the spot but in reality to take some altogether provocative risks of ending up in the loch himself.

We crossed the Caledonian canal again by the Laggan Swing Bridge and a mile further south left the Landrover Discovery by the Laggan locks and took to the hills on foot. Rounding the head of Loch Lochy I recalled that this was the scene of one of the fiercest of all clan battles.

It had been fought in 1554: the Frasers had been ambushed among the heather-clad hills on the lochside by their enemies the Macdonalds of Clanranald. The clansmen of both sides had shed their tartan plaids to free their arms for wielding their heavy broadswords, and hence the affray became known as *Blar-na-Léine* or 'the battle of the shirts'. It was a desperate affair. Of the five hundred Macdonalds, only a score or so are believed to have survived. Three hundred Frasers were also killed including their chief Lord Lovat, eighty were minor chiefs or heads of families and – the legend goes – all eighty of them left their widows pregnant; even more remarkable and ominous was the fact that all eighty posthumous children were boys – born to avenge their fathers.

The north-west shore of Loch Lochy, along which the Prince's route had run from Fort Augustus to Loch Arkaig, must always have been a bleak track. A steep and featureless slope runs at a sharp gradient down from the peaks of Glengarry Forest to the long, straight loch. There may have been some mixed vegetation on the slope in the eighteenth century, but now it is an almost unremitting belt of Forestry conifers, with a clear but stony path cut into the slope some hundred yards above the water. It is a long and unexciting slog on foot.

'I sometimes think', said Alasdair panting up the ridge ahead, 'that Bonnie Prince Charlie should have been an Inca prince from Peru and not a Scottish one'.

When I asked him what had given rise to this apparently inconsequential remark, Alasdair replied that he had been told at school that Inca roads – unlike European ones – followed the tops of the mountains and not the valleys. This was why, he added knowledgeably, it had taken so long to find some of their sites like Machu Picchu.

'Why did Bonnie Prince Charlie have to be such a glutton for punishment?' asked Alasdair. 'Surely he could have taken the low road occasionally.'

There was a good reason why he could not. In the mid-eighteenth century the highland glens had been considerably more populated than they were in the late twentieth century. And travelling along a populated route meant being observed. Loyal as the highlanders were – despite the reward of £30,000 offered for the Prince alive or dead – the Prince's escorts naturally preferred not to test that loyalty unnecessarily by exposing themselves to more people than need be. They therefore kept to the high routes. I explained this to Alasdair.

'That's odd', he said. 'Most places seem to have more people living in them now than 250 years ago.'

He was right. The Scottish highlands had gone against the trend in an almost unique way, and I knew that I should soon need to explain to Alasdair the phenomenon of the Highland Clearances. But for the moment we had more pressing things on our minds as we were approaching Achnacarry.

For followers in the steps of Prince Charles Edward, Achnacarry Castle is something of a shrine. It is the ancestral home of the Camerons of Lochiel. Some mention has already been made of the Gentle Lochiel – the Prince's most loyal and beloved supporter – and much more will be written about him before this tale is done, because he was to rejoin the Prince at a later stage in his travels. The original house at Achnacarry was – predictably – burnt by Cumberland's troops in 1746. Some English soldiery, who were probably looking for loot in the ruins of the house, came across the Gentle Lochiel's cook and gardener. They flogged these unfortunate retainers unmercifully, in an attempt to extract from them information about where Lochiel had buried his valuables – principally the family plate. Neither of them divulged anything and so they were sent 'with their backs cruelly flayed' in irons to Inverness. The castle, as it is to be seen now, was built in the early nineteenth century by the grandson of the Gentle Lochiel – another Sir Donald – to whom the estates had been restored in 1784.

The present head of the clan is Colonel Sir Donald Cameron of Lochiel, a Knight of the Thistle. He has constructed a clan museum in the grounds of Achnacarry. The clan museum was shut, but the kindly lady who looked after it would not hear of our going away without seeing it and opened it up specially for us. It was well worth it, abounding as it did with relics – including a broad sword – of the Gentle Lochiel. Everywhere the stark motto of the Camerons stared out at one from coats of arms and old documents: 'Sons of hounds, come and I will give you flesh'. The words of the march of the Cameron men are also written up on the museum walls. Two verses have a particularly poignant ring when one remembers how the arrival of Lochiel with his pipers at Glenfinnan had signalled the serious start of the Forty Five, and how the Camerons and their chief had suffered on the field of Culloden:

'I hear the pibroch sounding, sounding,
  Deep o'er the mountain and glen;
Where the light springing footsteps are trampling the heath.
  'Tis the march of the Cameron Men.

Oh, proudly they walk, but each Cameron knows
  He may tread on the heather no more;
But boldly he follows his chief to the field,
  Where his laurels were gathered before.'

We emerged from the museum to see the handsome present seat of the Lochiel, and – near the stable block in the grounds – the remains of the original castle burnt down by Cumberland's men. Heather and rowans sprout from the old stones, making the whole look like one of those romantic Follies that rich English landowners delighted to build as an ornament to embellish their carefully constructed vistas.

From Achnacarry you cross the river Arkaig to join a narrow but well-paved road that runs along the north shore of Loch Arkaig. Just before the road joins the loch, it passes the celebrated water-falls of Achnasaul, at the point where the forest track down Gleann Cia-aig (to be trodden by the Prince at a later stage in his flight) reaches the road. From there the road continues along the north shore for what has for centuries been known as 'the dark mile' on account of the heavy over-hanging trees which exclude any ray of sunshine.

As the road emerges from the trees, so it becomes narrower, with only periodical passing places. It hugs the lochside closely. As we made our way along this northern bank of Loch Arkaig we were haunted by the thought of the treasure that may still lie hidden and awaiting discovery there. The French privateering ship *Mars* which had picked up some of the Prince's supporters on 3 May (very soon after Culloden) had not only come to look for the Prince and his companions: it had also come – together with the *Bellona* – bringing a substantial sum of gold (35,000 *louis d'or*) to help finance the Jacobite cause. This money had first been handed over to Murray of Broughton and then had passed into the keeping of Cameron of Lochiel and later of Cluny Macpherson. Some of the money had been spent to support the rebellion; some was eventually repatriated to France to help finance Prince Charles Edward in exile; but a very large – if unquantified – part was left buried somewhere along the shores of Loch Arkaig. It is thought to be still there, and a few years ago some eighteenth century gold coins were found stuck in the hooves of cattle which had been grazing in the area, thus encouraging the idea that the treasure chest might have disintegrated and its precious contents be lying not far below the rocky surface.

'What a pity' said Alasdair 'that we didn't think of bringing a metal detector.' Feeling the weight of my shoulder bag, and guessing who would have ended up carrying that hefty bit of equipment, I didn't comment. But I did find myself looking out for landmarks that might have been chosen to identify the resting place of a cache of gold, and wondering whether one day some antiquarian bookseller in Edinburgh would find a crumpled chart – like that in Stevenson's *Treasure Island* – fallen out of some musty old volume and the treasure hunt would begin in earnest.

'Was Bonnie Prince Charlie very rich?' asked Alasdair, his mind clearly also still on the treasure.

'Like quite a lot of people', I said, 'he managed to be a big spender without every having very much money of his own. Not a happy formula in the long run.' I added rather didactically.

In fact, the Prince's finances were always something of a nightmare. In 1743, just two years before the Forty Five when the Stuarts in exile in Rome were largely being financed by the Pope, Prince Charles Edward managed to spend over 30,000 *livres* – an enormous sum – on personal expenses in the course of a year when his father was recorded as only spending 4,000 *livres* and his brother – Prince Henry – only 8,000. Horses, clothes, hospitality and sporting weapons were probably his main extravagances at that time. In the months before he sailed for Scotland, the Prince ran up big debts in Paris including to landlords, tradesmen and retainers.

During the Forty Five, the Prince borrowed money from anyone who would lend to him – notably from Lord Elcho. But in the months after Culloden, when his financial resources like his other supplies were always on a hand-to-mouth basis, he paid for everything he consumed wherever he could. It can be argued that the period of his flight was financially, as in other respects, his most honourable hour. After his return to France his finances, like other aspects of his personal affairs, went from bad to worse: debts accumulated and creditors got forgotten or ignored. No, the Prince's financial standards were not ones I wanted to enlarge upon to Alasdair as an example of heroics.

One has constant reminders along the twelve miles of Loch Arkaig that, depopulated as they may be, the highlands are nonetheless a major holiday attraction: every mile or so there is a clearing among the rocks and heather between the road and the loch just large enough for a caravan or a pair of tents. The waters of the loch, clear and clean, lap these small sandy bays. This is Scotland as the tourist brochures depict it.

But when the head of Loch Arkaig is reached, a sterner world opens up. At first we were on a gentle enough stoney track through forestry, with the river Pean glistening far below us. But when the conifers ended, so did the track. No vehicle can venture further, except just possibly a tracked 'weasle' or 'snow-cat' to extricate the carcass of a stag. We were now entering the upper part of Glen Pean, that 'cruellest road that cou'd be seen' – according to Colonel O'Sullivan – where even poor Burke got himself 'all nastied' in the treacherous boggy mosses and reeds.

Near to where the forestry ends there is a derelict bothy standing above a point on the river where stepping stones enable the traveller to cross dry-shod. We were approaching the bothy when we were stopped dead in our tracks. Something was growling at us from the heather; another step, and the growling gave way to barking; one step more, and we could see the guardian of the bothy – a diminutive wire-haired terrier. Alerted to our approach, a young woman emerged from the bothy in jeans and anorak, clutching cooking utensils and a rolled-up sleeping bag. She had slept there apparently alone, protected from the ghosts of the glen by her ferocious terrier.

We asked her about the route through the glen to Loch Morar and the sea – the route which she had taken from the opposite direction the previous day. How long was the walk? What was the going like? She smiled weakly. She wished she could tell us, but the rain had been so terrible, the visibility so bad, her feet so sore, her pack so heavy, that the whole experience was one long saga of weariness with no external check-points of time or geographical reference points.

'You see, it was horizontal', she said. 'The rain, I mean', she added as we looked blank. 'Not the path. Oh certainly not the path, that couldn't have been less horizontal. It seems silly', she went on, 'not to be able to describe the way to Loch Morar, but the fact is the whole thing has rather blurred already. I had to carry Humphrey, you see.'

We looked with concern towards the doorless opening to the bothy, expecting a pallid male companion to emerge in a weakened state of post-exhaustion. Could we do anything to help, I asked.

'Oh no, thank you, really. Humphrey's *much* better now, aren't you Humphrey?' She looked affectionately down at the glowering terrier. It was still giving occasional growls as we pursued our way up the glen, through the tufts of rough grass and along the river bank. We were to meet no other humans, or dogs, all day.

The going got considerably boggier the nearer we came to Lochan Leum an t-Sagairt, the next feature on the ordnance map. There were steep cliffs above us to the south and some smaller – twenty or thirty foot – crags to the north. As we picked our path – only occasionally going over the tops of our ankle-high walking boots – beneath the crags, we became conscious of a very putrid smell. Could it be the torpid water of the bog? My unspoken question was answered all too abruptly: breasting a slight crest of rocks, I almost fell over the corpse of a large stag. The hooded crows had done their worst: it was a horrid sight of flesh, innards, bone and hairy skin. Only the antlers – ten point I noted idly – retained the dignity of this former monarch of the glen. The rest was a charnal house.

Alasdair had come up behind me.

'I *was* feeling ravenous', he said. 'Now I think I'll forget about venison for the rest of the trip. In fact, I'm not sure I'll be able to face our beef sandwiches. Poor thing. What do you think happened to it? Old age?'

I looked up at the crags above us.

'More likely something frightened it up there and it jumped. Let's hope it broke its neck and it was all over quickly.' The thought of a proud stag lying crippled and dying as the hoodies hovered and pecked at its eyes was not a pretty one.

We pressed on to the little loch with the long and difficult name, while I found that line from Tennyson about 'nature, red in tooth and claw' ringing in my mind. When we got there, the green banks above the still waters looked inviting to rest, and the climbing of the last hour since the bothy had left us both hungry, despite our recent encounter with the odours of rotting meat. We devoured the beef sandwiches gratefully and there was no more talk of vegetarianism.

After the lochan, the slender river Pean was ever narrower and climbed more steeply. Soon we would reach the watershed; no longer would the streams run towards Loch Arkaig and its interlocking waterways with Loch Ness and the North Sea; they would run west to Loch Morar, and beyond that the Sound of Sleat and the Atlantic Ocean. But not yet.

Above us now loomed a strange configuration of rocks – a gateway to the west. We clambered up, around and through them, oblivious until later of the fact that a reasonable sheep track (though no sheep) ran along the hillside to our left. It was worth having taken the rough way, because we emerged directly on to the tiny and nameless loch that lay at the very watershed. Hemmed in by rocks and surrounded by gnarled deciduous trees (no vulgar conifers here), its waters lay green, rushy and murky. This was a haunt of hobgoblins or other sinister spirits: some Spenserian monster or enchantress – Duessa herself – might at any moment emerge from the caves and crannies around us to bathe her slimey figure in the motionless crème-de-menthe liquid of this mountain pool.

It was not a place to linger. Without a backward look over our shoulders we climbed up out of the crater-like cavity to the ridge westward and to our front. A glad sight met our eyes. Less than two miles ahead of us and clearly visible down the valley lay the deep

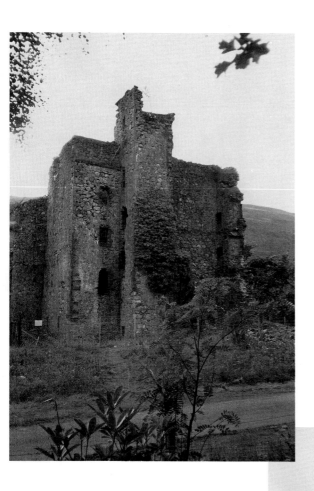

Invergarry Castle where Ned Burke
caught a salmon for the Prince's
supper, and the Caledonian canal
which passes close by linking the
lochs across Scotland.

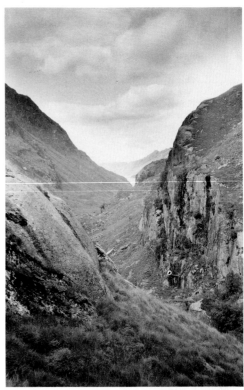

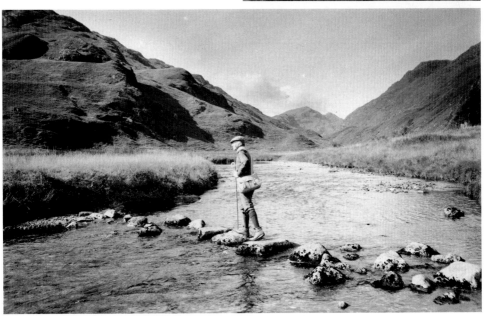

The author crossing the River Pean at the entrance to the glen and (above) the view from the head of Glen Pean down to Loch Morar in the distance.

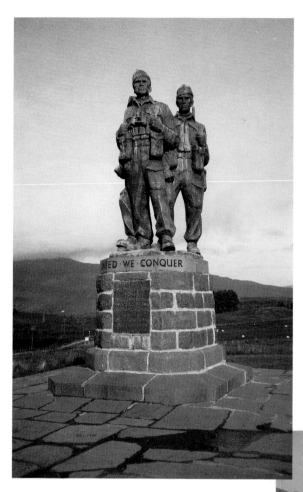

The Commando Monument close to Achnacarry in the heart of the mountainous region where they trained during the Second World War.

Fishing tackle at the harbour side on the Isle of Scalpay where the prince sheltered on his way to Stornoway.

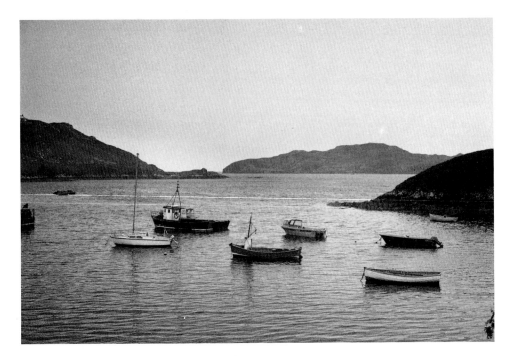

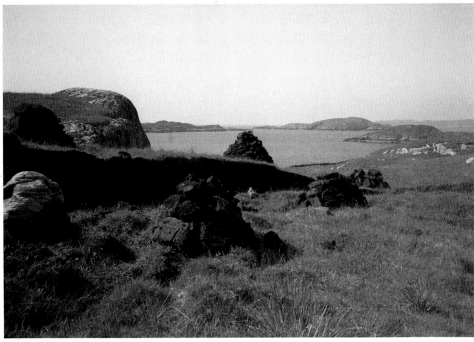

The island of Iubhard where the Prince had a comfortless stay off the coast of Lewes. Peat cutting (below) is still one of the main occupations on Lewes and Harris.

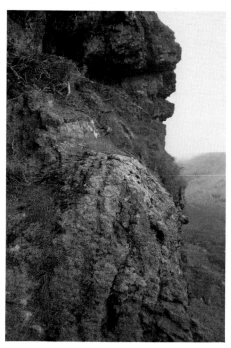

The eagle's nest above Corodale, and the author walking out of the glen where the Prince had spent three relaxed weeks shooting and drinking.

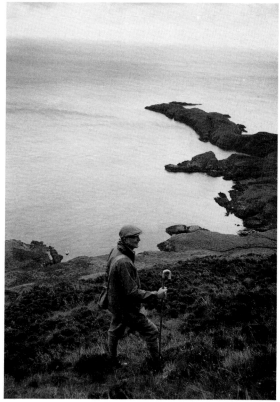

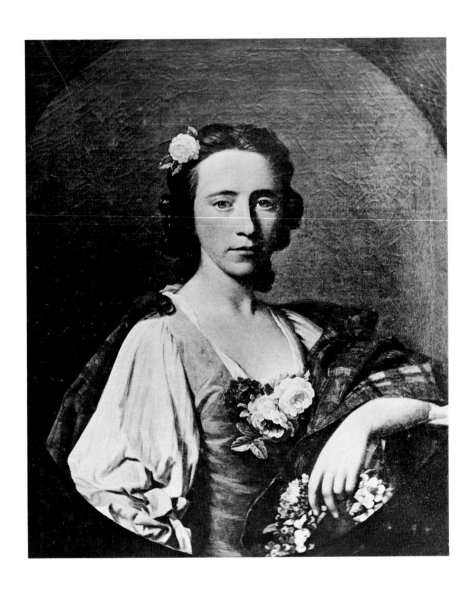

Flora Macdonald as painted by Allan Ramsay shortly after the Forty Five.

blue, healthy-looking waters of Loch Morar. A discernible path followed the glen. It was downhill all the way to our immediate destination. The crotchety Colonel O'Sullivan himself could scarcely have been more delighted at the prospect.

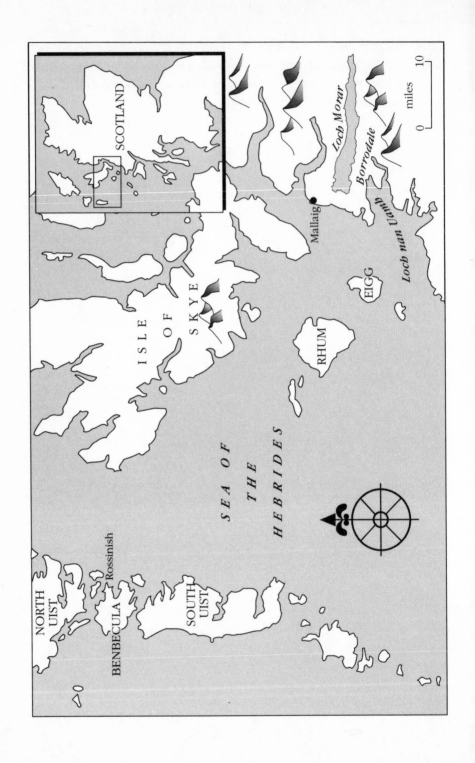

4

THE VOYAGE TO THE ISLES

T HE eight hours which followed Prince Charles Edward's embarkation from Loch nan Uamh were the most dangerous of his whole flight: there were many moments when he was nearer to capture – which would almost certainly have led to eventual death – but there were none when he was nearer to instant death. Romantic legend and song have immortalized his later voyage from the Hebrides to Skye with Flora Macdonald, but the toughest sea passage he had was that to the island of Benbecula on the night of 26/27 April.

It is immensely well documented. Of the Prince's five companions – O'Sullivan, O'Neil, Allan Macdonald, Donald Macleod and a Roman priest – four wrote or dictated accounts of the night's adventure; and one of the eight boatmen added his version. A fairly consistent picture emerges, although several of the narrators take pains to present themselves in the best light: for instance, Macleod stresses that he warned the Prince of the dangers of an impending storm; and O'Sullivan stresses how the Prince confided in him and 'whispered to him' at the moments of greatest tension. Only O'Neil parts company with the other narrators on an important point: he claims that the boat struck a rock on coming to land and was 'staved to pieces', while the other accounts make it clear that the boat remained intact. (As with the case of the Prince's horse at Culloden, eye-witnesses sometimes saw things very differently, particularly O'Neil who was inclined to over dramatize.)

The events were alarming enough with no embellishment. The

boat was not even out of Loch nan Uamh when 'a terrible cloud appeared' and prompted O'Sullivan to ask Macleod (who was the helmsman) whether they should turn back, but Macleod said it was not possible: it would be safer to go into the open sea beyond the loch and rely on the fact that 'the boat is a good one and we have good hands'. About half an hour later, the cloud broke and 'a most terrible storm arose which coming all at once was like to overturn us'. The open boat rapidly filled up with water. At this stage, O'Sullivan says 'every body was for makeing the first land', but Macleod pointed out that the only land within reach was the Isle of Skye (to the north of them) and that English men-o'-war were standing off the shore. The Prince replied (according to Macleod): 'I had rather face cannons and muskets than be in such a storm as this'. But Macleod was adamant that if they tried to land on the rocky shore the boat would break up and 'there was no possibility of saving any one life amongst them'. He told the passengers that the storm was only a squawl, but O'Sullivan recorded that in fact

'the wind continued and rather augmented, the sea become mountains, the weaves coming in every moment, all hands were at work to throw out the watter, there was not a soul in the boat but what were as wet as if they were dipt in the sea, we went like the wind, & just before it happyly, for the least side-wind wou'd overturn us'.

While all this drama was going on, the Prince remained calm and cheerful. He stood, holding on to a cross-plank for dear life, encouraging the sailors and the bailers. On one occasion a particularly savage wave knocked him off his feet flat against the far side of the boat, and when O'Sullivan and O'Neil rushed forward to pick him up they too were swept off their feet and thrown 'all three upon one another . . . waves covered the boat, & made it crack, so that all the sailors thought it was lost'. Macleod, despite his lifetime of sea-going (he was 68 at the time) was said to be trembling like a leaf. But the Prince, as soon as he had picked himself up, cried out 'there is no hurt' and set about urging the sailors to their oars, the chaplain to his prayers, and O'Sullivan to the task of encouraging and steadying

Macleod at the helm. So they continued through the night with 'neither pump nor compass nor lantern with them' and with the darkness so intense that they lost all certainty of direction.

When daylight came it was not much better, in fact 'the seas seem'd more frightfull' and although there was land on the horizon the pilot was not sure what land it was. Eventually Macleod recognized his whereabouts: he was approaching North Uist in the Hebrides and made for the channel between that island and Benbecula, but 'the nearer we came to land, the higher and more terrible the weaves are'. The coastline was strewn with little islands and rocks and the following wind was forcing the boat on to them. Macleod decided to lower the sail but the sheets were so wet that they jammed in the cleets and it seemed that the boat would be hurled at full speed on to the rocks. Everybody got forward into the bows and prepared to throw themselves out when the boat struck, but – at the very last moment – 'as if God set his hand to it, one man touched the seal (sail) and it fell in a minuit, when three or four men could not get it down a moment before'. The helmsman turned the rudder, avoided the rocks and brought the boat in under shelter of land at a point called Rossinish on Benbecula. They had survived.

It was hardly a joyous landfall. The wind was still so strong that they could scarcely stand on the shore and 'had all the peinnes (pains) in the world to get to a house that was not three musquet shots from us'. It was not much of a house, being in fact a shieling which Clanranald's shepherds used only in summer, and which was deserted and stripped of all furnishings. However, 'wet from head to foot, & black with cold' as they were, it was good to be ashore and to have any cover at all. Macleod and the sailors declared that in twenty-five years of sea-going in these parts they had never known such a night or felt in such grave danger. According to O'Sullivan, everyone was talking at once – Prince and sailors alike – and all felt the companionship of having lived through a notable ordeal. Even while they were congratulating themselves on their survival, they saw a ship driven past by the gale at a tremendous speed, despite having its top-mast broken and no sail up at all.

At last the practical Macleod called them to order: 'Come, come', (O'Sullivan records him saying) 'you'll have time enough to talke of that, let us get a fire made yu see the condition young Sinclair is in'. (Sinclair was the name by which they had agreed to call the Prince.) Fortunately they had some provisions which had remained dry in a chest on the boat: a little leather bag of meal, butter and cheese. A fire was made and an old iron pot 'with a holle as large as half a crown in it' was unearthed from the kitchen of the shieling, repaired with a bung of dirty rag, and put on the fire with half a sheep to stew. When the mutton was finished and everyone was still hungry, the Prince told his companions to shoot a cow – which he would pay for. This they did and 'all were happy'. The Prince lay down to sleep on a bedding roll made of the ship's sail.

All must have been relieved as well as happy, but none more so than Donald Macleod, the pilot, who had had his fifteen-year-old son Murdoch on board as one of the oarsmen. Murdoch Macleod had already shown himself to be one of nature's survivors, and his story – typical of many in the Forty Five – warrants a short digression.

When the Forty Five rebellion started, Murdoch had been a schoolboy at Inverness Grammar School. He immediately set about equipping himself to join the fray, and having bought a broadsword, dirk and pistol 'he ran off from school, and took his chance on the field of Culloden battle'. After the defeat he set about tracing out the route the Prince had taken, making enquiries among those who had helped the Prince on his way and following the same trail himself. So it was that he arrived at Borrodale on the shore of Loch nan Uamh shortly after the Prince met up with his father. 'And this was the way', Donald Macleod recounted later to Bishop Forbes, 'I met wi' my poor boy'.

Having fed, rested and dried their clothes by the fire for a day, the Prince decided that he would have to try to establish some contact with the nearest Jacobites. The local laird was Macdonald of Clanranald and one of the party – probably Allan Macdonald who was a relative of Clanranald's – was sent to his house a few miles away. He met Clanranald's second son who had been with the Prince's army but – like many another – had returned to his homestead when the Jacobite army retreated to Scotland, and had therefore been absent (without leave?) from the battle field of Culloden. Young Clanranald nonetheless came to pay his respects to the Prince as soon as he heard that the latter had been washed up, as it were, on his door-step. He came back again the next day bringing some welcome supplies – biscuits, and more meal and butter – but did not suggest that the Prince's party moved into the family house, possibly for reasons of the Prince's safety rather than Clanranald's. Macdonald of Clanranald came himself the following day to visit the Prince at the shieling and 'to kisse the Prince's hand but in privat'. His wife, Lady Clanranald, was to perform more practical services at a later stage in the Prince's travels.

The party had now been three days at the spot where they made their landfall and were anxious to move on. The Prince had decided on a plan: he would go on by sea to Stornoway on the island of Lewis and from there he would hire a small ship to take him on to the Orkneys and thence to Norway; he would then 'make the best of his way to France, to see if he co'd engage the King of France to send troops with him to Scotland'. The first step was to work his way up the Hebrides to Stornoway in the boat which had brought him this far. And that boat, far from being 'staved to pieces' (as the over-dramatizing O'Neil had claimed) was in good shape to take them on their way. On 29 April they set sail in her again. Troubles in plenty lay ahead, but no maritime hazards as severe as they had encountered between the mainland and Benbecula on that memorable night.

* * *

As Alasdair and I trudged down the swampy length of Glen Beasdale, at the end of our journey through Glen Pean and the Braes of Morar, we speculated about how we might find a boat to take us to the Outer Hebrides. The Caledonian MacBrayne steamers did not help: some sailed from nearby Mallaig to Skye and the Inner Hebrides, while others sailed from more distant ports such as Oban to the Outer Hebrides. We were going to need to persuade someone to take us on a special voyage.

The most promising place to charter a boat or hitch a maritime lift was undoubtedly Mallaig, and after a recuperative night at Arisaig we set out in the Discovery up the winding road along the broken coastline of the peninsula heading towards Morar and Mallaig – where the road ends in the sea. Our eyes had been continually attracted westwards, to the plethora of rocks and tiny islands off-shore; but when we turned inland just before reaching the village of Morar, it was to the east that our attention was diverted. We had a glimpse up the length of Loch Morar, stretching between the high hills we had penetrated the previous day, and in the foreground – green and inviting – clustered a group of gentler wooded islets. One of these had a close connection with the same Lord Lovat with whom the Prince had supped on the night of the Battle of Culloden, and from whom he had received the somewhat smug advice about remembering Robert the Bruce. We stopped the car, found someone prepared to hire us a rowing boat, and set off for the half-mile pull across to Eilean Ban – the nearest of the group of islands. As we rowed, I told Alasdair the story which was the reason for our detour: it concerned that old ruffian Lord Lovat, whose adventures after his meeting with the Prince had been every bit as extraordinary as his earlier lurid career.

Lord Lovat's eventual commitment to the Forty Five meant that after Culloden he was a marked man. That being so, it had not taken long before Cumberland's dragoons had arrived at Castle Dounie and, not finding Lovat at home, had set it on fire in the same way that they were burning the homesteads of all those highlanders who had – or even might have – supported the rebel cause. Lord Lovat was not only not at home, he had – once again – gone into hiding in the manner to which his earlier career had accustomed him. Indeed, he had taken the precaution some time before of preparing a secret retreat on an island in the middle of Loch Morar. It had been no easy matter to get the lame and over-weight chief to his hide-out. On one occasion he had had to disguise himself as an old spinning woman when English grenadiers were searching crofters' houses in the Fraser country. Subsequently he had been carried in a litter, by stout-hearted and strong-armed clansmen, over the same route which I – with so much scrambling and difficulty – had just taken from Loch Arkaig through Glen Pean to the shores of Loch Morar.

Once installed at his island retreat, Lord Lovat thought he was safe. But he had reckoned without a party of sailors from one of the

English warships patrolling the sea lanes between the Western Isles and the Scottish mainland in their search for Prince Charles Edward. These sailors had come ashore on the narrow strip of land between the sea and Loch Morar; seeing the wooded islands on the loch they had decided to commandeer a small boat and explore them – whether to look for Jacobite fugitives or for some more innocent recreation is not clear. As soon as Lord Lovat saw the boat heading for his island, he hid in his pre-arranged ultimate hiding place, taking into hiding with himself his travelling treasure chest containing six thousand guineas.

When the sailors started their exploration of the little island, one of them became intrigued by a large and ancient tree. On close examination, it turned out to be hollow and to harbour in its interior a fat, ugly old man sitting on a brass-bound chest. Lord Lovat, protesting volubly, was extracted.

Then began another long series of rides in a litter, handled no doubt with rather less consideration than when borne by his own clansmen, to Fort William, thirty miles to the south-east. Once there, though held in close arrest, the old fox started intriguing in the manner to which he was wont. He remembered that, not only was one of his own sons a godson of George I, but he himself had known the Duke of Cumberland when the latter was a child. He therefore wrote to the Duke a typically devious letter from Fort William, full of sentimental recollections of 'carrying your Royal Highness in my arms in the parks of Kensington and Hampton Court' and of veiled offers to turn King's evidence and 'demonstrate to you that I can do more service to the King and the Government'. Lovat was up to his old time-serving tricks again.

But this time it was of no avail: he had swapped sides once too often. He was taken by a slow series of horse-drawn litters and coaches to London where he stood trial for high treason. Continually calling for the return of his chest of gold coins, regularly insulting and provoking his judges, grumbling about the discomforts of his captivity, he made a recalcitrant prisoner to the end. Even on the way to the inevitable scaffold he exchanged insults with onlookers. His malice never deserted him: when a part of the spectators' stand surrounding the scaffold collapsed, injuring bystanders he muttered 'the more mischief the better sport'. He showed no sign of fear as he knelt at the block and became the last man to be publicly beheaded in England. The Old Pretender granted him the title of Duke of Fraser. Unprincipled he may have been; cowardly he was not.

Indeed valour – particularly of the martial variety – has always been a trait of the Fraser chiefs. The 16th Lord Lovat – another Simon Fraser – was to raise and lead into action in the Boer War the Lovat Scouts, winning among other distinctions the D.S.O. and becoming a Knight of the Thistle. His son – the 17th Lord Lovat – was a brilliant commando leader in the Second World War and also won the D.S.O. among numerous other gallantry awards; he was described by Winston Churchill as 'the gentlest man that ever slit a throat'. The tradition continues.

When Alasdair had exhausted himself looking for hollow trees on the island, and I had decided that the prospect of finding any stray gold coins from Lord Lovat's chest hardly justified prolonging our diversion from the Prince's route, we returned as we had come to the mainland and completed the drive to Mallaig. Here we dined in an agreeable hostelry overlooking the harbour. Although, despite the rowing, the day had been an easier one than the two previous ones spent walking through Glen Pean and its surrounding hills, I none-theless felt weary and glad to be offered a glass of Drambuie after dinner from the famous bottle with the slogan 'A link with the '45'.

Alasdair asked if he could try it too, He made the mistake of adding that he had read of Prince Charles Edward enjoying carous-ing with the officers at the siege of Gaeta 'and when he was there he was only fourteen – one year older than me – so why can't I at least try it?'

Some biographers of the Prince have dated his addiction to alcohol from that very period, or at least from before the Forty Five. It is true that he was reprimanded by his father for giving too much time to 'wine and games' (cards) on the Gaeta campaign, and there were more serious complaints of his drinking during the months he spent in Paris in 1744 and early 1745. In particular, MacDonnell of Glen-garry – a profligate companion – seems to have led him into some wild parties in the *ginguettes* around Montmartre when he was living there shortly before securing his passage to Scotland. But these appear to have been no more than youthful frolics, despite the heavy emphasis placed on them by some of his detractors.*

There are also reports of the Prince drinking heavily during the early part of the campaign in Scotland and on the retreat from Derby. But on examination most of these seem to stem from Lord Elcho's comments long after the events and following his quarrels with the Prince about money matters. The first real dependence on alcohol emerges – as we see in the tale of his adventures – as a warming comfort and stimulant after the cold and fatigue of his highland flight.

After the Forty Five it was another matter altogether. The casual carousing and semi-medicinal nips give way to increasingly damaging drunkenness: his personal relations suffered and so did his health. Louis XV was to be unamused by Prince Charles Edward's tipsy disparagements of Madame de Pompadour; the Cardinal York – as his brother Henry became – was deeply shocked by having an inveterate toper as his closest living relation; Clementia Walkinshaw – the Prince's mistress – and later Princess Louise of Stolberg-Gedern – his wife – were to experience the strain of living with one who was habitually drunk, especially at times of family quarrels. Finally and inevitably the bottle got the better of him.

But this was all far ahead. The boy who quaffed wine with the Spanish officers in the camp outside Gaeta showed no special weakness for the grape and was to be said – when he came to manhood – to have a strong head for spirits.

'I don't think you'd like it', I said feebly, pushing the Drambuie bottle away from Alasdair.

Of all the small fishing ports we were to visit in the western highlands, Mallaig gives the impression of being the most serious and busiest. Indeed, twenty years ago it was the largest herring port in Europe; then over-fishing set in and now it is on a strict quota. But there is still an air of bustle and activity: rusty little fishing boats spew their haul of white fish and shell-fish all over the untidy quay while trucks and barrows jostle their way between quay-side and

---

* Susan Maclean Kybett's *Bonnie Prince Charlie* (see bibliography) makes much of the Prince's early tendency to alcoholism.

rail-head. The kippers we were given with our breakfast the following morning were the fattest and freshest we encountered anywhere.

Finding a boat that could take us across the Sea of the Hebrides to
Benbecula or North Uist might not have been easy had we not had
an introduction to a fisherman who regularly sailed from Mallaig
round the west coast of Skye and into the Minch. The nearest point
to Rossinish (where the Prince had landed) that the boat could put us
ashore was Lochmaddy, a few miles further north on North Uist. We
welcomed this as we had arranged to hire a car there and could
therefore quickly get to Rossinish and start the serious part of our
Hebridean journey. What we had not reckoned on was that nature
would attempt to reproduce for us the weather that had characterized the Prince's crossing. As Alasdair and I sailed between the
spectacularly beautiful coastlines of southern Skye and the islands of
Eigg, Rhum and Canna, we saw little except the heaving waterline
over the rail of the boat, and the return to the sea of our breakfast
kippers.

5

THE STORNOWAY DEBACLE

O N 29 April the weather seemed calmer and the Prince's party was encouraged to embark at nightfall for the first stage of the voyage to Stornoway.

The embarkation at dusk and the night sailing were evidence of the hazards of being spotted in these waters in daylight. Indeed it was soon to become apparent that the sea-lochs and channels around and between the Hebrides were infested with Government shipping. The hunt was on, and the English were shrewd enough to realise that Prince Charles Edward was likely to be island-hopping in his quest for a French ship to carry him to safety. The islands themselves provided less cover than the mainland; once the Prince's presence was suspected on any island, it could be flooded with Government troops − combing the heather − while escape from one island to another was a good deal harder than moving across country on the mainland. All in all, it was to prove a mistake to have taken the road to the Isles.

But for the moment, one step at a time was enough. At dawn on 30 April, the Prince and his party landed at Scalpay, a small island off the east coast of Harris. A tenant of the Macleods, one Donald Campbell, took them in to his farmhouse. There was no special reason for a Campbell such as he, who was reported to be 'strictly loyal and well attached to the reigning family'* to offer shelter to the Prince; yet once having done so, he resolutely resisted suggestions

---

* Buchanan's *Travels in the Western Hebrides* (1793).

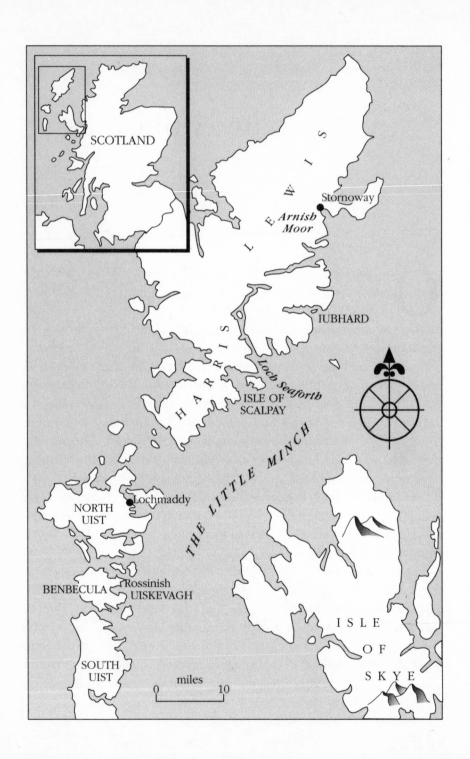

from a burly local resident who came over to Scalpay with a boat-load of armed men on the chance of finding the Prince and collecting the £30,000 award (which was the price the Government had now placed on the Prince's head) that they should capitalise on their windfall asset. The Campbells might be on the other side for their own good reasons, but – Donald declared roundly – they were not in the business of collecting blood-money once they had offered hospi-tality. The burly visitor was sent packing; but the news of the Prince's whereabouts was leaking fast.

The Prince for his part managed to make some small repayment to Donald Campbell, in his own characteristic way. One evening he was strolling along the shore near to where he had landed when he spied one of Campbell's cows stuck fast in a bog. Alone and unas-sisted he rescued the animal which (according to a report subse-quently given by Campbell's great-granddaughter) 'was afterwards sold for £2.10s., then an unheard of price in Harris'.

In all, the Prince passed four nights in Donald Campbell's farm-house, but all this while he was trying to arrange to get a boat at Stornoway. On 1 May, the Prince despatched Donald Macleod to hire a boat 'under pretence of sailing to the Orkneys to take in meal for the Isle of Sky, as Donald used to deal in that way formerly'.* Donald Macleod did not take the eight-oared vessel which he had produced on the mainland and in which the Prince had come to the Hebrides; but he managed to borrow an even smaller craft from Donald Campbell for the short voyage to Stornoway.

By 4 May he had sent a message back to the Prince on Scalpay to say that his mission was successfully completed: a ship was char-tered. The Prince immediately set out by boat to the head of Loch Seaforth and thereafter on foot with O'Sullivan, O'Neil and Burke. He was probably glad enough to get away from Scalpay. Despite the fact that the party were pretending to be shipwrecked merchants, and the Prince was pretending to be O'Sullivan's son – both named Sinclair, his cover was wearing very thin. There had been the awk-ward incident of the unfriendly callers, and even Donald Campbell's son – with whom the Prince went fishing but who had not been let in

* From Donald Macleod's own journal.

on the secret – was beginning to get suspicious that his father's guests were not what they were made out to be; he had asked 'young Mr Sinclair' some innocent questions about the capacity of the ship in which they were alleged to have been wrecked, and had got some very odd and unconvincing answers from the unnautical Prince.

But all was not well with the Stornoway scheme. In the first place the guide did not know the terrain between the head of Loch Seaforth and the port of Stornoway as well as he claimed. He missed the path and took the Prince and his small party blundering through ever deeper swamps and peat hags: in all they reckoned they covered 'no less thirty-eight long Highland miles' most of it in drenching rain and at night. The Prince was ill-attired for such exertions: his breeches and old riding coat had started 'as stiff as buckram from salt water' and soon were sodden from fresh water. He had 'not a shoe to his feet, all tore to pieces, they held only with coards that they tyed up with, his toes all quite stript'. O'Sullivan – whose distaste for Scottish weather and terrain emerges ever more clearly from his narrative – declared it to be 'the wildest country in the universe . . . not the least marque of road or path.' Eventually they reached the shelter of a croft on the outskirts of Stornoway.

The Prince sent a message ahead to Macleod in Stornoway to let him know that he had arrived and was ready to embark. It then transpired that the position in Stornoway was rather different from that which the Prince had been led to expect. Macleod (according to O'Sullivan and O'Neil – neither of whom seemed to care for him) had been drinking fairly heavily in Stornoway while trying to pro-cure a ship to sail to the Orkneys and Norway. It seems that the drink may have loosened his tongue more than was prudent, and the gossip soon spread that it was for the Prince that the ship was required, and that he was in the immediate vicinity with (some said) five hundred men at arms. An offer to buy a ship outright for £500 only increased the suspicions concerning for whom it was required. The promise of a ship was withdrawn and some panic spread through the little port.

In default of good news, Macleod sent provisions to the Prince, including brandy – the first time it occurs in the narrative – and saw him lodged reasonably comfortably with a Mrs Mackenzie of Kildun, who provided a good fire, warm milk, clean straw and blankets – all much needed. But matters were getting even worse in Stornoway. The Mackenzie clan as a whole who dominated the tiny community were determined that the Prince should move on – 'to anywhere he should think convenient' – before they were implicated as accomplices and risked losing their cattle or their lives. Unlike the stout-hearted lady of Kildun, the clan elders did not want to meet or succour a hunted Prince. Not even guides or pilots could be provided. The Minister of the church spread the alarm. There was even talk of raising 150 men to resist the Prince's entry to the port.

In the face of such united resistance, Prince Charles Edward decided to abandon his hopes of obtaining a ship and sailing to Norway. His hostess at Kildun – staunch to the end – slaughtered a cow she could ill afford to provide the Prince and his companions with a solid meal before they beat a retreat. Two of the boatmen who had rowed the Prince from the mainland 'ran away and left' at this point and even his indefatigable servant Ned Burke temporarily lost his nerve and suggested that they scattered and 'took to the mountains'. The Prince alone remained unrattled by the set-back; he chided Burke good-humouredly saying (according to the latter's own account):

'How long is it Ned since you turned cowardly? I shall be sure of (killing) the best of them ere taken, which I hope shall never be in my life'.

Then he turned his attention – characteristically again – to insisting that his hostess allowed him to pay in full the value of the cow she had slaughtered for his provisions: 'For', as Donald Macleod later commented, 'as long as there was any money among us . . . the deel a man or woman should have it to say that the Prince ate their meat for nought'.

It was one of the bleakest moments of the whole escape – the dashing of hopes, a cold repulse where he had looked for help, desertion where he had not expected it – yet Prince Charles Edward never wavered in his resolution and bearing towards those around him.

The Prince, who was already becoming disillusioned about the islands, wanted to sail across the Minch back to the mainland of Scotland. But the only boat they had at their disposal was the small one which Donald Campbell of Scalpay had provided, and the six remaining boatmen adamantly refused to risk their lives in it on the open sea where they reckoned that the least gale would overturn them. So there was nothing for it but to return to Scalpay. This time they did not make the overland march to the head of Loch Seaforth but attempted to sail direct down the east coast of Lewis.

They did not get far. Two men-of-war were sailing northwards up the Minch and the Prince's boat put back to shore to avoid being observed, making a landfall on the uninhabited island of Euirn (now called Iubhard) – about halfway between Stornoway and Scalpay. The Prince and his companions climbed up to a vantage point and had a good look: some thought the ships were English, some French. The Prince – always an optimist – was convinced they were the latter, and he proposed to the boatmen that they should sail out towards them, pretending to be fishermen, to get a better look. If they were in fact French, the boatmen should signal to them, get picked up and reveal that the Prince was awaiting rescue on the nearby island. But the boatmen – despite offers of money and rewards from the Prince – refused. Maybe they were nervous of being picked up and roughly questioned by an English ship. Or maybe they feared the rougher water in the mid-channel. They were in any case somewhat disaffected since the Prince had earlier tried to persuade Macleod to steer a course for the mainland, and not – after all – south to Scalpay, against their wishes, and the boatmen had only realised his intentions as they got further and further out into the Minch. Indeed they had been protesting to Macleod and the Prince about this trickery at the moment when the unknown men-of-war had been sighted. Their morale had been low since two of their number had deserted. So – for one reason or another – they dug their toes in and refused to execute the requested reconnaissance.

This was unfortunate indeed, since the unidentified ships were almost certainly the French frigates which had recently landed some gold to support the Prince's cause and which had picked up Sheridan and other Jacobites to take them safely back to France. Had the

Prince been picked up at this juncture, almost four months of hardship, danger and suffering would have been avoided. It is also more than likely that the Prince's addiction to brandy, which was to become more and more his support and comfort in the arduous months ahead, might not have developed; and had it not developed then the whole subsequent descent into alcoholism, which was to blight his later life in exile, might have been avoided. But equally it is true that had his epic journey in the heather ended a mere three weeks after Culloden much of the legend of Bonnie Prince Charlie would have been lost: the encounter with Flora Macdonald, the days disguised as a servant girl, the sojourn with the outlawed Glenmoriston men in their cave, the nights in Cluny's cage . . . all this lay ahead. Nonetheless, had Prince Charles Edward known on 6 May how close he was to rescue it would have been a bitter thought to bear.

As it was, as soon as the two ships were out of sight the Prince's party re-embarked and continued the voyage back to Scalpay. At five o'clock in the afternoon two other ships appeared in view and once more the boat sought the cover of the coast, further round the island of Euirn. There they found a fisherman's hut, which they had to break into for shelter, and they all set about cutting heather for bedding; later they also found a stack of fish lying on the shore. The Prince (according to Donald Macleod) took charge of the commissary. When Ned Burke became rather squeamish about using the remains of the butter that their hostess at Kildum had given to him, because it 'made a very ugly appearance' being all mixed up with bread in a dirty looking mess, the Prince adopted a more robust line:

'What', said the Prince, 'was not the butter clean when it was put there?' 'Yes', answered Ned, 'it was clean enough.' 'Then', replied the Prince, 'you are a child Ned. The butter will do exceeding well. The bread can never file (defile) it. Go fetch it immediately'.

(Donald Macleod, whose report of the conversation is the one quoted, went on to confess that he personally could not face the butter either as it was so filthy.) On another occasion at the same place the Prince concocted 'a cakey of his own contriving' of cows' brains and dough.

But however much the Prince might direct and help with the menial tasks of the camp, he still kept a certain distance between himself and his companions on the one hand, and the boatmen on the other. Donald Macleod, who more than anyone in the party bridged this social gap, was later to be horrified at the suggestion that the hired boatmen sat down to meals with the Prince's party:

'Na, good faith, they! . . . set them up wi' that indeed, the fallows! to eat wi the Prince and the shentlemen! We even kept up the port of the Prince upon the desert island itself and kept twa tables, one for the Prince and the shentlemen, and the other fir the boatmen.'

Be that as it may, Donald Macleod, Ned Burke and others had plenty of opportunity of observing and listening to the Prince at very close quarters and in uniquely informal circumstances. And they missed no occasion to memorise and later record what he said and did. Thus on Euirn Macleod recalled that he would drink to the toast of 'the Black Eye' which Macleod and others assumed to be a reference to the King of France's second daughter to whom the Prince referred explicitly on other occasions and for whom he was assumed to have a tender sentiment.

Political conversations also took place. The Prince spoke affectionately of King Louis XV of France and affirmed his conviction that the French King had his cause much at heart, intending to do all in his power to help him. But even in his most sentimental moods the Prince recognised that the Jacobite cause needed more than the personal goodwill of Louis XV, and he would frequently declare:

'Gentlemen, I can assure you, a King and his Council are two very different things.'

However much improvised meals, sentimental toasts and serious conversation might help him to pass the time on Euirn, there was no denying it was a bleak sojourn. They had to lie on the bare ground when they found it necessary to use their heather bedding as fuel for the fire, and to rig the sail of the boat over the ramshackle hut to keep the rain out. After four days of this, they decided once more to brave the risks of interception by English shipping and press on to Scalpay, where the Prince was anxious to see again the hospitable Donald Campbell.

Before leaving Euirn there was another instance of the Prince's determination not to exploit hospitality, be it voluntary or involuntary. The party loaded two dozen fish – from the stack of dried cod they had found – on their boat as provisions for the next stage of their journey, and the Prince left a pile of coins in place of the fish to compensate the unknown owner when he should reappear. (The gesture was invalidated by those canny Irishmen O'Sullivan and O'Neil who convinced themselves that the money would fall into the hands of vagrants who might happen to land there, and so it should be 'taken up again'.)

On 10 May therefore they sailed on. But when they got to Scalpay there was no sign of Campbell: he had 'gone a skulking' – that is had taken to the heather himself, fearing that his earlier services to the Prince would catch up with him in the form of arrest. Without Campbell, Scalpay had few charms, and the Prince sailed on the same day (still using Campbell's boat) but soon once more ran into difficulties. This time it was a sinister ship off Finsbay on Harris, which they only spotted when she was a mere two musket-ball's range away, that chased them for some distance and was only thrown off when they got into shallow waters where the deep-draughted warship could not follow. The practical Ned Burke commented that oars were proving a lot more useful than firearms. Then another ship in Lochmaddy on North Uist forced them again to put on all speed with sail and oars to get quit of the loch.

Progress down the coast was proving nerve-racking, and hardly surprisingly. Had they known it, these waters were already being patrolled by H.M. Ships *Greyhound*, *Baltimore* and *Terror* and had been joined on 4 May by the sloop *Raven*. On 13 May this squadron was further reinforced by H.M.S. *Glasgow* and the sloops *Trial* and *Happy Janet*; on 17 May H.M.S. *Furnace* – under command of the dreaded Captain Ferguson – joined the chase. Never before or since can the Western Isles have been so scoured by Government warships.

On 11 May, having been harried out of Lochmaddy, they were still at sea and provisions – including the requisitioned cod – had run out. So the boatmen made a 'dramach cake' of meal and salt water which the Prince ate with the rest of them and with a good grace. Indeed this latest culinary effusion prompted Donald Macleod to comment that in the Prince's case:

> 'Never any meat or drink came wrong for him, for he could take a share of every thing, be it good, bad or indifferent, and was always cheerful and contented in every condition.'

Certainly it was true that the Prince was not squeamish about rough or unfamiliar food. But it is less true that nothing upset his digestion. Only a week later he was to succomb to a 'bloody flux' (which was probably a form of dysentery) and to blame this on drinking milk; thereafter he stayed off milk and increased his consumption of brandy whenever he could get it.

Later the same day they put in at Uiskevagh on the island of Benbecula. They were back almost where they had started their Hebridean adventures two weeks earlier, and in scarcely less discomfort, in a poor grasskeeper's bothy, the doorway to which was so low that the Prince's companions dug out a passage to let him crawl in more easily. This primitive hut was the best shelter they could find for three nights.

The first two weeks on the Hebrides had not been happy ones. Not only was he back where he started, but options appeared to be closing. Escape to the Orkneys and Norway seemed more remote than ever; going back over their tracks and reactivating shelters and safe-havens was an increasingly perilous process, both for the Prince's party and for their hosts (as Donald Campbell's rapid exodus had illustrated); the sea-lanes were becoming more dangerous all the time. Few would have thought that this cat and mouse game could be kept up for more than days or weeks longer.

* * *

Any land must have been a welcome sight after nearly drowning at sea, and no doubt Prince Charles Edward's first impressions of Rossinish were favourable. But when we reached this least hospitable corner of the Outer Hebrides we felt that its charms were severely limited from most points of view except ornithology. We had sailed direct from Mallaig as the Prince had done, and had crossed the Sea of the Hebrides in a boat only slightly bigger than the Prince had sailed in, in seas only slightly calmer, and with qualms and queasiness no less than those felt by the unhappy O'Sullivan. Like the Prince and his party, we wanted to pass on to Stornoway just as soon as possible, but we realised we must visit – as he had done – the island of Scalpay on the way north. We therefore crossed to North Uist and took the ferry from Lochmaddy to Tarbert on Harris (the southern part of the island of Lewis); from here it is only five miles to Scalpay – the island where the Prince had been sheltered by the hospitable Donald Campbell.

Landing at Tarbert was an altogether happier experience. We sailed into East Loch Tarbert in drifting mist, but with intriguing outlines of islands all around us. As we landed the sun came through and – as we had no chance of crossing over to Scalpay the same day – we decided to explore our surroundings on Harris.

The Harris region of the island of Lewis is best known – often *only* known – to the outside world on account of Harris tweed, a fairly loose-spun and hairy material which has been popular for a century for jackets (especially kilt jackets), overcoats and women's suits; and in recent times also for furnishing fabrics and even automobile upholstery. Though most frequently recalled in heather-mixture or herring-bone patterns, many more sophisticated designs are also manufactured today.

Harris tweed has the reputation of being the quintessential crofters' industry, and the Harris Tweed Association make much of the local, hand-woven and traditional aspects of the production process. Indeed one of the responsibilities of the association has been to ensure that no power motors of an unacceptable sort are attached to looms, and this has been a condition of making the material with the internationally-recognised Orb trade-mark. The weaving is spread among crofters throughout Lewis from the two main mills in Stornoway and from other mills on the mainland.

Much of the industry is now concentrated in Stornoway: carding and spinning are two of the processes which take place in the mills, and quality control also has been centralized for a product that sells world-wide and for which 'repeat orders' strive to be identical in pattern and texture. But the personal touch remains: the Hattersley Domestic Loom, which is the one generally to be found in the island crofts, is powered by a foot-treadle; the weaver has to tie in broken threads and set up tweeds which arrive already warped from the mill. Thus much hand – and foot* – work remains. Although he may be tied to a specific mill for his supplies and for his outlet, the weaver works in his own time on his own premises. Like fishing and crofting, the weaving of Harris tweed has contributed greatly to the independence of spirit of the Hebridean islanders.

Knowing this, and also being aware that the manufacture of some sort of tweed was a very long-standing occupation in these parts which had been going on during the period of Prince Charles Edward's visit, we set out in the course of an afternoon to visit half a dozen such crofts where the looms were humming. They were scattered around the tiny rocky lochans on the east side of south Harris, and among those we stopped at was one at Liceasto where even the Hattersley loom was rejected as being too mechanised.

Anne Campbell, who weaves the Clo Mor ('the big cloth') at Liceasto appeared to have an almost missionary zeal for her work. She explained to us – with a very highland mixture of dedication and quiet charm – how she and her partners had learned their traditional skills from a Marion Campbell of Plocracpool, and how the whole process from sheep to tweed followed its age-long rhythm. She told us that this starts when the shearing takes place in July.

'This is still a communal activity, when all the village sheep are gathered from the moorland graziers and sheared, using hand-clippers. Some of the wool we use comes from my father's flock of black-faced sheep and the rest we buy from our neighbours.'

She went on to explain that the wool is dyed in the fleece over a

* Judith Ennew in her book *The Western Isles Today* quotes many weavers as describing the process as 'like cycling up-hill all day long'.

peat fire in the open air. The dyes include ragwort flowers and heather, which gives yellow; indigo for blue; peat soot which gives a yellow brown; and crotal, a flat grey lichen which is scraped off the rocks and yields a rich red-brown after long boiling. The different colours are blended together during the carding process, and then handspun for the weft using a traditional spinning wheel.

Our minds began to reel somewhat at the thought of all this homespun activity. Anne perhaps interpreted our confusion as doubt about whether such old-fashioned methods were really any longer appropriate.

'Although it takes three hours to spin the weft for each yard of tweed, we feel it worthwhile as it gives the finished cloth its special texture and softness', she explained, in a voice as soft and solemn as her tweeds.

Our eyes fell on the unusual-looking loom that stood in the weaving shed. 'Ah yes,' said Anne, 'that's a wooden beam loom; it has four foot-pedals and a hand-operated shuttle. Using it is very hard work and good coordination is necessary to keep up a steady rhythm and a constant tension in the cloth. Everyone used this sort of loom on Harris until the semi-automatic Hattersley loom came in in the 1920s. This is one of the last of the original sort still in use; we bought it from a Harris crofter and have restored it to working order ourselves.'

But the weaving was not the end of the process. Anne explained how the woven tweed was first washed in hot soapy water, then pounded vigorously by hand on a rough wooden board until it had shrunk and become not only thicker but softer. This 'waulking' process was traditionally done by women, who chanted local highland songs to keep up the rhythm of their pounding: special 'waulking songs' and poems have been preserved.

We left Liceastro feeling that we had stepped back into the eighteenth century, into the period we had come to the Western Isles to relive. Was all this antiquated labour worth while? As we handled some lengths of Anne Campbell's Clo Mor tweed, with its soft fleecy texture and its gentle evocative colours, we thought the answer was probably yes.

The following day we drove the five miles down East Loch Tarbert to the point where a boat taking two Land Rovers, three border-Collie sheep-dogs, two bags of new fish nets and various other vital supplies set out for the five minute crossing to Scalpay, with its fishing and crofting community of some 400 souls clustered around two little harbours – one on the north and one on the south shore. While we saw some black-faced sheep, we saw no cattle such as Prince Charles Edward had rescued during his four day stay on the island.

Gavin Maxwell visited Scalpay regularly in the early 1950s when he was running his shark fishing business from the island of Soay off Skye, and before he settled elsewhere on the coast to write *Ring of Bright Water*. The island he describes was one in which everything man-made fitted harmoniously into the beauty of the local scenery. I fear he would no longer feel this was so were he able to return. Although the natural beauties of the island remain undimmed from his time – and doubtless from 1746 for that matter – there are now a handful of ugly little 'rendered' box-like bungalows scattered haphazardly around the rocky coves. If they were whitewashed, in the traditional highland manner, they would not look quite so bad. On a Greek island such simple houses would – with their less angular construction and their blue or white washed exteriors – be a positive asset; here they did their best to destoy the harmony Gavin Maxwell had noted.

From Scalpay the Prince had sailed up Loch Seaforth to approach Stornoway, confident that he would find a boat to take him to Norway. We decided to follow the road up the western side of the loch and then to walk across country to Arnish Moor where he had found shelter with Mrs Mackenzie of Kildun. The point where we would leave the loch-side road to take to our feet was the line where the southern half of the Isle of Lewis ceases to become known as Harris and becomes Lewis proper. Visitors to the island find this artificial border inexplicable: the dividing line is not at Tarbert (where the island is almost cut in half by west and east Loch Tarbert) but at its widest point. When one travels from Harris to Lewis the position of this unmarked border becomes more comprehensible: there is a complete change of scenery. Everything south of the mythical line is wild and mountainous; everything north of it is flat and marshy.

We found Loch Seaforth deep, dark, sinuous and distinctly sinister as it took right-angle turns among the glowering hills. It was more like a Norwegian fiord than a Scottish loch. Having left the road, the hills and the loch behind us we found the squelchy terrain featureless and disagreeable.

The Prince had done the cross-country march at night and got very lost and very wet; even retracing his steps by day we nearly did the same and were relieved when we struck the road a few miles south of Stornoway, and were able to press on to this principal town of the Hebrides. A warm bath, a hot supper and a dry bed did something to compensate for the flatness of the surroundings and the austere look of this grey little town which had rebuffed Prince Charles Edward and seemed intent on doing the same to us. The tweed mills looked dark and satanic through the skudding rain.

The next day was a Sunday, and I have never seen anywhere so comprehensively shut as Stornoway managed to be. Nothing and no-one moved. Some of the Outer Hebrides – South Uist for example – are Catholic communities. But Lewis and Harris are Presbyterian, and not only Presbyterian but often Wee Free – the disestablished and most puritanical branch of the Scottish churches. Censure can fall on anyone who moves around, indulges in social activity (other than churchgoing) or – worse still – pursues any vaguely commercial activity on the Sabbath, such as running a ferry service or even a B&B establishment for visitors.

'I think', said Alasdair, 'we've got the feel of this place. And since they didn't let Bonnie Prince Charlie enter the town, I don't see why we need to hang around.' I saw no reason to disagree.

Our next objective was the island of Iubhard (called Euirn in the Prince's time) where his boat had been obliged to put in when they sighted some possibly hostile warships on 6 May. In fact, the Prince had had to spend four days there because when he tried to leave he was again chased back, to a different part of the island, by the appearance of more warships. Minute though the island of Iubhard is, it was clearly somewhere we should not miss.

This time we did not walk from Arnish Moor to the head of Loch Seaforth, but drove as far as the village of Balallan on the A859 road from Stornoway, and then took to a narrow B-road with occasional

passing places that wound in a leisurely way along the southern
shore of Loch Erisort and then turned south through a labyrinth of
lochans and low heather-covered hills. Eventually the road ended in a
ragged quay, surrounded by frames for drying or mending fish nets, at
the tiny clachan of Lemreway. There was no trace of life: it was still
the Sabbath. We climbed up to rocky prominence overlooking the
little harbour and unpacked our picnic lunch; a few black-faced sheep
munched the long coarse grass and moved cautiously away from our
proximity. Much to our surprise, one of these detached itself from its
lambs and sauntered over to where we had spread our rug; it looked
curiously at our sandwiches and when Alasdair held out a piece of one
it approached close enough to nibble it from his hand. We remembered being told that sometimes if a lamb were sickly when it was
young it would be reared in the kitchen of the shepherd's bothy and
fed by hand; this was probably one such which had retained its
confidence in humans.

There was no sign of life of any sort round the fishing quay of
Lemreway on this Sunday afternoon, and we were just beginning to
despair of ever reaching the island of Iubhard when a rowing boat
propelled by a diminutive boy nosed its way around the corner of the
bay. For a couple of bars of chocolate he agreed to lend us the boat to
row the few hundred yards across to the island, providing we brought
it back before five o'clock when he was going shrimping. In fact, we
were back by four; our walk over Iubhard had revealed it to be as
uninhabited (so far as we could see) and as bare as when the Prince
had left his pile of coins on the shore to pay for the cod he had
commandeered.

'How can anyone make a living up here, if he's not spinning tweed?'
Alasdair said thoughtfully. Many people in recent years had asked
themselves the same question.

Life in the Hebrides has probably altered less since the eighteenth
century than it has in any other part of the United Kingdom.
Although there have been many changes, crofting and fishing still
continue to be the background to life. It is true that while the crofts
and bothies, in which Prince Charles Edward so frequently took
shelter during his flight, were often made of peat, now they are
usually of stone. But a single cow and a score of sheep on a croft of

some thirty or fifty acres of sparse moorland is still a pattern of life that endures in these parts.

It has never been an easy pattern of life. Usually the crofters did not own, or even lease in any formal or legal way, their small-holdings; they traditionally complained that they were constructing dwellings which would only enhance the value of their landlords' property. In 1882 there was an ugly incident known as 'the battle of the Braes' following which Mr Gladstone's government had declared a state of emergency in the Highlands. A 'highland land league' was set up; five 'Crofting M.P.s' were elected to Parliament, and there was an outcry for the large sporting estates to be broken up into small-holdings for crofters. But none of these measures solved the problem. By 1887 matters got even worse: the 'Deer Park Raid' of that year on Lewis involved the slaughter of two hundred red deer by angry crofters encouraged by their Free Church ministers. Indeed, land raids in which crofters carved out areas for themselves from large estates, continued into the twentieth century.

The Western Isles were no less badly hit than the mainland by the highland clearances – to make way for large-scale sheep-farming – of the nineteenth century. In 1849, Lord Macdonald evicted more than six hundred people from Sollas on the island of North Uist. On Harris, the 78th Highlanders were called in to help the local laird with his evictions. Colonel Gordon of Cluny had an official transport ship sent to Loch Boisdale (the scene of some of Prince Charles Edward's most memorable adventures) in 1851 where a particularly brutal eviction took place; one contemporary* recorded:

'I have seen big strong men, the champions of the country, the stalwarts of the world, being bound on Loch Boisdale quay and cast into the ship as would be done to horses and cattle'.

Even long after these excesses, the process of depopulation was to continue in the Hebrides; as late as the 1950s and 1960s, when the population of Scotland as a whole was slightly rising, the inhabitants of the Western Isles shrank from 36,000 to 30,000.

* Catherine Macphee of Iochdar, as reported by John Prebble in his *The Highland Clearances*.

Often the crofters have also been part-time fishermen: this was
equally true of the eighteenth and the nineteenth centuries. In the
present century efforts have been made to make the fishing a more
professional business. The first Viscount Leverhulme bought a large
tract of the Hebrides during the First World War and extended
generous loans to fishermen who wanted to buy their own boats; he
improved harbour facilities and he even set up a very successful
national chain of fishmongers primarily as an outlet for the Hebridean
fishing fleet. But while MacFisheries flourished, the local fishermen
did not. They continued to catch herring and mackerel as their
forefathers had done in the eighteenth century and long before, but
they failed to take up the blue-whiting catch in the Minch which was
proving more profitable to mainland and foreign fishing fleets with
larger vessels. Life remained a struggle. Gavin Maxwell prints its
epitaph in his book *Harpoon at a Venture*:

'All that remained of Lever's plans
Were some half-built piers and some empty cans.
And the islanders with no regrets
Treated each other to cigarettes.'

Crofting and fishing, sheep and herrings, wool and tweed . . . these
were the characteristics of Prince Charles Edward's Western Isles
and also of our own.

From Iubhard we drove south again to Tarbert and picked up the
Caledonian MacBrayne boat back to Lochmaddy. The Prince had
made the voyage without putting in at Tarbert, but had again put in at
Scalpay, only to find that Donald Campbell had left the island and
there was no point in staying there. Indeed, he had spent very little
time in Lochmaddy either, because when he put in to the bay there
he had found another warship – presumably hunting for him – so
he had put out to sea again and finally landed back at Uiskevagh
on Benbecula – just opposite the barren strand on which he had
first landed in the Hebrides two weeks before. It had taken us less
than half that time to complete the same circuit, but we had not
been stranded on either Scalpay or Iubhard, even if we had made

some diversions to inspect the Harris tweed looms. Now we were to venture into wilder regions of South Uist where the Prince had enjoyed himself much better and where we were to do the same.

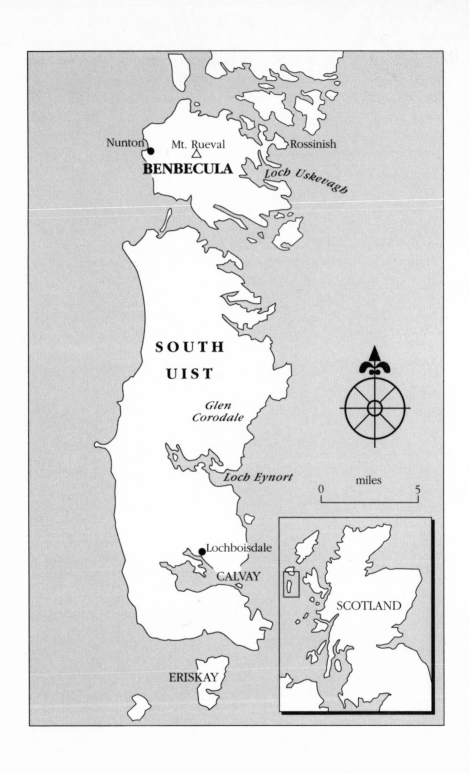

Nunton   Mt. Rueval   Rossinish
            △
BENBECULA   *Loch Uskevagh*

S O U T H

U I S T

*Glen
Corodale*

Loch Eynort

miles

0   5

Lochboisdale

CALVAY

SCOTLAND

ERISKAY

– 6 –

SKULKING IN THE HEBRIDES

AFTER the bleak bothy at Uiskevagh on Benbecula where the Prince's party had spent from 11 to 14 May, things belatedly started to get better. The Prince had sent one of the boatmen to inform Macdonald of Clanranald – the local laird – of his whereabouts, and Clanranald responded with a visit the following day, bringing with him two bottles of Spanish wine, some beer, biscuits and trout: 'never was a man welcomer, to be sure' – declared O'Sullivan. The Prince being at a low ebb at this point, O'Sullivan decided that the wine should be put aside for his personal use 'to cumfort him from time to time'; but the Prince would not countenance this 'and would not teast of it, if those that were with him did not drink as fair as he did of it'. The following day Clanranald sent the Prince a bag of shirts, stockings, shoes and a silver cup with a cover. The shirts were welcome replacements for ones which the Prince had previously given to O'Sullivan and O'Neil whose own shirts had totally disintegrated earlier. The silver cup and lid were also greatly appreciated since although – as we have seen – the Prince was not squeamish about what he ate and drank, he did not apparently relish drinking from the same wooden bowl as the rest of the party, and henceforth he always carried the cup and lid in his pocket – using the latter as a spoon and the former for his drams. However, he declined an offer of sheets, showing Clanranald his tartan plaid and declaring that as a highlander he needed nothing better. As so often, the Prince seemed impervious to discomfort but not unmindful of his dignity.

Things soon got better still. On 14 May the Prince and his party sailed and walked to Corodale in South Uist where they spent twenty-two days in a forester's cottage which was a distinct improvement on the grasskeeper's bothy at Uiskevagh. Here the prince relaxed probably more than at any time during his flight. He went shooting and fishing in a region where (according to Captain Alexander Macdonald who was with him) 'all species of wildfowl are in great plenty besides deer'. Macdonald records that he shot dozens of moorhens and was 'most dextrous at shooting all kinds of fowl upon the wing, scarce ever making a miss'. The years of elegant shooting parties in France and Italy had left the Prince with some accomplishments that could be put to good use in his present very different circumstances.

On one occasion when he had shot a deer and the faithful Burke had gralloched it and dragged it back to the camp to cut it up into portions for cooking and eating, a poor boy (who seems to have been a hanger-on in the camp) tried to pinch a piece of meat for himself, and got a swift cuff across the ears from Ned Burke. The Prince promptly read Burke a lecture on how 'the Scripture commands to feed the hungry and cleed the naked . . . you ought rather to give him meat than a strip'. The Prince paid for some clothes for the boy and declared that he would never see a Christian perish for want of food and raiment while he had the power to prevent it.

The Prince obviously enjoyed teasing Burke, whether it was for his faint-heartedness, squeamishness in cooking, or lack of charity to those poorer than himself – none of them characteristics which the stout-hearted, robust and kindly Burke demonstrated in any but the mildest and most ephemeral form. But Burke was a convenient foil for the Prince, and his detailed and circumstantial account of the Prince's most humdrum doings and sayings (given later to Bishop Forbes) has a special value since with him – less than with anyone else – was the Prince playing to the gallery. O'Sullivan and O'Neil – if they survived – were obviously going to repeat and dine out on the Prince's reactions and sayings; but the Prince could hardly have expected that the simple and uneducated Sedan-chair-carrier Burke would produce a record for posterity.

While the Prince was shooting and teasing Burke he was also

trying to obtain more funds to keep him going. He sent Donald Macleod (still in the boat borrowed from Donald Campbell at Scalpay) to the mainland with letters to Cameron of Lochiel and John Murray of Broughton, in the hope that Macleod might return with money – and with more brandy. He also desperately wanted news. Macleod returned after eighteen days. He had done well to find Lochiel and Murray at all: they had been 'skulking' at the head of Loch Arkaig, and gave him letters to the Prince recounting the dispersal of his supporters. But he had been less successful in getting money. Lochiel appears to have given him what little he had, but Murray declared he had so little it was not worth sending. However Macleod managed to buy 'two anchors of brandy' and so did not return altogether empty-handed to the Prince.

Meanwhile the consumption of brandy at Corodale was going on apace, particularly after the Prince had contacted Macdonald of Boisdale, Clanranald's brother, who lived only a few miles from the forester's cottage at Corodale. Boisdale was a more important land-owner and clan chief than Clanranald and his protection was essential if the Prince were to be safe where he was. Indeed, the Prince had been apprehensive about the reception he would receive from Boisdale who had not 'come out' with him, and to whom he sent O'Sullivan as an emissary. 'After a great deal of reasoning and reflections on what had past' Boisdale declared he would do what he could for the Prince and would make a further attempt at getting a ship from Stornoway. Boisdale was however at first reluctant to go to kiss the Prince's hand at Corodale, pleading that to do so might draw attention to where the Prince was hiding; but he agreed to meet the Prince elsewhere. After this, the Prince (still using the cover-name of Sinclair) and Boisdale (using the cover-name of Johnston) embarked on a daily correspondence, by which the Prince was informed of all local news and troop movements. This intelligence added greatly to the Prince's peace of mind and security during his relatively long – three week – stay at Corodale.

One of the other developments which helped to raise the Prince's morale at this juncture was the arrival of Clanranald with a complete suit of highland dress. Not only did he require new clothes because his old ones were 'tore to pieces and full of soate', but he derived great satisfaction from once again being properly attired as a highland chief. O'Sullivan recorded:

> 'When the Prince got on his new highland Cloaths he was quite another man. "Now" says he leping, "I only want the Itch to be a compleat highlander".'

He also got a tartan coat and waistcoat from Lady Margaret Macdonald, another local grandee who appears to have cherished a sentimental affection for the Prince, despite the fact she did not meet him as her husband was engaged in the Government cause. She also sent him newspapers which, taken together with the despatches he was receiving from Boisdale, added to his information about what was happening beyond the skyline of Corodale.

Among the other Macdonalds who visited him regularly at this time was Hugh Macdonald of Balshair. He became a favourite drinking companion of the Prince: indeed the latter's immediate reaction on seeing Balshair was normally to call for a dram as 'the first article of Highland entertainment'. Emboldened by his good reception, Balshair embarked on telling the Prince some of the hard facts of political life – as he understood them – in England and Scotland: of the people's dislike of both Popery and arbitrary government. The Prince reacted by making some cynical remarks about the religious convictions of most European rulers. This incensed Boisdale (who was also present) into telling him that his own predecessor as laird in these parts had 'fought seven battles for his (the Catholic) religion and yet after the restoration, he was not owned by King Charles at Court'. The Prince told Boisdale not to 'rub up old sores' and promised that in his own case it would be different. Balshair begged leave to doubt it, and said that despite the freedom they enjoyed in the Prince's company while he was on the run, they would have no access to him once he were settled in London. This provoked the Prince into declaring that 'if he had never so much ado, he'd be one night merry with his Highland friends' – hardly the most generous commitment in the circumstances, particularly coming at the end of what was recorded as a three day and night drinking session in which the Prince kept his end up with the notoriously hard-headed Boisdale.

It is pointless to speculate as to whether Balshair was justified in his suspicions that Prince Charles Edward would have proved forgetful of his highland friends and protectors. The Stuarts were not notable for their gratitude. But the Prince did – at least in the early stages of his subsequent life in exile in France and Italy – try to look after those of his campaigning comrades with whom he had not quarrelled. Lochiel, Ogilvy, Elcho, Glenbucket and others shared in his triumphal drive to Versailles to be congratulated by Louis XV on his safe return to France. He found regiments and commissions in the French army for some of his supporters, and gave rich gifts to Lochiel. But his companions of the heather had – by and large – little part in his subsequent life in Paris and Rome, and – had the course of history run differently – would probably have had even less part in his life in Whitehall and Windsor.

But the relatively happy and carefree days of Corodale were over. By 6 June the intelligence reaching the Prince's party – from his correspondence and from his daily contacts – was that the Government forces were closing in on him. General Campbell and Captain Ferguson, supported by elements of clans loyal to the Government, were landing troops in South Uist and intensifying the hunt in the region where they were convinced the Prince was hiding. There was a plan to sweep the island from north and south simultaneously.

The next two weeks were to be among the most confusing and unsettled of the whole flight, and one of the hardest periods to chronicle accurately because of all the feverish activity. First the Prince and his party quit Corodale for the small island of Ouia (or Wiay) off the coast of Benbecula where they stayed until 9 June, but then they heard that Government troops were following them. The Prince and O'Neil went to Rossinish and remained there three days until they heard that Government militia boats were patrolling nearby. Meanwhile Donald Macleod and O'Sullivan were left behind on Ouia where they stayed for a further two nights after the Prince had moved on to Rossinish. They then decided – on the basis of evidence that is not clear – that it would be best after all if the Prince returned to Corodale. With great difficulty Macleod and O'Sullivan sailed by night to Rossinish and picked up the Prince and O'Neil taking them on towards Corodale. Again, there was a narrow squeak with Government ships: the Prince's party reckoned that although one ship passed very close to them 'the rocks (along the coast) were so black that they could not distinguish us'. The ship passed on, but hardly had the party breathed a sigh of relief than they saw a boat full of troops being lowered and apparently being sent inshore after them. O'Sullivan thought they were 'lost without remedy' till he saw that the boat party were only looking for fresh water. Soon after this further rough waters forced them to seek shelter at Usinish Point, some two miles north of their destination. They passed the night in a cleft in the rock with Government troops only a mile or two in the other direction. The next day they sailed on past Corodale via Cilistiela in South Uist and reached Loch Boisdale on 15 June, where they took shelter in an old tower (traditionally Calvay tower).

Here they learnt to their consternation and surprise that Boisdale himself had been arrested by the Government forces; they had thought that his refusal to 'come out' in the campaign, the fact that he had 'kept back all Clanranald's men on the Isles from following their young chieftain', and the circumspection of his later contacts with the Prince, would have protected him. His arrest despite all this 'distressed the Prince exceeding much', not only because he had brought trouble on Boisdale but also because without him local protection and intelligence were likely to be much reduced. As Macleod put it:

'Had not Boisdale been made a prisoner The Prince need not have left the Long Isle (Uist) for all the searches – and very strict ones they were – that were made after him by the troops and militia; so well did Boisdale know all the different places of concealment throughout the Long Isle that were fittest for the Prince to be in, and so exact was he in sending timeous notice to the Prince . . . to be . . . in this or other place, at such and such times.'

Lady Macdonald of Boisdale was less good at sending intelligence reports, but she did what she could: she despatched four bottles of brandy to the Prince once she heard he was back on Boisdale land.

While the Prince was so hard pressed and everyman's hand seemed turned against him, Donald Macleod took the opportunity of their time together on Loch Boisdale to ask the Prince how he would deal with those who had been his enemies 'if he were come to his own'. In particular Macleod suggested that the Prince would feel bitter about Sir Alexander Macdonald and the Laird of Macleod, both of whom had detachments (or 'independent companies') operating with the Government troops in the region. These were the very two highland chiefs to whom the Prince had requested Donald Macleod – at their original meeting at Borrodale on the mainland – to take letters, and about whom in refusing – Donald had warned the Prince. The Prince appeared to bear no grudge:

'What would you have me do with them? Are they not our own people still, let them do what they will? It is not their fault for what they have done . . . besides, if the King were restored, we would be as sure of them for friends as any other men whatsoever.'

Donald Macleod thought the Prince might be choosing his words a little carefully, bearing in mind the name of his interlocutor, but nonetheless concluded 'the Prince had an excess of mercy and goodness about him at all times'.

Donald Macleod also found on a less philosophical level that the Prince was a great pragmatist. He used to smoke a great deal of tobacco and was always having to patch up broken pipes. In fact, Macleod declared that he

'never knew, in all my life, anyone better at finding out a shift than the Prince when he happened to be at a pinch'.

He added that at this stage the Prince would sometimes sing them a song to keep their spirits up.

But Donald Macleod's faithful and invaluable services to the Prince, particularly at sea, were drawing to a close. When it became clear that Boisdale was not to get an early release, the Prince decided that his safety required that the size of the party should be reduced. They were hemmed in at Loch Boisdale: two warships blockaded the mouth of the loch, and some five hundred red-coats were in the immediate vicinity. The party clearly had to split up and move on once again.

Before they could do so, they all had one more shock. At day-break on 20 June, when they had just got their tent down, they saw a man running down the hill towards them as fast as he could. He reported breathlessly that boat-loads of soldiers were heading for the land and that they appeared to know the spot on Loch Boisdale-side where the Prince was to be found. There was a move to abandon everything and take to the hillside, but O'Sullivan reported that the Prince remained totally calm and said:

'A Gad . . . they shall never say that we were so pressed that we abandoned our meat'

and he proceeded to carry on eating the *mouton* which was left.

But the moment of parting had come. The Prince called the boatmen together and instructed Macleod to give each man a shilling for each day he had been with him, in addition to subsistence money. To Macleod himself he gave a draft of sixty pistols to be drawn on John Hay of Restalrig when he met him on the mainland. (Hay had in fact been picked up in early May with Sheridan by a French Privateer and taken to safety in France.) This draft remained unpresented but when two years later Macleod was relating his experiences to Bishop Forbes he still hoped to be able to cash his draft one day.*

It was a sad parting.

He was also to part from O'Sullivan on 20 June. This was partly because the latter did not have highland dress and also probably because he was too old to keep up on the long marches through the hills. O'Sullivan had always been the one to bemoan most loudly the

---

* This was to be the least of Donald Macleod's subsequent troubles. He headed south but all the boatmen – except one – deserted him so he had to sink the boat. Even so, he reckoned he could have eluded the redcoats had it not been for the assistance they got from the militia consisting of Campbells, Monroes, and Grants who knew the hillsides as well as Macleod himself. Eventually he was captured on Benbecula on 5 July. He was taken, with two captured priests, to Barra and from there to Skye where – at Portree – Donald 'had the mortification of being neglected and disregarded by some of his own relations'. He was later interrogated and threatened with torture, and suffered terribly on the prison-ship voyage to London. He was released in 1747 and returned to Skye, being later presented with a fine silver-gilt snuff box depicting his epic voyage with the Prince.

heavy going and intolerable weather. It was a predictably sentimental farewell: O'Sullivan in tears and the Prince – according to O'Sullivan – holding him affectionately in his arms for quarter of an hour.
The Prince eased the parting by explaining that O'Sullivan had a key
role to play in his future plans: he was counting on him to produce a
boat to carry him over to Skye. O'Sullivan for his part gave the
Prince some advice about what he should do if he were captured: he
was

'never to own what he was, to go by the name of Champville and
give himself for a Lt. in the Daufins Regiment of foot'.

French officers, unlike Scottish 'rebels', were treated as prisoners of
war by Cumberland; but the Prince's chances of passing himself off
as such, when the whole countryside was looking for him, knowing
his features and knowing the reward that his capture carried with it,
were derisory – and O'Sullivan must have known it.

Although this was not the last that the Prince was to see of the
cantankerous but faithful O'Sullivan, it was the last he saw of him in
Scotland. O'Sullivan was picked up by a French cutter at the end of
June from South Uist, where he had come in hopes of rejoining the
Prince who was in fact on Benbecula by that stage. At the time of his
rescue, O'Sullivan was reported to be exhausted and suffering from
exposure. He was with O'Neil, who had gone off to have a final look
for the Prince, when – in the caustic words of Flora Macdonald's
subsequent account –

'the timorous Sullivan, having a fair wind, and not having courage
to stay till O'Neil's return, being resolved to take care of Number
One, obliged the captain to set sail directly, lest he should be
taken and should lose his precious life'.

Even then O'Sullivan was not home and dry: the French cutter was
pursued by a Government warship before it eventually found safe-
haven in Norway, from whence O'Sullivan made his way back to
France. There he was knighted for his services in the Forty Five
(and subsequently made a baronet by the Old Pretender). And it was

in France that he performed his last controversial service to Prince Charles.

It was a curious and none-too-honourable service. When the Prince had fallen ill at Bannockburn a few months before the Battle of Culloden, he had been nursed back to health by his then host's niece – a pretty girl called Clementina Walkinshaw. Some observers – among them Lord Elcho – thought that the Prince succumbed to her charms on that occasion to the extent of becoming her lover. However that might be, six years later – by then in exile in France – the Prince remembered her with sufficient affection to decide he wanted to send for her from a chapter house for aristocratic young ladies at Douai where she was currently living as a canoness. It was a delicate task to get in touch with her and to persuade her to abandon her religious life and come to live the life of a refugee with him as his mistress. Various people were approached and refused to undertake a mission that smacked of pimping; but O'Sullivan effected the necessary arrangements and soon Clementina was living with the Prince as he desired (incidentally, much to the chagrin of the English Jacobites as Clementina's sister was a lady-in-waiting to the Hanoverian Princess of Wales and the whole liaison was considered a grave security risk). The relationship with Clementina was to end in scandal and bitterness. O'Sullivan, whose military advice had so often been unpopular and disastrous during the campaign in Scotland, had thus rendered one further disservice to his royal patron. But for the present the enforced parting was considered a sad penalty of the pressure which was now mounting against the Prince and his tiny party.

And it was to get worse. While the Prince was 'skulking' in a cave on the hillside with O'Neil and a guide, some 700 men landed from government ships at Boisdale's house, and while 150 of them set about slaughtering cattle the rest searched and rummaged the house for the arms and Spanish gold that were thought to be hidden there. Eventually they re-embarked, to the relief of the Prince's party, but not before they had left a trail of havoc and desolation. Such scenes were in marked contrast to the Prince's own punctilious insistence on paying for every fish and every head of cattle he consumed.

There was a third parting that took place at this time which was perhaps the most personal wrench of all for the Prince. Ned Burke, his loyal man-servant, had to be left behind. The Edinburgh sedan-chair porter who had poached fish for him, who had cooked his meals, who had endeavoured to provide occasional clean linen and continual good humour, and who had been the butt for many of the Prince's good-natured jokes, could not be taken further. Many years later Burke was to recall wistfully that 'the Prince went off with two shirts under his arm': it was the best the faithful Ned could do for him. Burke too was to have a hard time of it before he eventually got back to his native Edinburgh.*

The Prince was now finding Loch Boisdale too hot to hold him. With only O'Neil, and Neil MacEachain to guide him, he crossed the hills to a hut near Ormiclate where he was to make contact with Flora Macdonald.

MacEachain, who had been with the Prince – on and off – since his arrival in the Hebrides, was a most unusual guide. Although O'Neil tended to ignore him, both at the time and in his narrative, MacEachain was no simple gillie or crofter. A native of Uist, he had been educated for the priesthood at the Scots College in Paris, returning to Uist in 1738 and ostensibly becoming 'a sort of precep-tor (tutor) to the Clanranald family'; it may well have been† that he also had a brief from the French Government to further Jacobite interests in this strategically important part of Scotland. Certainly he emerged during the Prince's months in the islands as the canniest

---

* After leaving the Prince, Burke went to North Uist where he nearly starved, living on shell fish for weeks on end, and was later refused food by his own brother (who was deterred from helping him by a government decree forbidding giving 'so much as a mouthful of meat to a rebel'). Starvation he faced with equanimity, but the thought of capture frightened him because, as he subsequently explained:

'by that time it was well known that he had been the Prince's servant, and therefore he was afraid, if taken, they would put him to the torture to make him tell all he knew, and he could not bear the thought of doing hurt to anyone'.

Burke remained tight-lipped until the Prince was safely in France: he is one of the most endearing of the minor characters in the saga of the months in hiding.
† As is argued by Alasdair Maclean in his *A Macdonald for the Prince: The Story of Neil MacEachain.*

and best-informed – as well as the most self-effacing – of his companions. MacEachain did not join in the drinking bouts with the gentry in Corodale, but was inclined to sneak off to seek information about militia movements for Boisdale and the Prince. Flora Macdonald was to have far more time for him than for the flashier and faster-talking O'Neil, despite the latter's attentions to her. The co-ordination of intelligence about the movement of French ships seeking the Prince, which were eventually to achieve his rescue, probably fell largely to the silent highlander with the French connections. In the most romantic chapter of his escape which was about to begin, the Prince would owe much to MacEachain as well as to Flora Macdonald.

* * *

The main reason why Prince Charles Edward felt so safe in Glen Corodale was because the glen was so inaccessible. He had on different occasions reached it by both land and water, but by land it was surrounded by high and steep hills with sharp rock faces, and by water the approaches were around rugged cliffs. What had been a protection for the Prince was a problem for his latter-day followers. We needed a boat for the sea-borne approach and we needed some advice about the best route through the hills if we were to come out safely overland.

We were lucky that while we were still at Tarbert on Harris we heard about John Joseph Macdonald of Loch Eynort. (He had to be given his full name to distinguish him from all the other Macdonalds around on South Uist.) Our Macdonald had a fish farm at the mouth of the loch and was said to be always in one of his boats somewhere around the rocky shores between there and Corodale bay. When we contacted him, he asked us why we wanted to go to Corodale: there were plenty of other glens just as beautiful and more accessible. Once we had explained our reason, far from treating us as perverse eccentrics he seemed much more inclined to help. We made a rendezvous for an early morning meeting on the northern shore of Loch Eynort.

Before Macdonald could take us to Corodale he had to visit the fish farm. We clambered into a rubber dinghy with a powerful

outboard and were soon scrambling onto a wooded platform, teth-
ered in the fast-flowing waters at the mouth of the loch, looking
down at 12,000 young salmon leaping and darting around in the
deep, netted enclosures alongside the platforms. We learnt about the
problems of sea lice and about the difficulties caused by jelly fish
which clogged the nets and obstructed the flow of oxygen to the
young fish. The feeding and inspection over, we chugged through
narrows beset by whirlpools out of the mouth of the loch and headed
northwards below the cliffs of Creag Mor. Here we saw a pair of
peregrines circling and swooping above us.

Three miles further up the coast we rounded a headland and
found ourselves in Corodale bay with its tiny shingly beach. (The
inviting long sand beaches of the Hebrides are all to be found on the
western – Atlantic – coastline, not here on the east facing the sea of
the Hebrides.) We anchored off some steeply shelving rocks and
scrambled ashore on to slippery seaweed, being glad to reach the
security of the heather-covered banks above us. I asked Macdonald if
he knew where the cave, which was marked on the ordnance survey
map as being 'the Prince's cave' on the north slope of the glen, was
to be found. He was dismissive about it: *that* cave, he said, had no
connection with the Prince. There was solid evidence to show where
the Prince had stayed in Corodale, he went on. I was intrigued,
knowing that the Prince was reported to have stayed in a forester's
house, and not in a cave, during those happy three weeks of shooting
and carousing in the glen.

But first, said Macdonald, we must climb with him up the wall of
heather and rock that lay directly above us so that we could see
where a pair of golden eagles had nested every year for as long as
Macdonald could remember. As we clambered and slithered, puffing
and sweating, up the dramatic gradient above us, we had the distinct
impression that Macdonald was watching us critically to determine
whether we were sufficiently competent on the hill to be left in
Corodale to find our own way back through the tangle of rocks,
precipices and bogs that lay between Glen Corodale and the road to
the head of Loch Eynort; he did not want to be responsible for
abandoning two strangers from the south until he was convinced that
they could look after themselves in these wild parts. Perhaps, we

thought, the eagles' nest did not exist: this was a mountain training or testing course.

Hardly had such thoughts gone through our minds than Macdonald proved them to be unjustified. He had stopped and was pointing upwards to a narrow ledge at the top of the rock face above us; the ledge carried what looked like two enormous and loosely-woven wicker baskets; one of them stretched up some four foot to the height of the overhanging ledge above; the other was only some two feet high. Macdonald explained that every year the eagles added to the nest of the previous year; this had the effect that their nest grew steadily higher till it hardly allowed room for the birds to enter at the top; this was why they had started constructing another nest alongside the original one. We should not approach any further; eagles were sensitive to human intrusion, and could be very fierce if they returned to their nest and found visitors. We promptly and eagerly agreed that any further advance would be quite inappropriate, having no desire to trespass on the preserve of a protected and rare species, and even less desire to argue the toss with a brace of seven-foot-wing-spanned predators – with beaks and claws at the ready – on a narrow sheep-track perched 200 feet above the shingle beach. We retreated cautiously.

'And now', said Macdonald, 'I shall take you to the forester's house where the Prince really stayed while he was here'.

We looked around in vain for any trace of a house. No masonry was visible above the heather and bracken. But as we stumbled across the hillside on the southern side of the glen Macdonald stopped us in our tracks: we saw all around us the foundations of a stone building of modest proportions. It was perched two thirds of the way up the hillside, commanding a comprehensive view of the glen and the little bay. No one would approach this point unobserved.

'This certainly looks like the place where the Prince might have stayed', I said, 'but what was the evidence you were speaking about?'

'Try rolling that boulder out of the way', suggested Macdonald, indicating a particularly solid and heavy cornerstone. I bent down and heaved at it. To my intense surprise it not only budged but rolled to one side; behind it there was a dark, deep hole.

'You mean the Prince could have hidden in there if he or his companions had seen someone coming – perhaps a boat putting in in the bay as we did?'

'Not just hidden, but hidden where he could escape', said Macdonald. He walked me some fifteen yards round the spur on which the forester's house had been built. Another big rock was set into the hillside. 'Now try to move this one.'

Once again the rock budged, though with greater difficulty than before. And once again there was a dark, deep hole behind it.

'Try climbing in', said Macdonald. I did. It was a tight squeeze; my knickerbockers were black with peaty soil; my shoulders almost stuck; I could see nothing till I lit a match.

What I could then see was a tunnel some fifteen or twenty yards long, emerging at the other moveable boulder inside the walls of the former forester's house. This had clearly been a carefully constructed bolt-hole. The Prince, together with one or two companions, would have been able to hide here even while an intensive search was going on. And if his pursuers chose to loiter or even to stay in the forester's house, then he would have been able to make a get-away through the escape tunnel. No ordinary forester would conceivably have devised such an exit. It was as near to an absolute proof as one could have wished that this was indeed the ruin of the house where the Prince had spent his weeks in Corodale.

'Very few people know of this', said Macdonald. 'I only showed it to you because you said you were interested in Bonnie Prince Charlie and were prepared to take the trouble to walk here if need be. Most of his followers don't get further than Glenfinnan and Portree. Just as well perhaps. They'd all get stuck up there in the hills and we'd be up every night rescuing them. But you'll be all right.'

We had passed his test. Macdonald was prepared to leave us here and was confident that – with the aid of map and compass (the weather looked none too settled and mist could come down very fast) – we would find our way back to the road before nightfall. He told us the best route to take. We were to follow the coast, travelling parallel but on the high ground until we came level with Bolum

Island; then we were to strike inland over the tops until eventually we emerged at the pass and could see down to the broken string of small lochs that flanked the north of Loch Eynort. If it was still clear, we could see our line of advance; if it were not, a compass bearing of due west would bring us eventually to recognizable features along the loch side. He bade us well and refused to take any payment beyond a refund for the cost of the petrol for the outboard. The tradition of highland guides, from which the Prince had benefited so greatly, did not seem to have been eroded by two and a half centuries.

We set out by the route Macdonald had recommended. As we waded through knee-high heather in Glen Liadale three red deer hinds started up ahead of us and disappeared over the horizon.

'It looks as if one could still live off the land here like the Prince did', I said. I reminded Alasdair of some of the Prince's feats at Corodale, and he looked at me suspiciously.

'How on earth did he manage to be so good at shooting and looking after himself in the countryside, when he'd been brought up in a palace in the middle of Rome?' Alasdair asked after some thought.

I suggested that the answer was that hunting and martial arts were very much a part of the education of any young princeling at that time. In Prince Charles Edward's case, he had started unusually early. He shot birds with a cross-bow at the age of six and was reported – by his cousin the Duke of Liria – to be even better at hitting balls in the air with arrows. When he was slightly older, his tutor and confessor – Father Vinceguerra – used to take him out for days at a time on hunting expeditions into the Alban hills: the two of them would live rough, shooting game, skinning animals and plucking birds, cooking what they shot over open fires in the forest, and sleeping out under the stars. It was the ideal training for the five months he was to spend in the heather some fifteen years later.

Military skills were not neglected either. When the Prince was just fourteen the Duke of Liria got the Old Pretender's permission to take his son to the siege of Gaeta, a city on the Italian coast south of Rome which was being attacked by the Spanish. It was not intended that the young Prince's life should be put at any great risk, and he was given the honorary rank of General of Artillery. But in the event he managed to get close to the action – in fact, right into the trenches in front of the town at the moment of the final barrage of shots before the surrender. He acquitted himself well and was noted as showing a cool head under fire. So not all the Prince's young days, as I explained to Alasdair, had been spent in urban courtly pursuits.

Hardly had the three hinds disappeared from view when we saw a golden eagle patrolling the skies above us and I wondered whether it was one of the ones from the nest we had seen earlier in the day. Once Macdonald's dinghy had chugged its way out of Corodale bay we were to see no other evidence of human life until we reached the road five and a half hours later. A present day figitive would feel as safe in this part of South Uist as Prince Charles Edward had done.

The final climb over the pass was a stiff one. We followed the line of the burn that ran down to Bolum Bay and were surprised at how this formidable torrent at the point where it reached the sea – too wide to cross with dry feet – had diminished to a mere trickle – often lost in high heather – a mile further up the glen. The view from the top was rewarding; the expected mist had not settled, and indeed the day had become progressively hotter and brighter. Having reached the pass, we could see our way right down to Loch Eynort and almost to the main road which runs down the length of North Uist, Benbecula and South Uist.

When eventually we reached the road and turned south to Loch Boisdale, within three miles we found ourselves passing Flora Macdonald's birthplace. The walls of the former house are partly standing and a cairnlike monument records its association with South Uist's most famous daughter.

Another six miles took us to the little port of Lochboisdale. It was here that the Prince had found himself surrounded on the 20 June 1746, with English ships sealing the mouth of the loch and with redcoats landing on the shore. It was here also that he had said farewell to O'Sullivan and the faithful Burke, and that he had had the sangfroid to finish his meal while all around him were fleeing to the hills.

Lochboisdale today retains its calm. Crofting and fishing remain the principal occupations, although there is a pleasant hotel and a police station which has the good fortune to occupy the most attractive site overlooking the harbour. When the highland clearances were under way in the last century, many of the crofters from this part (and from Glen Corodale) were resettled on the tiny nearby island of Eriskay where they took to fishing as it was no longer possible for them to find the room to raise sheep. One could understand the crofters' resentment: one would not wish to be moved away from Lochboisdale. As we wandered round the harbour, being careful to avoid tripping over lobster pots and coils of old rope, and then out towards Calvay island at the mouth of the loch, formerly guarded by a fortress and now adorned with a lighthouse, we wondered just where the Prince had taken to the hills with O'Neil as the English ships approached. His next destination was to be his rendezvous with Flora Macdonald at Ormiclate and this was our objective too. Like him, we hovered over our last meal at Lochboisdale – fresh salmon at the hotel in our case – and decided we would be sorry to have to leave.

It was while we were hovering over dinner that I innocently enquired whether there was any local malt whisky distilled on South Uist, as there was on some of the other Hebridian islands like Islay and Jura. The mention of whisky prompted those sitting around after dinner to regale me with their own versions of the best known story about the spirit's connection with South Uist and the smaller neighbouring isle of Eriskay. It was here in 1941 that the S.S. *Politician* went aground on the rocks with her cargo of 24,000 bottles of Scotch. Everyone who has read Compton Mackenzie's famous book, or seen the film 'Whisky Galore' based on it, knows the story of how the islanders relieved the wreck of as much of the cargo as they could stow away in hiding places on the islands before the Customs and Excise men could catch up with them. It seems the story was based – at least in part – on some of the real incidents that occurred: people are said still occasionally to unearth a case of the hard stuff in some long-forgotten hideout.

I told Alasdair of these events and reminded him that it was on

Eriskay that Prince Charles Edward had first set foot on the soil of Scotland.

'Knowing his tastes, I would say it was just 196 years too soon', was Alasdair's parting shot as he went upstairs to bed.

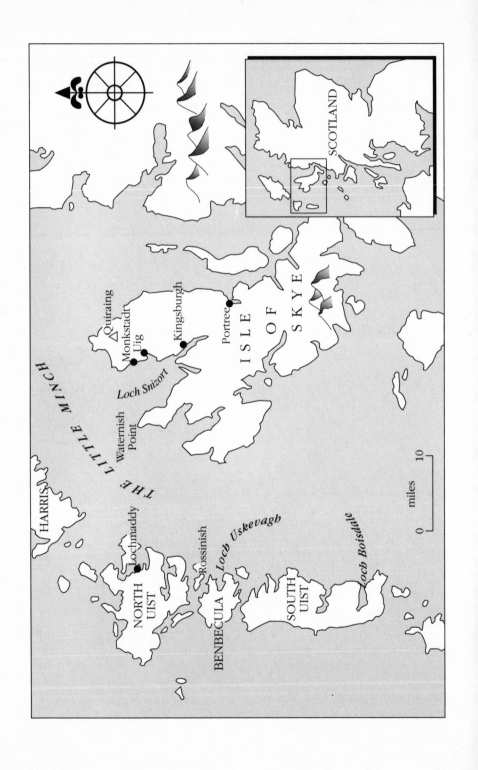

FLORA MACDONALD AND SKYE

S INCE the Prince had left O'Sullivan, Donald Macleod and Ned Burke behind him at Loch Boisdale, and set off with only Captain O'Neil and a guide to cross the hills towards Benbecula, it is now largely on O'Neil's account that we have to rely. He had not usually been the most accurate of reporters: it was he who had invented the incident of the horse shot under the Prince during the Battle of Culloden; it was he who had described the break-up of the boat that brought them to the Hebrides while others had recorded that it was intact; he had exaggerated the length and discomfort of some of their halts; and his hyperbole was to provoke the sharp subsequent comment of Ned Burke to Bishop Forbes:

'What deel needs a man mack mair wonders than we had. Faith we had anew o' them.'

But on the events immediately following 20 June, O'Neil is borne out by Flora Macdonald herself and his account seems impossible to improve upon:

'At nightfall we marched towards Benbecula, being informed that Scott* had ordered the Militia to come and join him. At midnight we came to a hut, where by good fortune we met Miss Flora

---

* Captain Caroline Scott, who commanded a company of Guise's Regiment and was already notorious for his ruthlessness in hunting down Jacobites and for his cruelty to those whom he captured.

Macdonald, whom I formerly knew. I quitted the Prince at some distance from the hut, and went with a design to inform myself if the Independent Companies were to pass that way next day, as we had been informed. The young lady answered me – Not – and said they would not pass until the day after. Then I told her I brought a friend to see her, and she, with some emotion, asked if it were the Prince. I answered her it was, and instantly brought him in.'

Flora Macdonald was in a very good position to know the movements of the Independent Companies (that is the clan units supporting the government forces) because her step-father – Hugh Macdonald of Armadale in Skye – was a captain in Macdonald of Sleat's company, which was currently in South Uist looking for the Prince. He was thus well placed to pass on news of troop movements to his step-daughter and others, and – even more important – to issue a safe-conduct to pass through the government checkpoints and cordons.

This was O'Neil's plan. He explained to Flora Macdonald that he:

'could think of no more proper and safe expedient than to propose to Miss Flora to convey him (the Prince) to the Isle of Sky, where her mother lived . . . The young lady's father being a captain of an Independent Company would accord her a pass for herself and a servant to go visit her mother'.

The Prince endorsed the scheme and urged it on Flora Macdonald, but she 'with the greatest respect and loyalty' declined. Both O'Neil's account and her own emphasise that she was reluctant to get so heavily involved, with all the implications for her own family if she were discovered. O'Neil spoke to her of 'the honour and immortality' that would rebound to her from such a glorious action (though even O'Neil could hardly have guessed how durable that immortality would be) and the Prince spoke of 'the sense he would always retain of so conspicuous a service'. She promised to sleep on it.

It was not an easy decision for Flora Macdonald. Added to the complication of compromising her step-father, and putting all her family at risk, was the fact that she was a strictly brought-up girl and embarking on an adventure alone with several men might be open to misinterpretation. Captain O'Neil, whom some historians consider may have been somewhat enamoured of Flora, is said to have countered this objection by offering to marry the lady if any imputations were made against her good character. Be that as it may, she reached her own conclusion the following day that her duty lay in helping the Prince – at whatever risk to herself, her family or her reputation. The Macdonalds were the staunchest of Jacobites and it became increasingly clear that the Prince himself always felt more secure with them than with any other highlanders. The subsequent sequence of events was most clearly recounted by Flora Macdonald (who dictated an account, in the third person, to Dr John Burton in Edinburgh a few years later) and is best described in her own words:

'After Miss Macdonald had (with some difficulty) agreed to undertake the dangerous enterprize, she set out for Clanranald's house, Saturday, June 21st, and at one of the fords was taken prisoner by a party of militia, she not having a passport. She demanded to who they belonged? And finding by the answer that her step-father was their commander, she refused to give any answers till she should see their captain. So she and her servant, Neil MacKechan, were prisoners all that night. Her stepfather, coming next day, being Sunday, she told him what she was about, upon which he granted a passport for herself, a man-servant (Neil MacKechan), and another woman Bettie Burk, a good spinster, and whom he recommended as such in a letter to his wife at Armadale in Sky, as she had much lint to spin . . . Armadale set his step-daughter at liberty, who immediately made the best of her way to Clanranald's house and acquainted the Lady Clanranald with the scheme, who supplied the Prince with apparel sufficient for his disguise, viz. a flower'd linen gown, a white apron, etc., and sent some provisions along with him.'

Meanwhile the Prince, O'Neil and MacEachain (acting as local guide) were getting increasingly anxious at the delay and lack of news from Flora Macdonald. They had been hiding in the Corodale hills, where they eventually received a message that all was well. O'Neil takes up the story:

'We determined joining her immediately, but the messenger informed us we could not pass either of the fords that separated the island we were in from Bebencula, as they were both guarded. In this dreadful situation a man of the country tendered us his boat, which we readily accepted, and next day landed at Benbecula, and immediately marched for Rossinish, the place of rendezvous, where we arrived at midnight, and instead of our protectress, found a guard of the enemy. We were constrained to retreat four miles, having eat nothing for thirty hours before. The Prince ordered me to go to the lady and know the reason she did not keep her appointment.'

The next few days were confusing and worrying for everyone concerned in the Prince's escape. Flora Macdonald stayed at Lady Clanranald's house at Nunton on the west – Atlantic – coast of Benbecula. The Prince who was not only desperately hungry, utterly exhausted (he fell asleep as soon as he sat down on a rock) and soaked to the skin, had to be content to sleep in a cowherd's bothy. Even this hovel was not safe, as the militia came there to get milk in the mornings. So there was nothing for it but for the Prince and MacEachain to spend the following day hiding behind a rock on the shore which gave no protection for them from the unrelenting rain which came down on them 'as if all the windows in heaven had broken open'. Things were a little better in the evening – though the midges were still tormenting the Prince – when a messenger from Lady Clanranald and Flora arrived with a hamper of wine and roast fowl. MacEachain made up a bed of heather for the Prince.

Everything depended on the news from Nunton: was a boat ready to take them to Skye, and was the coast clear of militia? The Prince and MacEachain moved up to a hill called Rueval, surrounded by small lochs and commanding a good view towards Nunton, to keep a look-out. The following day more messengers arrived. This time they were known to the Prince, being the same Macdonald brothers who had been with him on the original crossing from the mainland to the Hebrides in April. Like Flora's step-father, they were currently commissioned as officers in the militia and thus officially part of the force hunting for the Prince; but their clan loyalties surmounted their temporary occupation and any temptation of monetary reward. They reported that a boat had been found to take the party to Skye.

It was now MacEachain's turn to go to Nunton – leaving the Prince with the trusty Macdonald brothers – to see how the land lay. Lady Clanranald had finished the 'flower'd linen gown, white apron, etc.' for the Prince's disguise; more provisions had been collected; but it was still thought unwise for the Prince to come to Nunton house. Consequently Lady Clanranald, Flora and the rest of the party set out by boat round the north end of Benbecula to the Rossinish side of the island, where the Prince and O'Neil were waiting for them. A convivial meal ensued at which – Flora told Br Burton – she as 'his young preserver . . . sat at the Prince's right hand' in the bothy. The prospect of escaping to Skye must have seemed excitingly close.

The dinner, which had been cooked by the Prince and the Macdonald brothers, was rudely interrupted by bad news: one of Clanranald's herdsmen had run through the hills to tell that hardly had they left Nunton when General Campbell had arrived by sea in hot pursuit of the Prince and had landed 1500 men. The dinner party adjourned unceremoniously: taking what was left of the food, they bundled into a rowing boat and crossed Loch Uiskevagh, arriving at the far side at five the following morning to finish the cold remains of the supper.

Meanwhile Lady Clanranald had set off back to Nunton to brazen it out with General Campbell. When she arrived she found matters were about as bad as they could be. The dreaded Captain Ferguson was there and had had the temerity to sleep in her bed while she had been out on the hill with the Prince. The equally feared Captain Caroline Scott was also in the offing with yet more men. And what was worse, they all wanted to question her closely about where she had been.

Lady Clanranald was brought before Captain Ferguson and General Campbell to be 'strictly examined' about what she had been doing out on the hill so late. She said she had been visiting a sick child. She was asked where the child lived, how far away it was, and other specific questions. Somehow she managed to prefabricate a story that held up for the moment at least, and her inquisitors 'could make nothing out of the lady fit for their purpose'. But a few days later they realized that she had made a fool of them, and they returned to arrest her and her husband.

There was clearly now no time to lose if the Prince were to get away safely to Skye. The boat was ready. The disguise was ready. Flora was with the Prince on the north side of Loch Uiskevagh. But before going on to the next stage the party had to be further reduced. Now it was O'Neil's turn to be left behind: Flora Macdonald was adamant that she could not have more people with her than were provided for in the letter from her step-father: MacEachain as man-servant, the Prince – alias Betty Burke – as maid. O'Neil, who was the last of those who had left the field of Culloden with the Prince to remain with him, was to be shed from the party; inaccurate, and begrudging to MacEachain to the last, he recorded that the Prince sailed 'attended only by Miss Flora Macdonald'.*

This was the moment for the Prince to don for the first time his female disguise. He never made much effort to take it seriously, and Flora had some difficulty getting him into it, not least (as she reported) because:

'he proposed carrying a pistol under one of his petticoats for making some small defence in case of attack. But Miss declared against it, alleging that if any person should happen to search them the pistol would serve to make a discovery. To which the Prince replied merrily: "Indeed, Miss, if we should happen to meet with any that will go on narrowly to work in searching as what you mean they will discover me at any rate"'.

And so it was that at eight o'clock on 28 June they put to sea from Benbecula for Skye, on what was described as a very clear evening.

* Captain Felix O'Neil rejoined Colonel O'Sullivan – his fellow Irishman – and was very nearly rescued with him by a French cutter which had put in at South Uist looking for the Prince at the end of June. However, as we have seen, O'Sullivan insisted on the French ship sailing while O'Neil was absent. He was arrested shortly afterwards by Captain Ferguson and later confined in Edinburgh Castle. At one stage in his captivity he is alleged to have been confronted by Flora Macdonald who slapped his face and blamed him bitterly for 'her misfortune' (a most uncharacteristic action – if it happened). But he survived to record his own very self-centred account of events.

But they had not been rowing for long when the wind got up and the sea became tempestuous. The Prince sang to them his favourite song – 'The King shall enjoy his own again'. This was a popular song with most Jacobites, having been originally composed by the Cavalier supporters of Charles I during his imprisonment prior to execution, and resuscitated during the exiles of Charles II and James II. The best known verse ran:

'For who better may
Our high sceptre sway
Then he whose right it is to reign:
Then look for no peace
For the wars will never cease
Till the King shall enjoy his own again.'

When the singing was over, the wind remained high and the boatmen had to be active to keep the little vessel on course. Flora Macdonald, weary no doubt from the unfamiliar excitements of the previous few days and nights, fell asleep in the well of the boat; and when she awoke she found the Prince with his arms spread around her head to prevent the boatmen accidentally treading on her in the dark. This was perhaps the romantic high-spot of the whole escape, to be immortalized in the song 'Speed bonnie boat like a bird on the wing' (from which this book takes its title). However, that song was not written till long after the event, and is inaccurate in at least one detail of the third verse which relates:

'Though the waves leap, soft shall ye sleep,
Ocean's a royal bed:
Rocked in the deep, Flora will keep
Watch by your weary head.'

In fact, it was he who kept watch by her weary head. Indeed his solicitousness extended to keeping the last bottle of wine from their disturbed picnic for Flora 'lest she should faint from the cold and other inconveniences of a night passage'.

Fickle winds and fog made it difficult for the boatmen to tell where they were during the night, particularly since – as on the previous crossing – they had no compass. But before dawn (on 29 June) the sky cleared and the tiny boat made for Waternish, the north-western point of Skye, where they intended to land. However as they approached they found the point was occupied by Government troops who fired at them. They rowed away as fast as they could, fearing pursuit from the three boats they had seen with the troops on the shore. When they had put a safe distance between themselves and the point, they put in to a rocky creek and rested after the exertions of the night. But they did not stay long, guessing that the troops might alert others along the coast. As Flora Macdonald commented: 'It was lucky that it was calm then, for otherwise they must inevitably have perished or been taken'.

Leaving the Waternish peninsula behind them, they crossed the eight-mile-wide mouth of Loch Snizort and made their landfall at Kilbride on the western side of the Trotternish peninsula. Here Flora left the Prince at the boat and went ahead to spy out the lie of the land with MacEachain. She made for the nearby house of Sir Alexander Macdonald of Sleat, knowing that he was away from home – also serving in the Militia – and that his wife Lady Margaret was an ardent Jacobite. It was just as well that she had not taken the Prince with her on her reconnaissance because, when she reached the Macdonalds' house – Monkstadt – a Lieutenant Macleod of the Militia was installed at the house with his troops nearby. He immediately set about questioning Flora in the same sort of way in which Lady Clanranald had just been questioned at Nunton: where had she been, where was she going, why all this travelling in troubled times? She too managed to hold her own – for the present at least.

There was one piece of good luck about the timing of Flora's arrival at Monkstadt. Alexander Macdonald of Kingsburgh (to be known henceforth simply as Kingsburgh) was visiting Lady Margaret; he was her husband's factor and a man of resource who could be totally trusted. Lady Margaret decided she also needed help from another stalwart relative – Captain Donald Roy Macdonald – who happened to be nearby having his wounds from Culloden treated by a surgeon. Captain Macdonald rallied to her appeal, borrowed a horse from the surgeon and rode over to his kinswoman's house where he found a scene – as described in his own words – of considerable consternation at the turn which events were taking:

'When he came near them he dismounted, and Lady Margaret, upon seeing him, stept aside from Kingsburgh to meet the Captain and speak with him, spreading out her hands and saying, "O Donald Roy, we are ruined for ever". Upon this, he asked what was the matter? Her ladyship answered that the Prince was landed about half a quarter of a mile from the house, and that if he should have the misfortune to be seized there they would be affronted for ever . . . Lieutenant MacLeod was at that very instant in the dining room with Miss Flora Macdonald (she having left the Prince in women's clothes on the spot where he had come ashore); and, which still rendered the case worse and worse, that the Lieutenant had three of four of his men about the house with him, the rest of his command being only at a small distance from the house, as he was employed to guard that part of the coast of Skye, particularly to enquire at every boat that should come from the Long Isle if there were any rebels on board, etc. Kingsburgh coming directly up to them, they began to project what was fittest to be done, all of them agreeing that Lieutenant MacLeod's presence, with the whole of his command so near, threw a number of difficulties in their way, and made the case full of dangers, if not desperate.'

Lieutenant Macleod, whose presence in the dining room was causing such consternation, was – as Sir Fitzroy Maclean has pointed out in his admirable recent biography of the Prince – no simple foot-slogging soldier. Only recently he had been involved in highly delicate negotiations between the stay-at-home chief of the Macleods of Skye and the ambivalent Lord Lovat (of whom much has been written in an earlier chapter); the latter had found him 'a sneaking little gentleman', and no doubt Flora was having to choose her words extremely carefully if he was not to smell a rat. Her task was not made any easier by Lady Margaret flitting in and out of the room in an – understandable – state of high agitation.

Meanwhile the men outside – Captain Macdonald and Kingsburgh – were debating urgently what to do next. Clearly the Prince could not stay where he was: things were as perilous here as they had been in the Hebrides. Kingsburgh was all for the Prince sailing on, round the point of Trotternish, to the Island of Raasay. Lady Margaret joined them and said that she had heard there was a Government picket at Bornesketaig, past which they would have to sail if they were to round the point of Trotternish; this picket had a boat 'always ready at hand' to be launched in pursuit of suspicious voyagers. That put the lid on Kingsburgh's plan. It was now the turn of Captain Macdonald to suggest that 'the Prince should run the risque of making his way overland to Portree' some 20 miles away. He could stay at Kingsburgh's house that night before setting off. They all agreed that this seemed the least awful plan. Someone would have to go to break the news to the Prince who was, all this time, still lurking near the shore dressed in his flower'd linen gown.

It fell to Kingsburgh to do this. He had considerable difficulty in finding the Prince, until he resorted to the old highland ruse of waiting and watching for sheep movements. As soon as some sheep had given away where the Prince was hiding, Kingsburgh approached him. The Prince was alarmed by the sudden appearance of this unknown stranger, and sprang out at him with the cudgel which Flora had permitted him to keep under his petticoats. But Kingsburgh explained that he was a good and loyal Macdonald and produced some welcome wine as evidence of his credentials. The Prince accepted him. Prince Charles Edward must by then have been used to entrusting his personal safety to a bewildering succession of strangers.

Kingsburgh's house was about seven miles to the south. With MacEachain joining them, the three men – with the Prince still in his Betty Burke outfit – set out an hour before sunset to walk there. Flora Macdonald set out with a Mrs Macdonald of Kirkibost and the latter's maid by pony on the same track. Soon the mounted party overtook the walkers. Mrs Macdonald was in on the secret of Betty Burke and kept trying to get a good look at her; the maid, who was not in on the secret, had a good squint at Betty Burke too, and percipiently declared her to be 'of such impudent appearance' that she must be either a man dressed up or an Irishwoman. Flora Macdonald promptly declared that she was the latter and hurried Mrs Macdonald and her maid on their way. MacEachain realized what a bad job the Prince was making of his disguise and muttered 'For God's sake, Sir, take a care of what you are going, for you will certainly discover yourself'. Despite these warnings the Prince raised his skirts to an indelicate level when crossing a stream, and gave rise to further anxieties that the pious citizens returning from Sunday evening kirk might guess his secret. Susan Maclean Kybett, in her recent and hostile biography of the Prince, speculates that he must either have been drunk or 'in the throes of scorbutic euphoria' to have behaved in such a reckless way; but it seems more likely that he was just impatient to get on to a comfortable billet after several unusually hard days and nights.

It took them until eleven o'clock at night to cover the seven miles to Kingsburgh's house. His wife was already abed. Her maid told her that her husband had returned 'with company'. Hearing that the visitor was Flora Macdonald, she said that Flora should make herself at home and that she would see her in the morning. But – as Bishop Forbes was later to hear from those present – it was not to be a quiet night for Mrs Macdonald of Kingsburgh:

'In a little her own daughter came and told her in a surprize "O mother, my father has brought in a very odd, muckle, ill-shaken-up wife as ever I saw! I never saw the like of her, and he has gone into the hall with her." She had scarce done telling her tale when Kingsburgh came and desired his lady to fasten on her bucklings again, and to get some supper for him and the company he had brought with him . . . Mrs Macdonald went herself to get the keys, and I heard her more than once declare that upon looking in at the door she had not the courage to go forward. "For," she said, "I saw such an odd muckle trallup of a carlin, making lang wide steps through the hall that I could not like her appearance at all." Mrs Macdonald called Kingsburgh, and very seriously begged to know what a lang, odd hussie was this he had brought to the house; for that she was so frighted at the sight of her that she could not go into the hall for her keys. "Did you never see a woman before,"

said he, "goodwife? What frights you at seeing a woman? Pray,
make haste, and get us some supper.'

Kingsburgh refused to go for the keys himself, so his reluctant wife
had to brave the figure in the hall on her own. When she entered the
room, the Prince rose to his feet, went forward and saluted her with
a formal kiss. The unhappy lady then had a further shock, because
she felt 'a long stiff beard'. At last she began to suspect what was
going on and

> 'trembled to think that this behoved to be some distressed noble-
> man or gentleman in disguise, for she never dream'd it to be the
> Prince, though all along she had been seized with a dread she
> could not account for from the moment she had heard that
> Kingsburgh had brought company with him'.

She bustled out of the hall again in a terrible state and demanded
that her husband should tell her what was going on under her own
roof.

> 'Kingsburgh smiled at the mention of the bearded kiss, and said,
> "Why, my dear, it is the Prince. You have the honour to have him
> in your house." "The Prince," cried she. "O Lord, we are a'ruined
> and undone for ever! We will a' be hang'd now!"
>   "Hout, goodwife," says the honest stout soul, "we will die but
> ance: and if we are hanged for this, I am sure we die in a good
> cause. Pray make no delay: go, get some supper. Fetch what is
> readiest. You have eggs and butter and cheese in the house, get
> them as quickly as possible."
>   "Eggs and butter and cheese!" says Mrs Macdonald. "What a
> supper is that for a Prince?"'

At this, Kingsburgh reminded his wife that the Prince had been
living rough for a considerable time and was unlikely to be fussy
about his food. Furthermore, as he pointed out, any elaborate prep-
arations at this stage would have led the servants to suspect that the
guests were not what they seemed. With the food question solved,

Mrs Macdonald now found something else to worry her. Her husband had told her not only to hurry up with the meal, but also to make sure she appeared at the table herself.

> "'I come to supper!" says Mrs Macdonald. "How can I come to supper? I know not how to behave before Majesty." "You must come," says Kingsburgh, "for he will not eat a bit till he see you at the table; and you will find it no difficult matter to behave before him, so obliging and easy is he in his conversation."
>
> After he had made a plentiful supper, he called for a dram; and when the bottle of brandy was brought, he said he would fill the glass for himself: "For," said he, "I have learn'd in my skulking to take a hearty dram."'

The Prince sat up drinking for some time and did not emerge from his room in the morning. Flora Macdonald – in her own words – 'was in pain about the Prince's lying so long in bed lest he should be overtaken by his enemies'. Eventually she persuaded Kingsburgh to go into his room to rouse him, but Kingsburgh found him sleeping so soundly (it was his first night in a proper bed for some while) that he decided not to wake him but to let him sleep until evening, when it would – in any case – be safer to be on the move again.

When the Prince finally awoke it was getting dark and time to be setting off to Portree, with a view to getting a boat from there to the island of Raasay. Skye, like the Hebrides, was becoming too hot a spot for him to linger. Everyone agreed that the Prince did not take well to disguise: his movements were too masculine and clumsy, and there was some doubt about whether he was even prepared to try to dissemble very convincingly. As Kingsburgh had earlier declared, he was a very poor 'Pretender'. But it was necessary that he should at least set out from Kingsburgh's house in the floral dress in which he had arrived, if the suspicions of the servants were not to be aroused.

So the final dressing-up session took place. There was a good deal of larking around, with the Prince teasing Flora about forgetting his apron – 'a principal part of my dress' – and everyone subsequently agreeing that the Prince did not behave like someone who was in danger, but rather 'as cheerfully and merrily as if he had been putting on women's clothes for a piece of diversion'. As soon as he reached the cover of some woods on the path to Portree, he shed the women's clothes* with relief and changed into highland dress with a kilt – his preferred attire in his travels – which had been provided for him by Kingsburgh. At this point the Prince bade farewell to Kingsburgh, who had served him well in the brief period since he had landed on Skye. It was another emotional parting: it is reported that he wept and his nose bled as he said 'Alas, Kingsburgh, I am afraid I shall not meet another Macdonald in my difficulties'. The Prince went on with a guide by rough hill paths to Portree, getting once again soaked to the skin in the process.

Meanwhile Flora Macdonald was also on her way to Portree by a different route and on horseback. She was – once again – attempting to check that the coast was clear of militia and (as she herself put it) 'to gain intelligence and at the same time prevent a discovery'. She too was drenched by the customary wet weather in Skye before she reached – by her separate path – the inn at Portree. It was character-istic of the Prince that on being reunited with her – for what was to be their final encounter – his first concern was that 'our lady should be abused with the rain', and his second concern that he should find a dram. He at first declined to strip and change into dry clothes because he did not want to cause embarrassment to Flora who was also in the only private room they could secure at the inn. Later he remembered that he owed her a small sum of money – a crown he said, half-a-crown she corrected him – and insisted on settling up. He then tried to change a guinea into silver, which he thought would be more useful to him than a gold coin, and would have been prepared to take eleven shillings instead of the full twenty one, but was cautioned that he would arouse suspicion if he were too free with his money.

By now Captain Donald Roy Macdonald, who had gone on ahead from Kingsburgh's house, had made contact with the Macleods of Raasay and secured a boat for the short – four mile – crossing to that

---

* The women's clothes were hidden under a bush and his protectors subsequently burnt them all – except for the celebrated 'flower'd gown' which was rescued and reproduced by a dressmaker in Leith who sold copies to Edinburgh ladies of fashion with Jacobite sympathies.

island off the east coast of Skye. The night was far spent; the party was waiting to embark; the inn was not a safe place to linger 'for if any saw a stranger it would make them curious to enquire who he was'. The Prince bade farewell to Neil MacEachain.* He then tried hard to persuade Donald Roy Macdonald to accompany him to Raasay. 'I am anxious to have a Macdonald with me' he said, confirming his oft repeated sentiment of feeling more secure with Macdonalds than with any others, and doubtless also wearying of being passed – like a parcel – from one set of strangers to another. But Donald Roy pleaded his wounded foot 'which rendered him incapable of fatigue of any real service', and assured the Prince that there would be Macdonalds in plenty on Raasay.

Now the moment of parting from Flora had arrived. Unlike so many of the Prince's leave-takings, this was not an emotional one. He thanked Flora and declared 'for all that has happened, I hope, Madam, we shall meet in St James's yet, where I will reward you for all you have done'. She for her part remained sensible and unsentimental, recording in her subsequent report merely that while at the inn the Prince 'dried his clothes, took some little refreshment, and staid about an hour'. Then she saw him briskly on his way. With 'the bottle of whiskie to his belt at one side, and the bottle of brandy, the shirts and the cold hen in a napkin at the other side', he must have looked more like a travelling packman than a fugitive prince. As the inn-keeper was watching, they turned in the opposite direction from the boat and made a detour to conceal their intentions. The Prince, after a bare twelve days, had gone out of Flora Macdonald's life for ever.

But the repercussions of her heroic days as his protector were to

* MacEachain, probably because of his intelligence skills, managed to avoid capture after leaving the Prince and to lie low until he reappeared on the ship that eventually took the Prince to France three months later. He resurfaced in the Highlands on another Jacobite mission a few years later, probably again under French orders, and subsequently joined the French army and married a French girl. In France he had adopted the surname of Macdonald, possibly to identify himself more closely with the Jacobite cause or possibly because he found the French quite unable to pronounce MacEachain. He fathered a son in 1765 who in turn joined an Irish regiment in the French army and rose to distinguish himself at the Battle of Wagram and become one of Napoleon's Marshals, being granted the title of Duke of Taranto. O'Neil had little grounds for patronizing MacEachain.

be with her for the rest of her life. A few days later she was arrested and taken aboard Captain Ferguson's sloop *Furnace*. Ferguson had a rough way with prisoners, particularly those who might have recent news of the Prince's whereabouts. However, Flora was fortunate because 'General Campbell happened to be [there], who ordered Miss Macdonald to be used with the utmost respect'. This did not prevent her being shipped to London, incarcerated in the Tower and interrogated. But her brave and straightforward bearing made a very favourable impression on her examiners – and indeed on the public at large when they heard about her exploits. Hanoverian attempts to discredit her, which included the propagation of a story that she had slept with the Prince during their night under the same roof at Kingsburgh's house, were rightly scorned. After a year's detention she was released under the Act of Indemnity of 1747, was presented with £1,500 by her admirers, and was allowed to go back to Scotland – something of a heroine on both sides of the Border. She married Allan Macdonald, Kingsburgh's son; she had ten children by him; and she emigrated with him to North Carolina in 1774, sustaining a wound in the arm when their ship was attacked by a French privateer. During the War of American Independence her husband was made a brigadier in the British forces and Flora accompanied him on a number of campaigns until he was eventually captured; thereafter – having had their fill of the New World – they returned to Scotland in 1779 where she died at Kingsburgh in 1790.

Two independent witnesses fill out our picture of Flora Macdonald. One is Allan Ramsay, the Hanoverian court portrait painter. He painted her while she was still a young woman and she looks out at us today from his canvass, very much as she must have done at the heavily-laden Prince retreating from Portree – her eyes wide-apart, direct in their gaze, brave yet modest. The second witness is an even more improbable one: that urban and insular Englishman Dr Samuel Johnson. He visited her with Boswell in the course of their *Journey to the Western Isles of Scotland* in 1773 – just before she left for America. Johnson was captivated by her 'soft features, gentle manners and elegant presence' and, although he was to pre-decease her, it was he who wrote her enduring epitaph: Her name would be 'mentioned in history', and where 'courage and fidelity be virtues, mentioned with honour'. O'Neil had promised her immortality when trying to persuade her originally to befriend the Prince. It had been no idle promise.

* * *

O'Neil had described how, after the narrow squeak at Loch Bois-dale, he and the Prince had marched towards Benbecula and met Flora Macdonald in a hut en route. In fact, it has been recorded that the hut was at Ormiclate (about four miles north of Flora's birthplace at Milton). There is a castle and a ruin but no way of knowing just where the fateful meeting occurred. The land around Ormiclate is very flat and only a mile to the west stretches one of the long sandy beaches for which the Atlantic coast of the Hebrides is renowned. It was not weather for hovering on beaches, and in any case we might have been deterred by the ominous warnings on the ordnance map of 'danger areas' immediately to north and south: the major military base and airfield on Benbecula give much local employment, but have some disadvantages too.

In any case, the Prince had not waited there long before pressing on to the safer surroundings of Rossinish on the north-east corner of Benbecula. To get there, he and O'Neil had to wait until they could borrow a boat because they could not risk being arrested by the militia at the ford between South Uist and Benbecula as Flora herself had been only a few days before. We were able to cross by the causeway which now carries the north/south road at the point where the ford used to operate. Three miles to the north of the causeway we came to a cart-track to the right of the road which soon deteriorated into a footpath; this led after five miles to Rossinish, where the Prince and O'Neil had hoped to re-meet Flora Macdonald but found instead a party of militia in the vicinity which obliged them to spend most of the time there living rough on the shoreline, soaked by heavy rain. The same conditions greeted us and indeed, judging by the sodden appearance of the land all around us, would appear to be the normally prevailing weather. On every hand there were small lochans – almost more water than dry land – forming an area of utter desolation which continued unchanged on the southern side of Loch Uiskevagh. It was bad enough to be here for a few hours with the prospect of dry clothes, a hot bath and a solid meal at the end of the day; but the Prince had none of these prospects and it is little wonder that he grew somewhat tetchy during his time at Rossinish. Having sent O'Neil off to find out what Flora Macdonald was up to at Nunton, he and MacEachain spent their time climbing the little hill at Rueval and gazing towards Nunton in the hope of seeing some messenger with news of the boat that was to take them from the Hebrides to Skye. We too climbed the hill and could easily see – even though the unremitting rain – across the watery land-scape to Nunton. It was not one of the more exhilarating of highland views. As the evening came on, we too experienced the midges which had so tormented the Prince. Little changes – indeed little happens – on the Rossinish peninsula.

The Prince – like us – had looked in vain for any sign of interesting activity from the summit of Rueval; when eventually the boat for the escape was hired and the flowered cotton dress that was to be the Prince's disguise had been prepared by Lady Clanranald, it was deemed too dangerous for the Prince to come to Nunton, so Lady Clanranald, Flora and the rest of the party had come by boat round the north of Benbecula to rendezvous with the Prince's party at Rossinish. This had been the occasion when the celebratory dinner had been disturbed by the worrying news that General Campbell and his government troops had arrived at Nunton and were search-ing Lady Clanranald's house and, while she went back to invent her story about visiting a sick child, the rest of the party had transported themselves and the remainder of the dinner across the mouth of Loch Uiskevagh. The terrain the other side of the loch, as we knew from having made a diversion there the previous day, was just as bleak and cheerless as Rossinish. Other regions in which the Prince sheltered during his flight were equally remote and inaccessible, but nowhere we visited was as desolate as the region round Loch Uiskevagh. Wild fowl and water, clouds and mist made up the whole landscape which stretched away interminably in a series of inland lochs to the west and sea lochs – punctured by flat barren islands – to the east. It was not surprising that the Prince was restive there and glad to embark on his famous voyage 'over the sea to

Skye'. Our time in the Hebrides had also come to an end.

But we could not sail to Skye from Rossinish; it had taken Flora Macdonald and Lady Clanranald several days to organize a boat (admittedly in rather more complex circumstances) and we did not feel we could ask John Joseph Macdonald, who had taken us to Glen Corodale, to go so far from his home and his fish farm. In any case, it was not necessary: from Lochmaddy, at the northern end of North Uist, there was a sailing by the Caledonian MacBrayne ferry once a day to Uig on the north-west coast of Skye. Reference to the ordnance map showed that Uig was only two miles south of the spot where the Prince had landed (marked on the map as 'Prince Charles's point') just below Lady Margaret Macdonald's house at Monkstadt. The Prince had of course – apart from singing his lullaby to Flora – had an adventure on the crossing: they had been spotted and fired upon from the shore at Watternish point, where they had originally intended to land. The Caledonian MacBrayne boat also passed close by Waternish point as it crossed The Little Minch: the whole route could have been designed with our interest in mind.

Lochmaddy, as we had already discovered, was not as appealing a little harbour as Lochboisdale, but nonetheless had a good general store and post office, and it came to life at the hour when the MacBrayne ferry put in. Before embarking I went to the store to see whether I could find a replacement for my tall stick – or crummock – with its crooked handle which I found invaluable not so much for climbing as for descending mountain sides.

'If you really want a good stick, you should go and see Callum Robertson; he lives up at Newton right at the very top of the island, and no one makes a bonnier stick' I was told.

We had an hour or so before the ferry sailed and there seemed no possible better way of spending it than making a visit to Callum Robertson. We found his cottage with some difficulty; it lay close to a small hillock called Dunrossil – a name which had been adopted as the title of Shakes Morrison, the famous Speaker of the House of Commons in the 1950s, when he had been created a Viscount; the present holder of the title has a house there where he spends a considerable part of the year. Callum did not seem the least surprised at someone coming – out of the blue – to talk to him about sticks. He showed us a photograph of a set of four sticks, with rams' horn carved crooks as their handles, which he had made for the Prince and Princess of Wales and their two sons. The only problem was that it was getting harder to get hold of the right rams' horns; fewer rams were dying on North Uist as farmers hired rams from the mainland rather than buying their own; some of the horns had defects and could not be shaped and carved. He showed me some beautiful wooden handles which he had carved into the shape of thistles, salmon or other highland emblems. He would make me one and was sure he could persuade Lord Dunrossil to bring it south for me on one of his trips to the House of Lords. (This was not quite so improbable a suggestion as it sounded since Dunrossil was a friend of mine.)

It seemed impolite to ask Callum Robertson how he came to know Prince Charles and Princess Diana, since he had been too modest to volunteer any information on the subject. It was only on the ferry the next day that we learnt how Prince Charles had come to the tiny isle of Berneray – within sight of the hillock of Dunrossil outside Callum Robertson's cottage – to lead a simple life among the crofters and to relax from the official and social activities that necessarily dominated his ordinary existence. Doubtless it was on such a visit that the royal commission for crummocks had been lodged.

Prince Charles's voluntary visit to these parts had a curious echo of Prince Charles Edwards's enforced one. Both Princes had been pursued: Prince Charles Edward by the red-coats, and Prince Charles by the Press. And both sets of pursuers had offered the highlanders financial inducements to betray the whereabouts and privacy of the Royal visitor. The reward of £30,000 offered for Prince Charles Edward's capture has already been mentioned; but it is less well known that journalists offered the inhabitants of North Uist up to £1,500 for the use of a boat to reach Berneray on a Sunday so that they could photograph the latter-day Prince in his relaxed hide-away. Although this sum would have represented a month's wages for many a highlander, none were prepared to betray the Prince's privacy – least of all on the Sabbath. As the newshounds found, the rowing boats of North Uist remained at anchor. If there was no profit for the highlanders, at least there was no retribution of the sort meted out to those who had sheltered the earlier visitor.

'Prince Charles seems to have caused a good deal less bother to the islanders than Prince Charlie', Alasdair remarked with some truth as we climbed to the upper deck for a final view of the Outer Hebrides.

Sailing by MacBrayne ferries is an essential, enjoyable and characteristic part of the whole experience of visiting the Western Isles. They are a life-line to the islands in every sense: food and mail, local lairds and visiting tourists, containers of sea-weed and bevvies of sheep-dogs all jostle each other on deck; there are comfortable saloons with generously proportioned windows for watching the passing islands and hills; a dram can be obtained at the bar to help pass the two-hour crossing.

The sea-weed lorries – or kelp lorries as they are more correctly called – particularly intrigued Alasdair. 'What on earth can it be used for?' he asked. I told him I understood it had alkaline qualities which were valuable in the manufacture of such things as soap and glass, and that it had been a major product of the Highlands until early in the last century when the demand had fallen off at about the same time as the crofters had been losing some of their other means of livelihood (as their land was given over to large-scale sheep grazing). We noticed the kelp changing colour as it dried out on the surprisingly sunny crossing. Alasdair told me that was bad news: he had been talking to one of the kelp-lorry drivers and had been told that the cargo was paid for on weight and so the more dehydrated it became the less it weighed and the less it was worth. A sudden cloud-burst just before we docked at Uig doubtless cheered the drivers up.

Uig is a minute and charming little port, typical of many scattered around the Western Isles and Skye with its solid quay – designed to withstand all weathers – and its random piles of lobster pots and fishing nets. Disembarking was an orderly and friendly business, achieved like many things in that part of the world with a minimum of shouting and hassle but with equally little waste of time. Once ashore, we passed through the straggling village fringing one side of the bay and drove north for a little over two miles until the turning to Monkstadt. There is still a working farm on the site of Lady

Margaret's house and – all round it – ruins of the earlier habitations. Monkstadt must have been quite a sizeable establishment at the time when Flora Macdonald turned up there to find Lieutenant Macleod of the Militia installed in the dining room: the ruined stables and farmyard stand some way from what are clearly the remains of the original 'big house'.

From the house it was half a mile's walk over bare, windswept and treeless grazing to the rocky coast. It was not hard to find the narrow pebbled beach where the Prince had landed and where he had been left to wander or shelter on his own, while Flora scouted out the lie of the land at Monkstadt, until Kingsburgh surprised him – wearing his flowered linen gown and waving his cudgel – some hours later. We were puzzled that Kingsburgh should have found it difficult to locate him, and had to resort to looking for sheep movements, as there was remarkably little cover along the open exposed coast.

Our night near Monkstadt was one of the most comfortable we were to have on Skye. A mere two miles further north was Kilmuir House, the home of Mr and Mrs Phelps and a former manse; they had decided that life on the Isle of Skye had more to offer than in the south and had moved up lock, stock and barrel, sent their children to the local village school and undertaken a substantial programme of improvements to Kilmuir House to make it the best of the many excellent bed-and-breakfast stops that we encountered. Over kippers at breakfast we discussed the next day's plans.

Prince Charles Edward had not spent a night at Monkstadt, but had pressed on the same evening seven miles further south to Kingsburgh's house at – naturally enough – Kingsburgh. Before doing the same, we thought we ought to take a brief look at two places in the immediate vicinity which were connected with the Prince's story although they did not directly feature in it. The first – only a mile further north – was Flora Macdonald's grave and monument; here, a few paces from a group of traditional crofts which have been converted into a museum of rural life on Skye, stands a tall Celtic cross bearing the quotation from Dr Johnson which has been referred to earlier. Flora's long and exciting life – which had taken her to the Tower of London and to the Carolinas during the War of American Independence – had begun at Milton on South Uist where we had been two days before, and had ended here in the north of Skye; it was somehow satisfying that this most highland of Scottish heroines should have chosen to end her life where she began it.

The other place which we wanted to visit before moving on had only a hypothetical connection with Prince Charles Edward. The Quiraing is the north of Skye's answer to the Cuillins in the south: it is a mountain formation of awesome grandeur and striking beauty, surrounded by lofty rock features with such suggestive names as the Prison, the Needle and the Table. The Prince did not reach here; our only justification for making a detour ourselves was that it seems likely that Lady Margaret Macdonald, Kingsburgh and others who were entrusted with the Prince's safety on this stage of his flight may well have had the Quiraing in mind as an ultimate fall-back haven if it proved too difficult or dangerous to reach Raasay or to return to the mainland. As the barely-discernable footpath we were following wound ever further into the craggy hills, I certainly felt that were I ever to be on the run like Bonnie Prince Charlie or like John Buchan's hero in *The Thirty Nine Steps*, I would feel far more secure from pursuit here in the Quiraing than on the bare shore at Monkstadt or among the gloomy waters of Benbecula.

The following day we turned our backs on the charms of the Quiraing and fantasizing about what might have happened: we took the road south from Monkstadt – the road which the Prince had travelled dressed as Betty Burke – to Kingsburgh. Apart from a well on the road, at which the Prince is reputed to have refreshed himself, and a burn which we guessed might have been the one so inelegantly forded by the Prince in his woman's garb, it is an unremarkable road, and Kingsburgh House had none of the haunted quality of Monkstadt. The same could not be said of the next leg of the journey. Although the Prince set out from Kingsburgh's house still in his Betty Burke outfit (so as not to confuse the servants who had seen him arrive as a woman), he quickly changed into a man's kilt and took a path to the east of what is now the main A856 road, where he would be less likely to encounter other travellers. Flora Macdonald who was also travelling the same day to Portree (or rather, the same evening – the Prince did not wake up from the comforts of a proper bed until the daylight was already fading) felt more secure and was able to travel by pony on the main track which the road now follows.

As we trudged along a rough track, vaguely parallel with the main road to Portree, Alasdair was obviously still thinking about the Prince's change of attire which had taken place in this exact locality.

'If Kingsburgh lent him a kilt, as we're told, then surely it must have been a Macdonald tartan one; but the Prince would only have been able to wear a Royal Stuart tartan one', said Alasdair.

He had a point. I said I didn't suppose the Prince was too fussy at that particular moment about what sort of tartan he wore: he would have been glad enough to get out of the wretched flowered linen dress. But Alasdair's remark led us on to a more general discussion of tartans – of who could wear them and the significance of the different varieties.

Tartans as we know them today – even the varieties known as 'ancient' – are of less antiquity than is generally imagined. But undoubtedly many were well established by the early eighteenth century. One witness to this is Martin Martin, who was factor to the chiefs of the Macdonalds of Dunvegan and who toured the Western Isles some forty years before the Forty Five. He found:

'Every Isle differs from each other in their Fancy of making Plads, as to the Stripes in Breadth, and Colours. This Humour is as different thro the main Land of the Highlands, in-so-far that they who have seen those Places are able, at the first view of a Man's Plad, to guess the Place of his Residence.'

Since different districts were dominated by separate clans, it followed that the tartan of a 'place of residence' would also be a sept or clan tartan. Indeed there are letters extant from the seventeenth and eighteenth centuries on the subject of bringing individual septs into harmony with the tartans worn by the rest of their clan. But strict uniformity was seldom if ever achieved and contemporary portraits show even brothers and close relatives wearing distinctively different variants of sett (pattern) and colour.* Clan chiefs frequently

* Jeremiah Davidson's late eighteenth century portrait of The Macdonald Children and some of the Grant family portraits of the same period are cases in point.

sported their own modifications of clan tartan, and some still do. The famous painting by the Swiss artist Morier of the Battle of Culloden is meticulous in its treatment of the red-coated uniforms of Barrell's English regiment; but when he paints the Jacobite clansmen, for which captured highlanders are said to have been used for models, no less than twenty-two different varieties of tartan can – it is claimed by Neil Grant – be distinguished, and none of them bear any close identity with recognized existing tartans. It has to be acknowledged that it was not until the formation of the highland regiments of the British army that any really strict uniformity and consistency of tartan was maintained.

There were nearly forty years after the Forty Five when the wearing of all non-regimental tartan was proscribed in the highlands, as part of a conscious effort by the government to break the Jacobite spirit and the old clan affiliations. After this break, most of the tartans were reconstituted when – as happened by the turn of the eighteenth century – the vogue for all things highland set in, aided by Sir Walter Scott's romanticizing of Scottish history. Not content with establishing regimental and clan tartans, the latter were augmented by modified versions for different occasions: dress tartans and hunting tartans proliferated. Nothing improper was felt about devising new tartans for new purposes: Prince Albert himself designed the Balmoral tartan which is still worn (much more frequently than Royal Stuart) by members of the Royal Family; and a 'Johore Tartan' was even designed for a regiment of the Indian army under the British raj.

Having exhausted the subject of tartans in our discussion, and having exhausted ourselves with our long walk, we reached Portree in the early evening. The capital of Skye is clustered round a splendid natural harbour and the multi-coloured row of houses along the harbour front suggests a Nordic version of Portofino. We naturally made straight for the Royal Hotel which boasts that, even if the present unremarkable building was not the scene of the Prince's farewell to Flora Macdonald, it is at least on the site of that memorable parting. There is little more that can be said of the connection.

The Prince did not sleep in Portree; having said his farewells to Flora Macdonald, he embarked later the same night for Raasay. We were glad enough to sleep in a comfortable hostelry and postponed our sailing to the island of Raasay until the following day.

When we did sail it was on a small vessel called the *Tri Star* which plied the Sound of Raasay regularly with visitors anxious to see seals and porpoises. The skipper of the *Tri Star* told us that if we were lucky we might see something much rarer than either. The white-tailed Sea Eagle had long been a native of the Hebrides, but its gregarious nature and propensity for following ships and swooping for fish in their wakes made it an easy target for those who viewed it as a predatory menace: the Sea Eagle had become extinct in these parts. Now however, the skipper told us, some pairs had been reintroduced to Skye from Norway and were already breeding here. The Sound of Raasay was their favourite haunt and, with their superior wing-span, they chased the less uncommon Golden Eagles further inland. Such Golden Eagles we had already seen more than once, but we were less lucky with the elusive Sea Eagles. We could not win every time, said Alasdair philosophically.

– 8 –

IN MACKINNON COUNTRY

THE island of Raasay was the wrong place to have gone from Skye. To start with, it was an uncomfortably small island: 'too narrow and confin'd in its bounds' (as the Prince quickly realised) to provide the necessary cover. And what made matters worse was that the limitations of the island were emphasised by the fact that it had already been laid bare by Captain Ferguson's force of redcoats and militia in the weeks following Culloden, as a retribution for the Macleod's – fairly minimal – support for the Prince. Three hundred homes, most of them turf bothies but including the laird's stone house, had been razed to the ground; 700 sheep and 280 cows had been wantonly slaughtered; all of the boats that could be found – some thirty – had been holed and sunk. The island was a morgue: anything that stirred was all too conspicuous.

Be that as it may, the Prince landed there early on 1 July and the Macleods found him 'a mean, low hut' at Glam where at least he could shelter from the rain which was once again bucketing down. While they were taking refuge there, an incident occurred which well illustrated the Prince's reluctance to authorize or countenance any unnecessary bloodshed in the interests of his own personal safety. Captain Malcolm Macleod, who was with him at the time, subsequently recounted to Bishop Forbes exactly what passed:

'At that time there happened to be in Raaza a fellow who had come into the island upon pretence of selling a roll of tobacco; but after he had sold off his tobacco he continued strolling up and

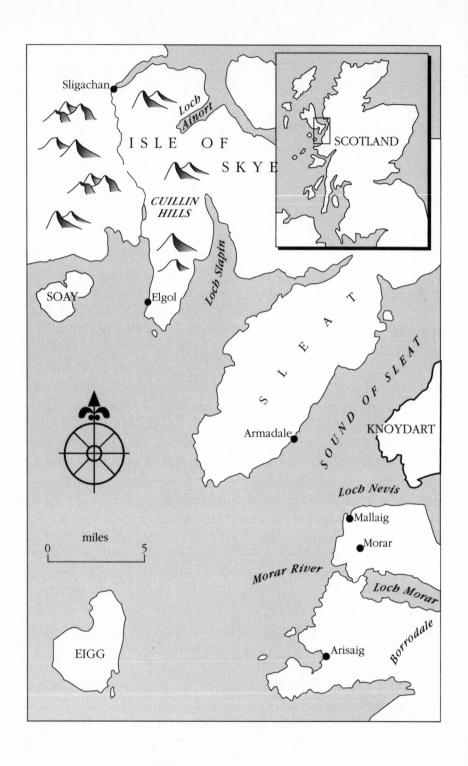

Sligachan

Loch Ainort

ISLE OF SKYE

CUILLIN HILLS

Loch Slapin

SOAY

Elgol

SLEAT

SOUND OF SLEAT

KNOYDART

SCOTLAND

Armadale

Loch Nevis

Mallaig

Morar

Morar River

Loch Morar

miles

0   5

EIGG

Arisaig

Borrodale

down the island in an idle way without anything to do, for no less than twelve or fourteen days, which made the people of the island suspect him to be a spy. When the Prince and his friends were in the hut, Malcolm Macleod happened to see this stroller coming towards the hut, which he took notice of to the Prince, and told him withal what kind of fellow he was suspected to be. The Prince not liking the thing so well, Malcolm said he should take care that the fellow should not go back again, for that he would immediately go out and shoot him through the head. "Oh no", said the Prince, "God forbid that any poor man should suffer for us, if we can but keep ourselves in any way safe." And he would not allow the Captain to stir, though their apprehensions behov'd to be the greater that the hut was not upon any road. But the fellow happened to pass by it without looking into it.'

So the immediate crisis was avoided, but Raasay still felt too exposed for comfort.

It was not long before the Prince decided they should cut their losses and return to Skye. Captain Malcolm Macleod who had taken them over to Raasay now agreed to bring them back. About seven o'clock in the evening of 2 July they re-embarked; the small party included the young laird of Raasay 'who could not think of parting with him so soon'. As so often in the Prince's adventures, no sooner were they at sea than a storm brewed up. Indeed, according to Macleod:

'the sea became so rough and tempestuous that all on board begged he would return; for the waves were beating over and over them, the men tugging hard at the oars, and Captain Macleod laving the water out of the little boat. The Prince would by no means hear of returning, and to divert the men from thinking on the danger he sang them a merry Highland song'.

Three hours later they landed again on Skye, this time at a place called Nicholson's Rock near Scorobreck in Trotternish. It was a difficult landing and the Prince lent a hand to haul the boat up the beach, getting soaked to the skin by the waves as he did so. He was clearly utterly exhausted when they eventually reached a cow-byre to camp for the night. He was too fatigued even to accept the offer of dry clothes, and when eventually he fell into a fitful sleep it was only to wake with a start every few minutes and to stare in dazed non-recognition at his companions. He also cried out in his sleep 'Oh poor England!' He was fairly close to delirium and to final collapse.

But by the next day he had rallied and was asking Macleod 'if he was a stout walker' and 'if he could walk barefooted'? By barefooted it turned out that he meant with shoes but without stockings – 'the way I used to walk at my diversions in Italy'. Macleod rather testily said he was pretty good at walking but he couldn't tell how good he was without stockings as he'd never tried it, nor (he seemed to imply) did he intend trying anything so silly.

This inconsequential conversation was, of course, the prelude to the Prince suggesting a long walk across southern Skye with Macleod to reach the Mackinnon country. When Macleod cautioned him of the dangers of falling into the wrong hands, the Prince replied 'Why, Macleod, I now throw myself entirely into your hands, and leave you to do with me what you please. Only I want to go to Strath, Mackinnon's country. I hope you will accompany me . . . .'. But however much the Prince might protest that he left everything to Macleod, he declined to accept his advice to go by sea and insisted on marching across country. As he rightly pointed out, 'there was no doing anything in their situation without running risques'. The Prince further aggravated Macleod by suggesting that he knew the way himself, provoking Macleod to say 'I am sure I must know it much better' and to go on to warn him of the length of the march – some twenty-five miles – and of the necessity of going by rough byways to avoid people. Finally the Prince even rejected Macleod's advice to wait until nightfall before setting out, and insisted on 'setting out immediately . . . along the ridges of high hills, and through wild muirs and glens'.

It is easy to be critical of the Prince's headstong determination to decide where, how and when he was going. Mrs Kybett in her *Bonnie Prince Charlie* makes much of his imperious way of deciding on his movements, and suggests that this was responsible for his failing to make contact with the various French ships sent to collect him. But that Prince Charles Edward attempted to keep some control over his destiny is hardly surprising. He had been passed on from familiar Irish companions to less-familiar Scottish ones, from clan to clan, from person to person, and from island to island. He must have had a keen awareness of the dangers closing in on him. That he chose to make his own decisions was only natural: he had been accustomed to command. And that he should prefer to choose – wherever possible – those in whom to confide his trust was no less natural; it had earlier been the Irish or the Macdonalds, now it was the Mackinnons, soon it would be other Macdonalds and Lochiel again. The Prince had a lively sense of whom he could trust and of when a place was getting too hot for him; had it been otherwise he would hardly have survived five months in the heather.

Now that he was embarked on another long overland march, it was again necessary to him to adopt the personality and dress of someone else. Female disguise had not been a success. This time, Macleod suggested he should take on the name of Lewie Caw and the guise of his servant. He should

'walk at some distance behind him; and if at any time he happened to meet with any persons to converse with them, as he was well known in the island, that the Prince should show no concern at all in his face, but sit down at a small distance . . .'

The Prince also insisted on carrying the baggage at all times.

Theirs was an intimate journey together. The Prince unburdened himself of many things on his mind. He spoke of Lord George Murray's disinclination to obey orders, and of his own incredulity at the barbarities of Cumberland's troops after Culloden. Later he contested Macleod's advice not to drink cold water when he was hot and sweating, as it would be bad for his health. 'No, no,' said the Prince, 'that will never hurt me in the least. If you happen to drink any cold thing when you are warm, only remember, Macleod, to piss after drinking, and it will do you no harm at all. This advice I had from a friend abroad.'

Speaking more generally of his health, the Prince admitted that he had had 'a bloody flux' (probably dysentery) in South Uist and that 'it was not possible to be altogether in good health considering the many fatigues and distresses he was obliged to undergo'; but Macleod commented that he made little of his ailments and 'always bore up with a surprising stock of spirits'.

One thing however which did indicate that the Prince was in some distress on the march was that he kept 'fidging' – or fidgeting. Macleod investigated and discovered that the royal personage was covered in lice: 'he took some fourscore off him'. It was hardly surprising as the Prince had lived rough and slept in his clothes for many weeks now. Mrs Kybett comments – somewhat uncharitably in the circumstances – that the Prince was careless about his personal hygiene, and that he slept in his clothes even when he did not need to; this seems to take little account of all those exhausted arrivals and hurried starts that characterized the Prince's travels.

The Prince also waxed philosophical on the long, arduous walk with Macleod. The latter recorded his remarks verbatim for Bishop Forbes:

'Macleod, do you not think that God Almighty made this person of mine for doing some good yet? When I was in Italy, and dining at the king's table, very often the sweat would have been coming through my coat with the heat of the climate; and now that I am in a cold country, of a more piercing and trying climate, and exposed to different kinds of fatigues, I really find I agree equally with both. I have had this philibeg on now some days, and find I do as well with it as any the best breeches I ever put on. I hope in God, Macleod, to walk the streets of London with it yet'.

The talk of clothing reminded the Prince that the waistcoat he was wearing – made of scarlet tartan with a gold twist button – was too grand for Lewie Caw, and he changed it with Macleod's old plain one, saying as he did so that he hoped to give him a better one some day. A little later the Prince was prevailed on to pocket his periwig and to tie a dirty white napkin round his head and top it with a highland bonnet, as a further measure of disguise. A suggestion by the Prince – probably not meant to be taken seriously – that he should blacken his face, was rejected by Macleod, who commented that whatever the Prince did he could not conceal his regal bearing. The Prince himself acknowledged the problem, but put it more modestly: 'This is an odd remarkable face I have got that nothing can disguise it'.

They had passed through some very wild country while these conversations had been in progress. Indeed, at one stage the Prince had remarked to Macleod that he was sure that the Devil himself would not be able to find them in such a God-forsaken spot. But as they approached Strath they were beginning to meet people again. The very first they encountered were two Mackinnons who had 'been out' with the Prince in the Forty Five. They immediately confirmed the truth of the Prince's remarks about his own unmistakeable face by recognizing him for whom he was, and weeping bitterly 'to see him in such a pickle'. Macleod cautioned them to keep their observation to themselves, and – true to their old loyalties – they did.

Now it was again a question of approaching a house where help might be found, and leaving the Prince outside until the reaction of the inmates was determined. Macleod went to the house of his brother-in-law – John Mackinnon – at Elgol, where he found the master of the house away but his own sister at home. She assured him that no government forces were in the immediate vicinity, and so Macleod and 'Lewie Caw' were admitted and welcomed, Macleod not telling his sister the true identity of his supposed servant but merely indicating that he too was on the run from the redcoats. Mrs Mackinnon instantly took a liking to the lad and seems to have suspected that he was a gentleman.

The Mackinnons' simple country serving-girl was less impressed by Lewie Caw and a scene ensued which provided a welcome touch of low comedy to the otherwise tense drama. Macleod, having explained that he and his companion had fallen into various bogs in the night and that they were consequently muddied up to the tops of their thighs, needed cleaning up. He subsequently told the tale in his own words:

'The Captain [Macleod] desired the servant lass, who could talk nothing but Erse, to bring some water for his feet, which she did; and being much fatigued he desired her to wash his feet and legs. When she was washing them he said, "You see that poor sick man there, I hope you'll wash his feet too. It will be a great charity, for he has as much need as I have." "No such thing," said she, "although I wash the master's feet, I am not obliged to wash the servant's. What! he's but a low countrywoman's son. I will not wash his feet indeed." However, with much entreaty Malcolm prevailed upon the maid to stoop so low as to wash poor Lewie's feet. While she was washing them she happened to use him right roughly, and the Prince said to Malcolm, "O Macleod, if you would desire the girl not to go so far up."'

John Mackinnon at this stage turned up on the doorstep of his own house and Macleod, having sounded him out about whether he would – hypothetically – be prepared to help the Prince, and having received the reassuring answer 'I wish with all my heart we had him here, for he would be safe enough', told the startled host that he did indeed have the Prince under his roof at that very moment. But Mackinnon's resolve to pretend that he thought the Prince was Lewie Caw was quickly undermined by finding – when he entered his own house – that his young child was being carried round the room on the Prince's shoulders with the latter declaring to all who cared to listen: 'I hope this child may be a captain in my service yet'. Prince Charles Edward was never able to sustain another role for very long.

Now once more the talk turned to finding a boat – this time one that could take the Prince from Skye to the mainland again. The Prince and Macleod had resolved not to involve the old laird of Mackinnon – the chief of the clan – in their plans since, although he was deemed to be 'a mighty honest, stout, good man', he was thought to be too old and doddery for such work. However, in the event John Mackinnon, while on his way to find a boat for him, ran into the laird and found 'he could not keep the matter from him'. The Mackinnon of Mackinnon rose to the occasion and immediately took charge of the situation. Old and doddery he might be: incapable or faint-hearted he was not. Soon a boat was procured and Macleod decided that his own role in the drama was now completed: having delivered the Prince safely across Skye, he would hand over his charge to Mackinnon and his clansmen.

As always, the Prince was reluctant to part with one who had won his trust and affection: as with so many others – O'Sullivan, O'Neil, Macdonald the boatman and Donald Roy Macdonald among them – he tried to persuade him to stay, but Macleod insisted. Macleod explained that his own disappearance from home would be much remarked upon by now and might result in a search which would uncover the Prince. The latter accepted the situation and gave Macleod a silver stock-buckle (that he must have been keeping about him for just such an eventuality) and ten guineas; Macleod took a lot of persuading to accept the money, pointing out that the Prince was not much in funds at that moment. But the Prince pressed the money on him, and even insisted on writing a note to another Macleod – Murdoch – whom he thought had been expecting to meet him and who would be disappointed if he had no direct word from him. Malcolm Macleod was to meet the same fate as most of those who helped the Prince and parted from him: he was captured a few days later.

The crossing from Skye to the mainland was safely made and the Prince with the two Mackinnons – John and the laird – landed on the south side of Loch Nevis, near Mallaig, at four in the morning on 5 July. Most habitations had been destroyed and there were militia in the vicinity; there was nothing for it but to lie low and sleep in the open for three nights. On 8 July the laird of Mackinnon with one of the boatmen set off to look for somewhere better – possibly a cave – to shelter.

While they were gone, the Prince and John Mackinnon with three oarsmen rowed up the loch, and very nearly met with disaster. They turned a point and found themselves almost on top of a moored boat attended by five men 'with red crosses over their bonnets' – the badge of the government militia. The militiamen challenged them and then gave chase in the boat. The Prince was all for landing and trying to make off on foot. But John Mackinnon was adamant: he must stay in the boat, as their best chance of escape was to out-row the pursuers. The Prince was

> 'sitting low down on the bottom of the boat betwixt John Mackin-
> non's knees . . . with John's plaid spread over him . . . enquiring
> now and then how they kept their distance from the red crosses'.

John Mackinnon and his oarsmen meanwhile pulled manfully, but at
one moment it looked as if they would have to shoot it out with the
militiamen and Mackinnon told his men to aim well. At that point
the Prince characteristically intervened to plead that they should not
'take any life without absolute necessity'; Mackinnon crisply commented that 'if they were forced to come to blows it was necessary
that none should get off to tell tidings'. But eventually Mackinnon
and his men pulled ahead and, as soon as they had a good lead, they
put in to shore at a point where the trees came down to the water
and where they reckoned the militia would not dare to pursue them
on foot for fear of being ambushed. The calculation proved correct,
and shortly the Prince's party had the satisfaction of seeing the
boatload of red crosses abandon the chase and turn for home. When
Mackinnon congratulated the Prince on his narrow escape and apolo-
gised for having overborne the Prince's wish to land earlier, the
Prince explained that his fear had been that they would be captured
on the water and

> 'that he would rather fight for his life than be taken prisoner, but
> that he hoped God would never so far afflict the King, his father,
> or the Duke, his brother, as that he should fall alive into the hands
> of his enemies'.

It was now becoming urgent to find someone who could give them
shelter, guides and support. It was going to prove difficult. After the
Prince had slept briefly on the hilltop from which they had spied the
militiamen's retreat, they again rowed across Loch Nevis to the
Knoydart (north) side to look for old Macdonald of Clanranald, who
was thought to be sheltering at the house of Macdonald of Scotus.
John Mackinnon left the Prince on a small island while he made a
reconnaissance alone himself.

They were right in thinking that Clanranald was in those parts; in fact, Mackinnon caught up with him just as he was entering Scotus's house. But it was not a happy encounter. Clanranald pretended not to recognise Mackinnon, and when firmly accosted replied:

'Oh, Mr Mackinnon, is this you? I did not know you. How do you do? It is not easy to know people that come to visit us now.'

Mackinnon explained his mission. The Prince was close by and wanted to know from Clanranald to whom he could turn for support and shelter; Mackinnon made it clear that he was not expecting Clanranald to run any physical risk on the Prince's account, nor even to receive him personally; it was merely local advice he was seeking. Clanranald, who had been helpful enough back on Benbecula a few weeks earlier when he brought provisions to the Prince in his hiding, now exploded:

'What muckle devil has brought him to this country again? . . . The troops upon hearing of his motions, will be sure to follow him fast and raze us all to the ground, leaving us nothing that they can either carry off or destroy.'

Mackinnon was astonished at this outburst and remonstrated with him: to whom could the Prince turn in his need if not to his friends? He was only asking for advice about any person in whose hands he would be safe. Clanranald was not to be budged:

'I tell you, Mr Mackinnon, I know of no person into whose hands I can put him. But if my advice or opinion can be of any use, it is that you should directly return with him whence you came . . .'

It was now Mackinnon's turn to explode:

'If this be the best advice you have to give, Clan, you had better keep it to yourself . . . I plainly see you are resolved not to do the smallest service to the Prince in his great distress, and that you only want to be rid of him . . .'*

* John Mackinnon quoted this whole exchange at length to Bishop Forbes in the infirmary in Edinburgh in 1761, adding it and other details to the account which the assiduous bishop had already obtained.

It was a curious exchange. Old Macdonald of Clanranald had been a loyal supporter: he and his brother – Boisdale – had provided one of the happier and safer interludes in the Prince's flight, and he had extended numerous courtesies including the gift of the much-appreciated silver drinking cup. What had soured him? It seems a classic illustration of the recognised fact that courage is an expendable commodity. Clanranald had had enough. His brother had been arrested. His friends and clansmen had been harassed. He felt old, tired and frightened. He had braced himself to help Prince Charles Edward before; he could not face it yet again. When Mackinnon reported this disheartened response to the Prince, the latter took it philosophically enough: 'Well, Mr Mackinnon, there is no help for it. We must do the best we can for ourselves'.

Faced with this rebuff, the best plan seemed to be to walk eight miles south to see if they got a better reception from another Macdonald – Macdonald of Morar. On the journey an incident occurred which Mackinnon was to describe as 'comical'. The Prince was again dressed as a servant – this time Mackinnon's. When they came to a ford of the deep and fast Morar river, Mackinnon asked their guide (who was unaware of the identity of the Prince) to give his servant a pick-a-back over the river. The response was reminiscent of that of the serving girl who had declined to wash the Prince's mud-spattered legs a few days before: 'The devil be on my back he comes, or any fellow of a servant like him'. Mackinnon did not press the point, but contented himself with escorting the Prince – arm in arm – across the Morar river. The Prince was getting better at concealing his 'royal air'.

Macdonald of Morar's house, like so many others, had been burnt down by Captain Ferguson, and he was living in a bothy with his wife (who was a daughter of Lochiel) and his children. The visitors had a friendly reception. Morar's wife wept at seeing the Prince come to such dire straits, but she warmed up some salmon. Morar led them to a nearby cave where he settled the Prince comfortably, who slept for ten hours.

But the next day Morar's attitude changed: 'he became all at once very cool and backward'. It transpired that he had encountered old Clanranald and – taking his cue from him – now said there was nothing he could do for the Prince and he did not know of anyone into whose care he could entrust him. This was too much for the Prince; hitherto he had been resilient in the face of hardship and rejection, but he now turned bitterly on Morar and said:

'When fortune smiled upon me and I had pay to give, I then found some people ready enough to serve me, but now that fortune frowns on me and I have no pay to give, they foresake me in my necessity . . . O God Almighty! Look down upon my circumstances and pity me; for I am in a most melancholy situation . . . I hope, Mr Mackinnon, you will not desert me to and leave me in the lurch . . .'

The old chief of Mackinnon imagined that these last words were directed at him and, with tears in his eyes, declared roundly: 'I will never leave Your Royal Highness in the day of danger'. The Prince promptly explained that he had not been referring to the chief, who was too old to be expected to make further sacrifices, and – in any case – in whose 'zeal for me and my cause' he was well satisfied. This prompted John Mackinnon to jump in with his own protestation that 'with the help of God I will go through the wide world with Your Royal Highness, if you desire me'.

All these recriminations and reassurances did nothing to solve the immediate problem of where the fugitives were to go. It was the Prince himself who decided: 'I am pretty sure', he said, 'honest old Aeneas Macdonald will be ready enough to do all he can for me'. Aeneas lived at Borrodale, some seven miles further south; it was with him that the Prince had stayed when he first landed on the mainland of Scotland the previous year. This was beyond the limits of the country which the Mackinnons knew and therefore a more local guide was necessary. The Prince asked this last favour of Macdonald of Morar who made up for his earlier unhelpfulness by offering his young son as a guide on the overnight march of 9/10 July. The Prince enquired whether the boy already knew him and, on being assured that he did not and therefore presumably would not compromise himself, readily accepted.

Yet another night march ended in the discovery of yet another

house burnt down by Captain Ferguson – this time that of Aeneas
Macdonald. He too was living in a bothy and he too knew of a nearby
cave on the beach in which the Prince could hide. But Aeneas was
no reluctant host like Morar had been; he stoutly declared to Mackinnon that he would not fail to take care of the Prince and 'shall
lodge him so secure that all the forces in Britain shall not find him
out'.

The Mackinnons – the old chief and young John – had now done
all they could for the Prince. It was probably with considerable relief
that they handed him on to Aeneas, John declaring: 'I have done my
duty: do you yours'. When the parting came John asked the Prince if
he might ever hope to see him again; the Prince replied that if it
pleased God that he should safely reach the Continent he had every
resolve to raise an army and return to Scotland, even if he had to 'go
and beg assistance of the Grand Turk'.

The Mackinnons then set out to go home to Skye; but like so many
of the Prince's erstwhile companions, they did not get far. The old
chief was captured the very next morning at Morar's bothy. John was
lying up near the boat and managed to get away in it overnight on 11
July; but he had no sooner set eyes on his own land again at Elgol in
Skye than he too was arrested by a party of militia. He was soon
handed over for interrogation to the barbarous Captain Ferguson,
who had one of Mackinnon's oarsmen stripped and flogged with the
cat-o'-nine-tails, and who threatened the same treatment for Mackinnon if he did not divulge the whereabouts of the Prince. Mackinnon
gave nothing away and was transferred to H.M.S. *Furnace* where,
like a number of other Jacobite prisoners, he was rescued from the
brutalities of Ferguson by General Campbell, to whom he declared:

> 'he knew nothing about the Prince, that he had not conducted him
> [more than] a gunshot from the shore, and had left him with a
> little boy they met accidentally, who had gone along with him as a
> guide'.

General Campbell then reminded Mackinnon that he could have
secured a fortune – the £30,000 reward – for himself and his family
by handing over the Prince. Mackinnon answered this with a frank
declaration of his feelings:

'to be plain with Your Excellency, what a base unworthy action it would have been in me who had been in his service, had received his pay, and broke his bread, to have given him up! I would not have done it for the whole world. And had I done it, I dare say Your Excellency would have looked upon me as a monster and a wretch.'

General Campbell – like so many of his clan a stout soldier and an honest gentleman – far from hiding his approval of these sentiments called for a bottle of wine and drank a glass with Mackinnon, to the satisfaction of everyone present except the vicious Ferguson.

The old chief of Mackinnon for his part was imprisoned for a considerable time. When eventually he was discharged – no doubt in part because of his age – the English attorney-general stressed the generosity of the Hanoverian king – George II – in releasing him and sending him back to Scotland. To this Mackinnon memorably replied:

'Had I the King in my power as I am in his, I would return him the compliment of sending him back to *his* own country.'*

He was an engaging character, and perhaps this is why the legend grew up that Prince Charles Edward entrusted to him the secret recipe for his own favourite liqueur – still marketed as Drambuie.

* * *

Prince Charles Edward had found the island of Raasay inhospitable: the houses burnt, the cattle slaughtered and the sparse population reeling from the vengeance of the redcoats. We found it a green and smiling island where we would have liked to have lingered longer, but the Prince had returned the day after his arrival to Skye again and the long marches ahead of us dictated that we did the same.

From the vicinity of Portree in the centre of Skye to the peninsula

* This remark is sometimes attributed to one of the other Mackinnons, but seems characteristic of the old chief of Elgol.

of Elgol in the south is a good twenty five miles walk. Captain Malcolm Macleod who accompanied the Prince had warned him it was a rigorous as well as a long walk. We had read what he said to the Prince: we had been warned too. The route ran through and round the Cuillins. The Prince found these forbidding mountains: he commented that the Devil himself would never find him in such a God-forsaken spot. His attitude was typical of his century: the period when wild and outlandish mountains were to be regarded as exhilarating and inspiring did not arrive until half a century later with Walter Scott and the Romantic Movement. But for those of us brought up with a twentieth century attitude to scenery, there can be few more spectacularly beautiful mountain walks in the world than that on which we were about to embark.

The first seven miles down Glen Varragill (where the road now runs) brought the Prince and brought us to Sligachan, a renowned climbing centre for the Cuillins. The Prince had had to skirt the little settlement there as it had a hostile garrison. We were able to refresh ourselves at the Sligachan Hotel before the long march that lay ahead of us, up Glen Sligachan by a well-marked path into the heart of the Cuillins.

The first hour's walk was along the broad bottom of the glen where the path followed parallel with the river Sligachan. In contrast to most of the hill walks which we had done on the mainland or in the Outer Hebrides, we passed a fairly steady trickle of people coming in the other direction; these were serious hikers – laden down with hefty back-packs from which obtruded handles of cooking pans and poles of tents – who had been traversing the Cuillins by the main track from the south coast of Skye to Sligachan; we envied them their clearly marked path and its proximity to the spectacular and highest peaks in the range. Our own route – as always dictated by the considerations that had influenced the Prince – was to be harder to define and to take us eastwards, away from the most dramatic rock formations.

After an hour we left the glen to traverse a swampy half-mile of moorland grass and spagnum moss before beginning a more rigorous climb following the steep banks of a burn called Allt na Measarroch on the ordnance map; this twisted and writhed its way up the hill ahead of us – punctuated by the flash of small waterfalls – to the saddle of the range. It was one of those deceptive and all-too-frequent saddles that presents a recurring skyline to the climber: each time such a skyline is reached – after much puffing and sweating – it turns out not to be the true skyline but just another ridge on an ever-longer convex slope. Eventually however we were rewarded by arriving at a brief plateau which looked across another wider burn ahead of us – the Allt Coire nam Bruadaran – towards a high ridge flanked by bare rock-faces which were for the attention of roped and cramponed alpinists rather than holiday hikers or mere hill-walkers like ourselves. Less lofty these might be than the spectacular peaks of the central Cuillins, but they looked forbidding enough to us. Fortunately our route did not lie across them but down to the burn below us and along its cascading banks to the head of Loch Ainort, then along the south bank of Loch Ainort (now the path of the A850 road) to the tiny clachan of Luib, and then south down the length of Strath Mor to Loch Slapin and the Elgol Peninsula.

This was the marathon march that the Prince had completed with Malcolm Macleod in the course of the one night of 3/4 July; it was crossing these 'wild muirs and glens' that he had philosophized with Macleod about everything from the intentions of the Almighty towards himself, to the importance of 'pissing' after drinking cold water on the march; and it was at the entrance to Strath Mor that the two Mackinnons who had been in his army the previous year recognized him – despite his disguise as Lewie Caw – and lamented the sad state of his appearance.

Strath Mor is a long and gloomy glen, lowered down upon by slaggy slopes, even on a day of sunshine and showers. We passed no cheerful hikers here but, just as I was recounting to Alasdair the Prince's remarks on this leg of the journey about preferring his kilt to the best breeches, we were overtaken by a remarkably well-turned out highlander – perhaps the son of some neighbouring laird – who swung past us in a Mackinnon kilt and goat-skin sporran. It was the latter (more appropriate to a highland gathering than a chance encounter in a remote glen) that most intrigued Alasdair.

'That's a very fancy piece of kit. It's really cool. What's it for?' he asked. We had a long slog ahead of us, so to pass the time I told him

all I knew about the chequered history of the sporran both as an item
of dress and as the catalyst for a curious and callous event in Scottish
history.

The sporran has always served a useful purpose as a purse, since a
kilt has no pockets and nor – by rights – do tight tartan trews. In fact
early portraits – notably that by Raeburn of Sir John Sinclair at
Ulbster as Colonel of the Rothesay and Caithness Fencibles at the
end of the eighteenth century – often show sporrans being worn with
trews. At the height of the highland revival in the nineteenth
century, the long horse-hair type of sporran, with numerous swing-
ing tassels, was much in favour; indeed this flamboyant variety of
sporran, with its silver mountings, is still in use in highland regiments. For civilian use, the leather sporran, with leather thongs or
tassels in place of the original purse strings, is more generally preferred. But sporrans have often been an evocative subject, and never
more so than in 1779 when they were one of the main provocations
leading to the mutiny of the Argyll Fencibles. The facts of that
bizarre affair* – ending in floggings and a death sentence – give the
flavour of the way in which the highland regiments were abused in
their early years.

The Argylls were stationed in Edinburgh Castle: bored by garrison
duties, resentful of their pay being in arrears and disgruntled at
being given 'absurd' goat-skin sporrans in place of the plain deer-skin
ones that were their traditional wear. Their chagrin was increased by
being expected to pay for these fancy and unacceptable sporrans by
deductions from the little pay they were receiving. They also took
against their ammunition pouches and belts, which were clumsy and
uncomfortable. They refused to wear the offending articles and
threw them out of their barrack windows.

Eventually their commanding officer, Colonel Lord Frederick
Campbell, marched them out of Edinburgh Castle to the links of
Leith. There they were peremptorily ordered to take up their
rejected sporrans and pouches. When they declined to move, six
mounted troops of the 10th Dragoons suddenly materialised from
the edge of the links and cut out six highlanders from the front rank

* They are comprehensively set out by John Prebble in his book *Mutiny: Highland
Regiments in Revolt 1743–1804.*

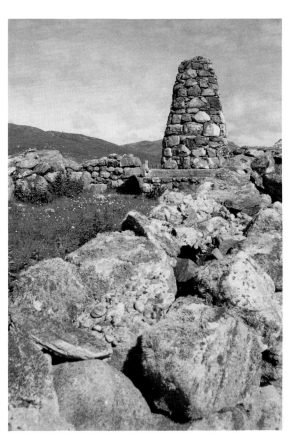

The cairn marking Flora Macdonald's birthplace at South Uist and (below) the harbour at Uig close to the point where Flora Macdonald landed with the Prince on Skye.

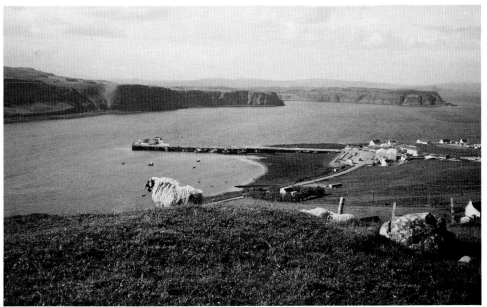

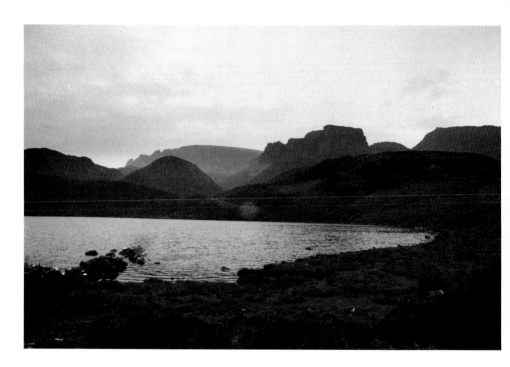

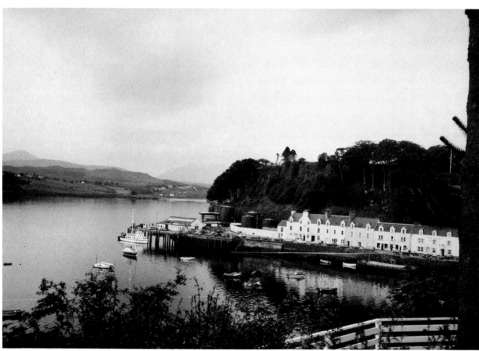

The Quiraing in northern Skye and (below) Portree harbour where Flora Macdonald parted from the Prince.

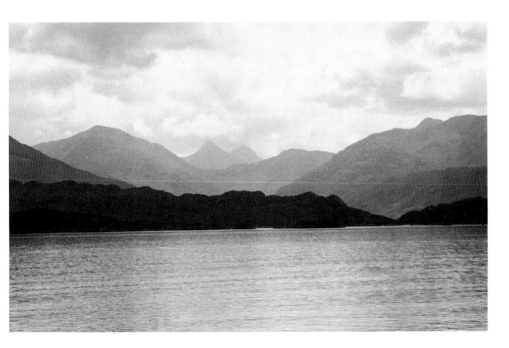

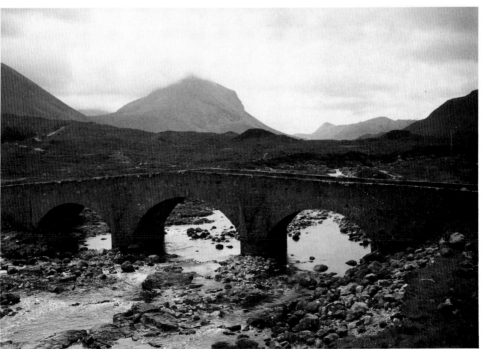

Two views of the Cuillins which the Prince would have seen: above, from the Elgol Peninsula and, below, over the old bridge at the entrance to Glen Sligachan.

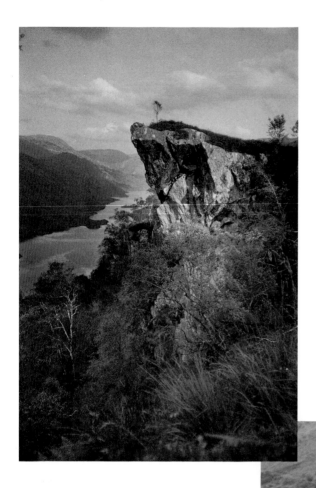

The view from the cave above Moible in the Braes of Morar where the Prince was hidden before he broke through the cordon around Moidart. Below, a young specimen of the highland cattle that still roam freely in these parts.

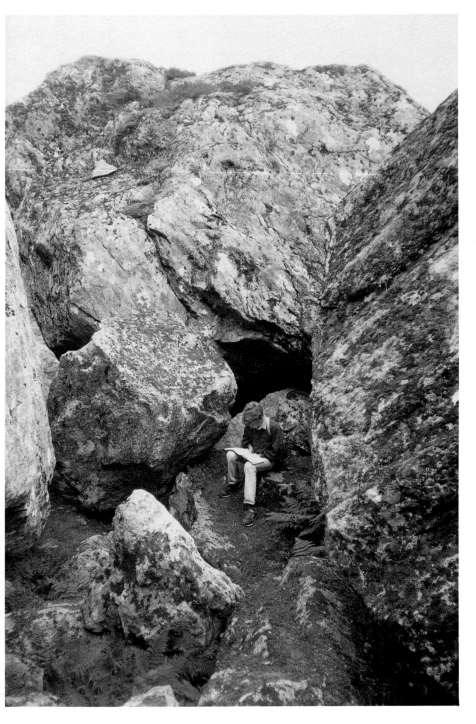

Alasdair studying his map at the entrance to the Glenmoriston men's cave in which the Prince rested 'as comfortably . . . as in a Royal palace.'

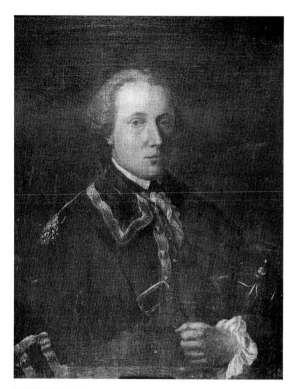

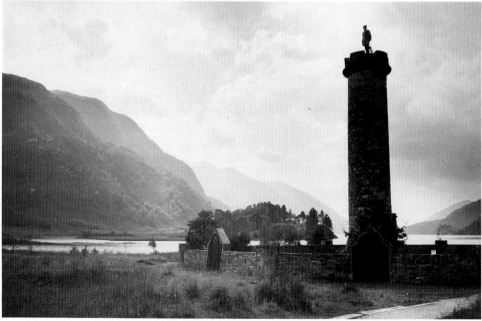

The Gentle Lochiel whose arrival with his clansmen at Glenfinnan, the scene of the memorial column below, signalled the start of the Forty Five.

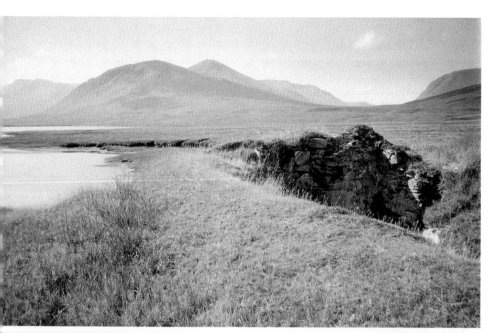

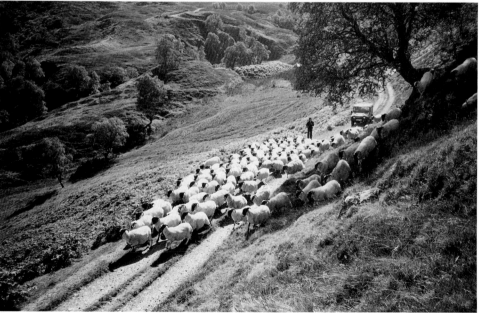

The remains of the shieling, above, where the Prince was nearly ambushed by mistake by Cameron of Lochiel, and where subsequently the Prince cautioned him not to kneel lest they should be overlooked from the surrounding hills and arouse suspicion.

Below: Sheep have been using General Wade's road over the Corrieyairack Pass from the Prince's day until the present.

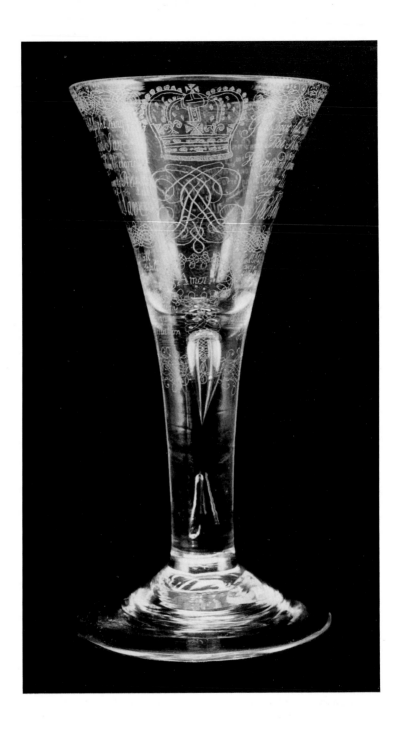

An Amen glass of the sort used by Jacobites to drink to 'The King over the water'. Of such supporters who failed to rally to his army, the Prince said 'I shall do for them what they have done for me: I shall drink their health.'

and herded them up to their colonel. Lord Frederick, after a hasty consultation with his commanding general (who – like the dragoons – happened to have prepositioned for the manoeuvre) ordered an immediate field court martial. Four of the men were promptly convicted of insubordination (two were acquitted, presumably to demonstrate that it was 'a fair trial') and sentenced to be flogged on the spot. The dragoons obliged the stunned highlanders to form a hollow square and witness the barbarous punishment in all its gory detail. This was a form of punishment unknown in the Highlands and the impact of the spectacle was all the more horrifying.

When news of what had happened on the links at Leith reached the few Argylls who had been left behind in Edinburgh Castle, mostly because they were sick or – ironically – on guard duty, they erupted in wrath and panic. Incited by one or two of their number who were bolder or more foolish than the others, they raised the drawbridge of the castle and declared that they would hold it against all comers. Indeed they probably could have held it, with judicious use of cannon and grapeshot, for long enough; but the sight of advancing dragoons frightened the ailing and half-hearted mutineers; the few officers and sergeants left within the castle eventually managed to lower the bridge and let in the dreaded dragoons who soon rounded up the mutineers. An even grimmer court martial followed: one man sentenced to be shot and another to receive a thousand lashes with the cat o' nine tails. A distaste for goat-skin sporrans had resulted in violence on a scale that would have been ludicrous had it not been so tragic.

If Alasdair wished he had not raised the question of sporrans, he politely gave no sign of it and limited his comments to wondering how so fine a regiment as the Argylls – of whom he had heard much on visits to Inveraray Castle – could have had such terrible officers. He was, I could see, already convinced of the axiom that there are no bad troops but only bad officers.

By the time we reached the head of Loch Slapin evening was closing in and, although we had not covered much more than half of the Prince's stoical night march, we were glad to find our prepositioned car. We spent the night a few miles further east, as also pre-arranged, with a Mr & Mrs Macleod at their cottage – offering

bed and breakfast – at Heast. The Macleods were determined to
make a living in the part of the world to which they belonged, and
were ready to turn their hand to whatever local employment made
that possible; our host had, in his time, woven tweed, fished profes-
sionally for lobster and langoustine, and raised sheep on the hillside
above his cottage, where the three hill-farmers of the hamlet
between them had the grazing over some 3,000 acres. He walked us
over the hill with his Border-Collie sheep-dog and a young puppy;
the older dog was loyal, canny and skilled but jealous of the attention
its master paid to the puppy. He could not leave the two together,
Macleod explained, as the older dog had killed an earlier puppy (not
his own) which had presumed too far on the older dog's prerogatives.
Alasdair was shaken by this tale of savagery: his previous experience
of Border Collies had been seeing shepherds taking them into a little
kirk in the Borders where they had been permitted to sit at their
masters' feet – silent and apparently attentive – throughout the
Sunday service.

The next day we drove down the narrow road, with its generous
provision of passing places, past Strathaird House (a Mackinnon seat)
to the end of the road at Elgol. Whether it was at Strathaird (as some
local tradition maintains) or nearer the village of Elgol itself (as the
contemporary record implies) that the Prince was subjected to the
indignities of having his thighs scrubbed by Mackinnon's cross and
class-conscious maid was unclear to us, but Elgol was certainly the
scene of the Prince's first meeting with the old Mackinnon chief and
his departure by boat for the mainland.

Elgol asserts its link with Prince Charles Edward in the same
fashion as many another location in the highlands and islands that
features in the tale of his escape: it has a cave designated 'Prince
Charles' Cave' on the ordnance map. The contemporary accounts of
the Prince's brief time – less than twenty-four hours on 4 July – with
the Mackinnons at Elgol do not suggest that he had to take refuge in
a cave, but the tradition is that he awaited the boat that was to take
him back to the mainland at a cave standing above high-water mark
on a small rocky bay a mile to the south of the village. The walk there
was one of the most beautiful of our whole expedition: we followed
the headland cliffs, that fell sheer to the sea, and looked across the

mouth of Loch Scavaig to the spiky silhouette of the Cuillins rising through wisps of cloud to a bright morning sky. A little further west, between us and the Cuillins, lay the island of Soay – almost cut in half by its deep harbour – where Gavin Maxwell had struggled so hard in the 1950s to establish a shark-fishing industry. But while gazing at the wonders of the scenery we also had to watch our feet: deep crevasses in the cliff face, in some cases so narrow as to be easily overlooked, cut across our path and invited a plunge hundreds of feet to the rocks and sea below. The Prince had embarked at night, and he must have been glad of the local knowledge of the Mackinnons to steer him safely to the cave, the final approach to which was down a steep track and involved back-tracking a few yards along the beach at the foot of the cliffs.

It was from here that the Prince left Skye for good and it was time we too returned to the mainland. Not having the assistance of the chief of the Mackinnons, we found it difficult to procure a boat at Elgol; it was also unnecessary, as from nearby Armadale there was a MacBrayne ferry sailing to Mallaig – the same destination as the Prince.

It was good to be back in Mallaig again. We installed ourselves in the same cosy, hospitable and slightly prim B&B overlooking the waterfront where we had stayed before setting out for the Hebrides and Skye. Everything in the house was spotless, and almost everything was pink: the curtains, the sheets and the shaggy loo-seat cover. The breakfast-time kippers were as plentiful and plump as before. Our feeling of well-being was only chilled by the daunting view of the hills of Knoydart which greeted us when we ventured out in a rowing boat on Loch Nevis to speculate as to which particular stretch of wooded shoreline had provided shelter for Prince Charles Edward after he had been chased by the militia with their red crosses in their bonnets: these hills of Knoydart were to be the terrain we had to penetrate and cross in the next few days. They looked as formidable as the Cuillins and much less frequented.

The Prince had been less hospitably received at Mallaig. He had had to spend three nights in the open air and then, when trying to find shelter on the other side of Loch Nevis, had been very nearly captured by the boat-load of militiamen; he had been rejected by old

Macdonald of Clanranald, and – still accompanied by the Mackinnons – had walked the seven miles south to Morar and sought a
haven there from the local laird – Macdonald of Morar. The latter
had received him at his bothy, but sent him for greater safety to
sleep in a nearby cave.

This was another cave we felt we should try to find. It was described as being near the mouth of the Morar river, in the face of a
cliff some twenty-five feet high, and near a pleasant white sandy
beach. It was low tide when we reached Morar and set off on the
south side of the wide river-estuary, walking over firm sand. But the
tide was coming in fast, and we had to take to the cliffs, edging our
way round them on narrow ledges, gripping with our hands as well
as our feet. For once my long stick was a definite disadvantage, and
Alasdair – with both hands free – was able to negotiate the route
with greater speed and safety. He led the way down and into a dark
cavern some twenty paces deep; another cave, almost as deep, was
close by, and we imagined that the party might have made use of
both. Rain came on and we collected some broken herring boxes
from the beach and lit a fire to warm ourselves in the cave, feeling a
closer kinship than usual with the beleaguered Prince.

From Morar the Prince had had to move on overnight on 9/10 July
to yet another protector: Aeneas Macdonald of Borrodale who lived a
further seven miles down the Arisaig peninsula. On the site where
Aeneas's house used to stand, there is now a luxurious highland
hotel; enquiries at the reception revealed that the land which old
Aeneas had owned, and on which the bothy where he received the
Prince had stood, still belonged to the same property. So did the
pastures leading down from the hotel to the sea; and on the lower
pastures by the coast yet another cave – that in which Aeneas
Macdonald had hidden the Prince 'so secure that all the forces in
Britain should not find him out' – was identifiable. It was a tranquil
and lovely spot, but we had had enough of hunting for caves for a
while.

We decided we should escape briefly from the Prince's route to
visit a nearby place of relevance to his story at an earlier stage (just
as we had taken time off to visit Flora Macdonald's birthplace and
grave). We would drive down the A830 from Borrodale towards Fort

William and stop at the memorial tower in Glenfinnan where the Prince had raised his standard the previous year. The tower, topped with the figure of a highlander, stands in its spectacular setting – the focus of every camera and ten thousand postcards. Opposite, across the road, is a small shop and standing exhibition telling the story of the Forty Five.

As we looked at the portraits and postcards of Prince Charles Edward round the walls of this tiny museum, Alasdair remarked that he must either have found it very tiresome having to wear such elaborate highland dress, or he must have been as vain as a peacock. There is some reason to think the latter was the case. Even before he came to Scotland, the Prince had affected highland dress in Rome. Not content with the normal colourful tartans and crimson coats, he had them trimmed with gold braid and ermine. Indeed, the Prince had always had a weakness for brilliant waistcoats of purple, scarlet, sky-blue or yellow satins and brocades; even in an age of foppish dressers, they were much remarked upon. Before he embarked for Scotland he had been in the habit of wearing shoes with two-inch high heels to add to his stature. As soon as he returned to France he was to appear in a rose-coloured velvet coat lined with silver tissue. To one so fond of dressing-up and fine clothes, the months of thread-bare breeches and dirty linen must have been a keen additional hardship of the flight. I looked back at the decorative portraits.

'All highland dress is elaborate', I said loyally. 'And of course when he was being painted he would have worn the lot.' The lot, in the Prince's case, tended to include the ribbon and star of the Garter and the cross of St Andrew – all set in diamonds.

'And just look at his hair', Alasdair went on. I explained it was a periwig: full-bottomed ones had gone out of fashion at the time Prince Charles Edward was growing up. For a while, as a young man-about-town in Rome, the Prince had dispensed with any wig in favour of his own hair, but there had been an embarrassing occasion when a visiting Irish officer had interrupted the Prince with his fair locks in paper curlers: Lord Dunbar had had to remonstrate with the officer to keep quiet about a practice which might have seemed – even to his contemporaries – as less than altogether manly. I saw no reason to tell Alasdair about the curlers.

As we emerged from the exhibition area an enormous charabanc drew up and disgorged some forty English tourists. This was one of the highspots of their Scottish tour; they had obviously not been wasting their shopping time in Fort William or wherever had been their last stop; almost to a man or woman they were decked out in tartan shirts or skirts, in blue bonnets and clan badges. The snippets of conversation we overheard revealed that 'Charlie was their darling': they were Jacobites to the core.

'Did many of the English join Bonnie Prince Charlie?' asked Alasdair. I could see the thought that had provoked the question, and on the drive back to Borrodale I tried to explain to him why the answer to his question had been such a disappointment to the Prince at the time, and a puzzle to many people ever since. The reasons were complex and highly political, and I skirted rather lightly over some of what follows.

When English sentiment is, and has traditionally been, so strongly in favour of the Stuarts, it is perhaps remarkable that – with the exception of the ill-fated Manchester regiment – there was virtually no English support for Prince Charles Edward during the Forty Five. Since it was this cold reception south of the Border (coupled with the failure of French support to materialise – a failure which is examined elsewhere in this book) which so obviously surprised the Prince himself and which embittered him towards the English and Welsh Jacobites* throughout his time in the heather and thereafter, it is perhaps worth looking more closely at what happened.

At first sight it seems very odd that no-one 'came out' for the Prince in England, where there was widespread discontent with the Hanoverians. The Whigs who formed the government, and who were the mainstay of the regime, excluded the Tory opposition from all key posts in the armed forces (where Tories often had to give up their expensively purchased commissions without compensation), in the legal profession, in the Bank of England and the chartered companies, and even in the countryside where they could not – for instance – be Lord-Lieutenant. In politics, since Tories were for so long excluded from government, many of the country gentry felt

* The Prince was subsequently to remark: 'I shall do for the Welsh Jacobites what they did for me: I shall drink their health.'

they could not afford to stand for Parliament while there was so little chance of recouping election expenses with the perquisites of office. The alleged justification for excluding the Tories from so many fields of patriotic activity was that they could not be trusted as they were potential Jacobites – a line of reasoning that came near to converting many to Jacobite sympathies who might otherwise never have held them.

In addition to these responsible elements who were opposed to the Hanoverians, there were many less reputable elements. Debtors saw the prospect of having their debts annulled by a Jacobite counter-revolution (indeed many of Prince Charles Edward's Scottish supporters were head-over-heels in debt*); the powerful smuggling gangs – some of Mafia-like proportions – supported all anti-government forces and passed information to the French about British naval movements in the Channel; those who had forfeited lands and property after the earlier Jacobite risings had little more to lose and everything to gain from a successful coup.

There were also philosophical doubts about the foundation and nature of Hanoverian Whig rule. The National Debt – a new-fangled device – was considered immoral by many. A peace-time standing army – as opposed to a militia – was considered by some as un-English and smacked of Cromwell's Commonwealth. The cynical corruption of Sir Robert Walpole – who died only in 1745 – with its condoning of placemen and graft, revolted many Englishmen. Across the social spectrum therefore there were people in England who were disillusioned about the House of Hanover and its ways: small wonder the Stuarts looked for some support south of the Border.

But they looked in vain. The hard fact was that however potent might be the desire for change in some quarters, vested interest in the *status quo*, coupled with fear of the unknown, were even more potent. Those in any sort of authority – whether concerned with local or central government – owed their position and income to the

---

* That impoverished Jacobite Lord Kilmarnock said on the scaffold that 'if Mahommed had set up his standard in the Highlands, I had been a good Muslim . . . for I must eat'.

patronage of the Hanoverian Whig regime; and it was these people who were least likely to risk upsetting a system that was working so satisfactorily to their advantage. While the Establishment held fast, less effective and influential elements in society – be they those who had lost jobs and estates, or debtors or malcontents – were not well placed to destroy that society.

There was also the fact that the Jacobite association with the Scottish highlands was a two-edged weapon. It added greatly to the romantic appeal of the movement – particularly in the eyes of posterity – but it also added greatly to the general apprehension about the movement in England. The Highlands were largely *terra incognito* to eighteenth century Englishmen (hence in part the success of Dr Johnson's *Journey to the Western Isles of Scotland*) and there was a very real fear of the wild, kilted, Gaelic-speaking warriors who came from those savage parts. There were plenty of honest English burghers who believed that the clamour-wielding highlanders slew their foes indiscriminately and even – it was said – were not averse to eating children when hungered after battle. The horrors of the English Civil War were only a hundred years before, and few wanted to risk precipitating another civil war in England's green and pleasant land.

What Prince Charles Edward and his supporters in France and Scotland failed to realise was that if the mould of Hanoverian England – set firm by sixty prosperous years since the Glorious Revolution – were to be broken, it required of them a massive effort of intrigue, diplomacy and public relations. A nation-wide net-work of contacts had to be established; bribes, promises and reassurances had to be applied; secret sympathisers in high places had to be activated; malcontents had to be stirred up. The half-hearted initiatives of the Old Pretender's court were just not enough, based as they were on a few equivocal collaborators such as Bolingbroke. In fact, the diplomatic and espionage initiatives lay firmly with the Hanoverians: while Sir Robert Walpole and the Duke of Newcastle in the English cabinet were receiving regular secret reports of Jacobite activities and plans in France, the Stuarts were woefully uninformed about events of importance to them in England. Walpole could boast to Thomas Carte

'How else can I learn the Jacobite designs but from the Jacobites themselves? Nobody else could inform on them.'*

because the Jacobite ranks were riddled with informers; and when information was not being sold to Walpole, he was having no difficulty in cracking the codes and ciphers used by the Jacobites in their correspondence between France and the united kingdoms of England and Scotland.

On the sole occasion when Prince Charles Edward complied with the advice of his commanders by sending a spy into England from his headquarters in Edinburgh (before the march south in 1745) he chose John Hickson whose indiscretions led him to be captured with secret messages from the Prince in his pockets; Hickson promptly told his captors all he knew to save himself from torture. Not only did the Prince thus learn nothing of Hanoverian troop movements, but he was himself made the victim of disinformation by the government: one of their agents – Dudley Bradstreet – persuaded the Jacobite commanders at Derby that an English army 9,000 strong stood between them and London at Northampton, when in fact no such army existed; this successfully planted deception was a major factor in ensuring the Jacobite retreat. (After the failure of the Forty Five the Hanoverian espionage effort was not wound up: notable achievements at penetration of the Jacobite plans and at monitoring the movements of Prince Charles Edward were achieved by Alistair MacDonell of Glengarry – known to history as 'Pickle the Spy'.)

Nothing that Prince Charles Edward did from France or Scotland, and nothing his father did from Rome, served effectively to activate the potential Jacobite supporters in England and Wales. South of the Borders Jacobites remained content to pass their wine glasses over their tumblers and drink romantically and safely to The King over the Water.

* Quoted by Frank McLynn in his *The Jacobites*.

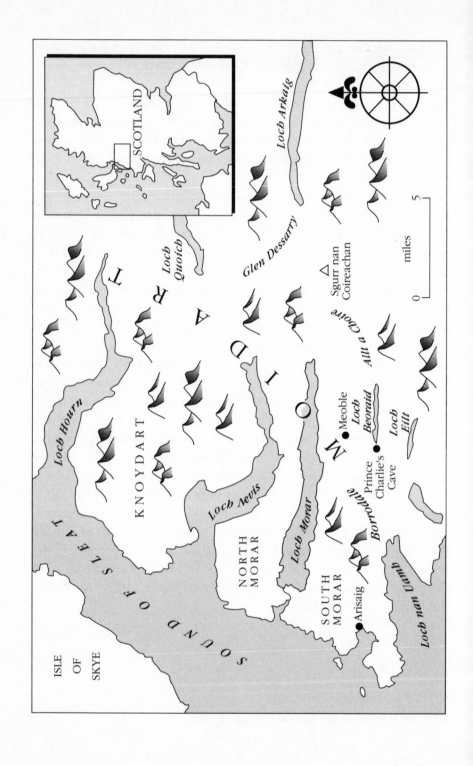

9

BREAKING
THROUGH THE CORDONS

WHEN the Prince heard of the Mackinnons being captured he realised that the hunt would be rapidly closing in on him. It was therefore thought best that he should move from the hut in a wood near Borrodale where he had spent the past three days (the beach cave having not been found necessary). Consequently on 13 July he went four miles east to hide in greater seclusion 'in an inaccessible cave, known to very few of the country people', which was described as being 'upon a high precipice in the woods of Borrodale'. The Prince had sent a message from Borrodale to Major Alexander Macdonald of Glenaladale asking the latter to join him. Glenaladale, who had fought and been wounded at Culloden, promptly answered the call and joined the Prince on 15 July in the inaccessible cave. The following day however Aeneas Macdonald got a message from his son-in-law informing him that 'it was whispered about the country that his royal highness was with them'; the messages went on to urge that they should not risk staying where they were any longer, but should go to a place of concealment he had prepared near Meoble in the Braes of Morar. No place seemed safe for more than a day or two.

The fact was that General Campbell, Captain Ferguson and Captain Caroline Scott knew well by now that the Prince had returned from the islands to Arisaig and they were positioning a cordon around the whole region and intensifying their patrolling of the surrounding waters. On 17 July, Aeneas Macdonald's son, who had been sent out to reconnoitre before any fresh move was made, 'visibly saw the whole coast surrounded by ships-of-war and tenders, as also the country by other military forces'. They later learnt that the English and militia camps were in a direct line from the head of Loch Eil in the south to the head of Loch Hourn in the north, thus cutting off the whole of Moidart – the three fingers of lands projecting into the Sound of Sleat (South Morar, North Morar and Knoydart) in which the Prince now was and had been since his return to the mainland. Furthermore the camps were

> 'within half a mile's distance of one another, their sentries being placed within call of one another, and patrols going about every quarter of an hour to keep the sentries alert, that so his royal highness might be surely catched should be attempt to pass through them'.

The next few days were to be a cat and mouse chase. It was clear that Clanranald's country – where they were – was no place to linger and they therefore decided to 'leave it with the utmost despatch, especially since it was impossible to join young Clanranald, the enemy being absolutely between them and the place where he was' (Clanranald subsequently wrote). The Prince set out on 18 July with Major Macdonald of Glenaladale, his brother and the son of Aeneas Macdonald of Borrodale; he left behind Aeneas Macdonald himself and his son-in-law. The plan was to work their way northwards travelling along the west side of the cordon and slip through it where they could. Glenaladale's brother was sent ahead to gather intelligence and a rendezvous was arranged at the top of Sgurr nan Coireachan – a 3,000-foot peak overlooking Glen Dessary and Loch Arkaig from the west – at ten o'clock that night. It was an ambitious plan, but at least had the merit that at the top of a mountain it would be impossible to miss each other and there would be a good field of view in the morning.

But it was not to be so simple: for one thing, the cordon was not a single line of camps and troops, but seems to have been sited in depth. On the way there they climbed the lesser peak of Fraoch-Bheinn to get a view of what was going on, and saw cattle in motion on the hillside below them. Major Glenaladale went ahead to investigate. It was what they had feared: his own tenant farmers were moving their cattle to keep them clear of government troops, five or six hundred of whom had reached the head of Loch Arkaig 'in order to inclose his royal highness in Clanranald's country, while the search was going on very narrowly within it'. One of the tenants' wives, seeing her laird's predicament but not knowing the Prince was with him, milked a cow and brought the milk up to them on the hilltop; the Prince's head was rapidly wrapped in a handkerchief and he was declared to be 'one of the Major's servants that had got an ache in the head'. The milk was most welcome, but the realisation that government troops blocked the route they had planned to take 'pretty much disconcerted their measures', as Glenaladale subsequently commented.

Worse was to follow. The next messenger brought in reports that a hundred Argyllshire militia were already at the foot of the very hill (Fraoch-Bheinn) on which they stood. They set off northwards without waiting for their hoped-for guide but instead 'trusting in the Great Guide that directs all'. They walked hard over the rough hills until about eleven o'clock at night when, passing through a small gully between two hills at Coire Odhar, they observed a man coming towards them down one of the hills. The Prince and Borrodale's son fell back while Glenaladale went forward 'to examine whether he might be friend or foe'. To their surprise and delight he was not only a friend, he was the very guide for whom they had earlier been waiting as long as they dared. This guide – Donald Cameron of Glen Pean – claimed to know the disposition of the government cordons and to be able to lead them through them. Glenaladale takes up the tale:

'Upon this they pursued their way through roads almost impassable even in day light, and travelling all night they came at four o'clock in the morning . . . to the top of a hill in the Brae of Lochharkaig, called Mamnynleallum, from whence they could (with the help of a prospective glass) discern their enemy's camp, being not above a mile distant.'

Being informed by the guide that the hill on which they stood had been searched the previous day by the government troops, they felt they could assume that there would not be a second search that day, and that they could safely lie up there; and so 'choosing the fastest place in the hill they took a little rest'. In the course of their rest, they had another stroke of luck: Glenaladale's brother, who had been sent ahead to spy out the land and – when he had not returned – had been assumed to have been captured, practically stumbled into the Prince's hide-out. 'The Great Guide that directs all' certainly seemed to be on the Prince's side that day.

When night fell, they plucked up courage to move on again – still northwards – and by one o'clock in the morning they reached Coire nan Gall on the borders of Glengarry's and Lochiel's country and to the west of Loch Quoich. Here they had hoped to find some of Lochiel's people who could have given them food; but there was no-one and 'as they had entirely run out of provisions, excepting a very small quantity of oatmeal . . .' they pressed on for an hour to 'a fast place in the face of a hill at the head of Loch Quoich' and there two of the party set off to look for some food while the others rested. All they came back with to eat were two small cheeses. But they also brought back news – grim news: 'about one hundred of the redcoats were marching up the other side of the hill his royal highness lodged in, in order to destroy and carry off such of the poor inhabitants as had fled to the hills for shelter.' There was nothing for it but to sit it out where they were all the following day and set out again about eight o'clock in the evening. The small cheeses were an inadequate day's sustenance after such a strenuous night and before another such.

However that might be, the Prince and his party 'travelled stoutly till it became dark' and climbed to the top of Druim Chosaidh from which they observed the fires of a military camp directly ahead of them. They sneaked past this in the dark, coming so close to the sentries that they could distinctly hear them talk. They climbed yet another hill and

'no sooner was his royal highness at the top than he and his small party spied the fires of another camp at the very foot where they were to descend'.

Again they veered off, this time into craggy country to the west. Now they were getting into very precipitous and dangerous terrain. It would have been tricky going in broad daylight; on a dark night it was distinctly treacherous. Major Macdonald of Glenaladale subsequently described the most nearly-fatal accident:

'crossing a small rivulet that gushes out of a spring, as I think, and glyded over a precipis att the very place we crossed it, Donald Cameron crossed first, the Prince next, and in crossing, missed a step, and 'tis altogether possible he would fall down the precipis, which we took to be very high, if he had not been very full of life, and that I caught hold of one arm and Donald Cameron of the other and recovered him in a tryce'.

Bad as this moment was, the night – it was 20/21 July – ended in triumph. At some time between one and two in the morning they passed between two more sets of sentries in Glen Cosaidh: they had broken through the cordon of redcoats around Moidart. General Campbell, Captain Ferguson and Captain Caroline Scott with their ships, their regular troops with their red coats, and their auxiliary militia with their red crosses, were all behind them. The Duke of Cumberland himself had abandoned the hunt on 18 July, setting out from Fort Augustus for England and wider acclaim; he left the disgruntled Lord Albemarle as commander-in-chief in Scotland.

Dangers in plenty lay ahead, but never again was the Prince to be surrounded as he had been during the previous weeks in Morar and in the hills between Loch Arkaig, Loch Quoich and the coast. The net had been holed. The trap had not snapped on them.

* * *

By the time we had finished talking about the English Jacobites we had driven the whole length of Loch Eilt and were back in the braes of Morar. We spent another night at Arisaig before commencing the long return march through the hills of south Morar towards Glen Pean and the even wilder mountains to the north: this was the area where the cordon had been pulled tightest round the Prince.

The following morning early we left the A830 road at Arieniskill and climbed by a narrow but clear track up the side of the Allt na Criche burn towards yet another of the caves where the Prince had hidden away. This time it was that place of concealment offered by Angus MacEachine in the braes of Morar near Meoble. Although marked clearly enough on the ordnance map as 'Prince Charlie's Cave', like so many others, it proved more than usually elusive. When eventually we found it, or at least a cave which we persuaded ourselves must have been it, there was a magnificent view across Loch Meoble and down the River Meoble to the cluster of farm buildings also of that name. There were distance views from the neighbouring peaks, and one could well imagine how Aeneas Macdonald's son 'visibly saw the whole coast surrounded by ships-of-war and tenders, as also the country by other military forces' when he had been sent ahead to reconnoitre this region.

It was from here that the Prince set out to break through the cordon surrounding the whole Moidart peninsula. The line he took from the cave above Meoble was almost certainly along the north shore of Loch Beoraid where now a reasonable path leads ever deeper into the higher hills. Rocks and precipices crowd in on the walker and the path up the Allt a Choire finally expires altogether as it approaches the peak of Sgurr nan Coireachan. Up here in the heart of Lochaber one is about as far from human habitation as in any part of the British Isles: it is country for red deer and not for people.

While lying in the heather and eating my sandwiches – my 'piece' as a gillie would call it – I surveyed the hillside opposite. It was too high for sheep and to the naked eye there seemed to be no life there. But as I looked more closely, I thought I could detect shapes among the rocks which had softer outlines than the others. Further scrutiny through binoculars confirmed my impression: deer were grazing. At first I could pick out only a few, and none with antlers: these were the females – the hinds. But then I saw, not far off but standing somewhat detached from the hinds, what I was looking for – a stag.

He stood as stags should – erect, his head pointing up wind, alert to danger, and looking as if he might have been posing for Landseer. I studied his head and tried to count the points of his antlers, wishing I had brought a telescope – the traditional stalker's equipment – rather than binoculars with their wider field of vision but less intense magnification. Each antler seemed to have five forks: a ten-pointed, a 'good' head, but not in the rare class of a Royal (twelve points) or the legendary class of an Imperial (fourteen points).

As I lay watching him stand motionless I recalled a day many years ago when I had spied just such a ten-pointed on the hills west of Inveraray in Argyll. I had been out with the last Duke of Argyll's head stalker – Angus, I seem to remember he was called. He had contemplated the ten-pointer long and tenderly through his spyglass: 'Och', he had finally declared, 'he's a wee bitty too good for ye'. I had known what he meant: the stag not only had a good head but was in the prime of life. Such stags, if they were to be shot at all – and Angus mostly ensured that they were not – were for Americans who were paying a fortune for the privilege of a trophy, or for visiting royalty. For ordinary guests, the ideal stag was an old one which would not survive another winter on the hill. For such a beast, a quick bullet through the heart or the lungs (the target area is about the size of a football, at the base of the neck) was a more merciful end than a lingering one among the snows of winter when, hungry and possibly lame, an aged stag attracts the sinister attentions of 'hoody' crows looking covetously at its eyes and hoping for its carcass.

What Angus preferred to shoot, and what in fact we had shot on that particular day, was a 'switch'. This was the term applied to a stag which, instead of growing two balanced antlers each with an equal number of points, had grown one antler as a single horn – like an antelope. In the rutting (mating) season when stags fight each other to establish their claim to their own groups of hinds and their own territory, they run at each other, clashing antlers and pushing until the weaker or lighter stag gives up and runs off. In this process a switch is a dangerous menace: instead of the relatively harmless clash of equal antlers – albeit attended by some splintering of horn – which normal stags indulge in, the switch slips its single horn through the branched antlers of its opponents – inflicting terrible wounds and often blinding its adversary. A single such defective beast could maim a score of stags in a season. For this reason Angus considered that the only good switch was dead switch.

Deer stalking is almost as old as the Highlands themselves. In ancient times, when the Highlands were much more heavily forested than now, a man with a bow and arrow would have stood a good chance of getting within range of a deer. But on the open heather-clad and boulder-strewn hillsides of modern times, the rifle (or earlier the musket) is the necessary weapon. Prince Charles Edward and his companions must have scoured the glens for deer in their hungrier moments, but more often he seems to have been content with a salmon or a sheep – far easier prey.

The great days of deer stalking date from Queen Victoria's fondness for the Highlands and Prince Albert's passion for the sport. Like a lot of 'continentals' he did not quite get the point to start with, and showed a disconcerting propensity to blaze away at grazing beasts from the windows of Balmoral. But once he had been properly initiated, he trekked over the hills and glens indefatigably, relishing the long climbs, the long crawls along the beds of burns or peat hags, and the whole physical marathon that lies between the initial sighting of the stag – perhaps at a range of more than half a mile – and the final panting, heart-thumping shot from a range of about a hundred yards. He had learnt – as doubtless Prince Charles Edward had done before him on his simpler hunting forays in the Hebrides and Badenoch – that it is no easy matter to cover the ground between sighting a stag and getting within safe range ('safe', because to shoot from too far risks injuring rather than killing the stag, and to leave a 'wounded beast' on the hill is the ultimate deer stalking crime).

A stag's sight and hearing, especially when on the alert in the rutting season, is quite as sharp and acute as a human's, and added to these faculties the stag has a sense of smell far transcending the human: he will catch a glimpse of a pale human face if it is not shaded by the peak of a deer-stalker cap; he will spot a tweed-clad bottom protruding from supposedly 'dead ground'; he will hear the scratching of heather on an anorak (hence the fact that true stalkers stick to tweeds – practicality being as important as elegance); he will observe a disturbed sheep and assume danger in any such unexplained factor; but most of all, he will – literally – get wind of any approaching human who is rash enough to approach from up-wind of him, so a stalker needs to study the direction of the wind as keenly as a yachtsman. And when a stag is puzzled by any such strange sight, sound or smell, he does not stop to ponder or investigate: he takes to flight with one bound, and will then leap or run for many miles before stopping to take stock of the situation. A disturbed stag is a lost stag for the stalker; and once the stag is on the move the hinds will follow and a situation ensues which is described as 'setting the whole hill in motion'. There are no second chances for stalkers.

Prince Albert's passion was infectious. The Victorian aristocracy flocked to the Highlands; they built lodges there; they acquired tartans; they had their portraits painted – in poses resembling Prince Albert's – by Landseer. One of the fashionable addresses of Oscar Wilde's hero in *The Importance of Being Ernest* is 'The Sporran, Fifeshire, North Britain'. Nor did the enthusiasm for deer stalking and the Highlands fade away. In the 1920s, John Buchan wrote the greatest classic of deer stalking – *John Macnab* – about three famous and fashionable London figures who set out to poach salmon and deer in the Highlands as a way of adding a spice of adventure to their otherwise sedate and secure lives. In the course of recounting their adventures, Buchan imparts much of the lore of stalking. He describes the head stalker's approach:

'Wattie managed to move both circumspectly and swiftly. He seemed to know by instinct when a hind could be bluffed and when her suspicions had to be laboriously quieted. The two men went for the most part on their bellies like serpents, but their lowliness of movement would have been of no avail had not Wattie, by his sense of the subtle eddies of air, been able to shape a course which prevented their wind from shifting deer behind them . . . After that it seemed advisable to Wattie to keep to the water, which was flowing in a deep-cut bed. It was a job for a merman rather than for breeched human beings, for Wattie would allow of no rising to even to a kneeling position. The burn entered at their collars and flowed steadily through their shirts to an exit at their knees. Never had men been so comprehensively and continuously wet.'

And Buchan's heroes have a very proper sense of the right stag to shoot and of how to shoot it. Palliser-Yeates is caught poaching a stag on the Glenraden forest by the daughter of the house, who comments to herself:

'He was beyond question a sportsman. The stag was just the kind of beast that a sportman would kill – a switch-horn, going back in condition – and he picked him out of a herd of better beasts. The shot was a workmanlike one – through the neck.'

Lord Lamancha, one of the two other amateur poachers, goes for a more ambitious but equally acceptable target:

'The third stag was no heavier, but he had a head like a blasted pine – going back fast, for the beast was old, but still with thirteen clearly marked points and a most noble spread of horn. "It's him," Wattie crooned. "It's the auld hero . . . and if ye dinna kill him he'll perish next winter, belike, in a snaw-wreath, and that's a puir death to dee."'

Buchan's aristocratic adventurers were as at home on a Scottish hillside as in the leather armchairs of their exclusive London clubs.

All this I had in mind as I peered through my binoculars at my ten-pointer. The longer I looked at him, the more handsome he seemed, standing four-square into the wind. There was no doubt about it: Angus would have declared him too good for me. On the other hand, Angus always saw that one got a satisfying stag. I remembered how once he had pointed out to me what appeared to be an over-large hind. He had declared it to be a 'hummel', which was apparently a stag whose hormones had got somewhat confused, resulting in its growing to great bulk but with no antlers and either no ability to service the hinds or a disturbing ability to reproduce itself and breed more hummels. Angus declared that hummels were bad for the forest: they should be shot for their meat, but not as sport by guests of the Duke. He would despatch them himself.

Angus had very strict ideas on the protocol of venery, and indeed on protocol altogether. He would not speak, if he could help it, at all until the stalk was over and the stag had been gralloched (gutted) with a long-handled knife by him; thereafter he would not be averse to accepting a dram from one's flask and even volunteering an occasional remark while one waited for the pony – led by a diminutive boy – to come up to carry the carcass back to the castle larder. Usually his remarks would be confined to the finer points of the stalk or the stag or the weather; but one of his conversational sallies has remained in my mind as an example of the outlook of a highlander whose horizon is healthily bounded by his own environment.

'His Grace was saying you live abroad, Sir?'

I confirmed this was true (I was in fact on leave from a distant embassy at the time). Angus sighed.

'I hear abroad's in a bit of a mess these days', he said.

It seemed to me then to be a fair comment on the state of the world outside Argyll: it still does.

I had rested long enough, ruminating on stags and stalking. There was much ground to cover before nightfall.

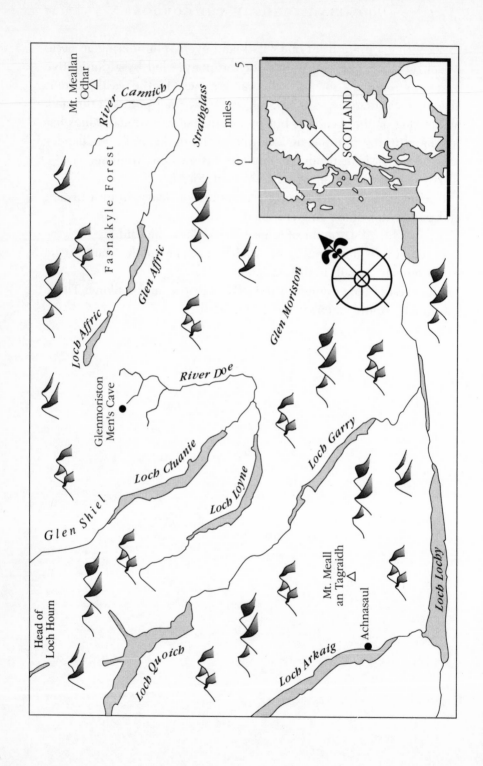

10

THE GLENMORISTON MEN

P RINCE Charles Edward had broken through the cordon surrounding Moidart, but the extent to which he and his companions were still in enemy territory was borne in on them
soon enough. They had spent what remained of the night of 20/21
July in a fold of hollow ground, well concealed by tall heather and
branches of young birches, on Coire-Sgoir-Adail at the head of Loch
Hourn. Once more the existing guides – Donald Cameron of Glen
Pean and Alexander Macdonald of Glenaladale – were nearing the
limits of the county they knew, and it was necessary to find those
with more local knowledge to guide the Prince further. Accordingly,
at around eight o'clock the following evening, Cameron and Glenaladale climbed out of the hollow ground and set off to find fresh
guides. The latter recounted what happened next:

'No sooner did they get out of the fasthold than they found they
had lodged all day within a cannon-shot of two small camps, and
spied a company of redcoats getting in some muttons to a cot and
chusing out some for slaughter.'

They promptly withdrew to their 'fasthold' and told the Prince how
close to his enemies he had been sleeping. There was nothing for it
but to wait until dark and then set out – without a local guide –
northwards towards Glen Shiel. Their route lay through the pass of
Coire Mhalagain, close to steep precipices, and was not made easier
by the fact that dark clouds obscured the full moon and produced

what John Macdonald (who was also still with them) described as 'the darkest night ever in my life I travelled'.

They reached Glen Shiel at three in the morning 'quite exhausted with hunger and fatigue'. Somewhere on the route they had met a certain MacGrath, who had given them some butter and cheese which they eagerly devoured despite the fact that both were 'exceeding salt'. They then hid up for the rest of the day on a rock above the river that ran through Glen Shiel. It was 'exceeding hot in the face of the mountain' and they all suffered appallingly from thirst, no doubt aggravated by the salt they had consumed. But although the river was only forty yards below them, and although they 'were all seized with such a druth that we were like to perish before sunset', Glenaladale would not allow anyone to slip down to the river to drink or collect water. They sweltered it out. (It is thought that this event inspired the incident in Robert Louis Stevenson's *Kidnapped* when David Balfour and Alan Brek lie panting with thirst all day on top of a rock while redcoats search the heather below them.)

But they had one great piece of good luck that day. While they were talking about how they would manage for guides,

'a Glengarry man appears towards them who that morning had been chased by the troops (they having killed his father the day before) from Glengarry to Glenshiel. Upon seeing this man, the Major [Glenaladale] knew him . . . to be a trusty fellow'.

It turned out that the Glengarry man had earlier served in the Prince's army. It was decided to 'make use of him as a reserve in case they should be disappointed with the intended guide'. Meanwhile Donald Cameron of Glen Pean, now uncomfortably far north of Glen Pean, was allowed to return home to look after his beleaguered family.

The question of guides was obviously related to what direction they wanted to go in. The original thought had been to head north to Poolewe, on the west coast, to meet a French ship that had been reported to be there looking for the Prince. But while the party was hiding in Glen Shiel a messenger arrived at seven o'clock in the evening at a 'place appointed' with the disheartening news that the

French ship – like so many before it – had 'gone off'. There was nothing for it but to change plans and to make use of the Glengarry man who was being held in reserve. The latter 'most cheerfully' took on the task and was brought to the Prince, who had remained in hiding while these delicate contacts were made with his companions.

Again, it was a night departure with them heading eastwards this time – towards Glenmoriston. This night had a peculiar drama of its own. They had not been going long when Glenaladale 'clapping his hand to his side' realised that he had lost a purse with the gold coins which the Prince had given him for their expenses. They retraced their steps and found the purse which had been left behind at a spot where MacGrath's young son had brought them some milk. But on examining the refound purse it was discovered that an inner purse, in which the gold had been, was missing. They concluded that it must have been deliberately removed and the obvious suspect was the MacGrath boy. Glenaladale and John Macdonald decided they must retrace their steps further – all the way back to the MacGrath's bothy in Glen Shiel. It was already midnight when they reached it, and Macdonald has described the scene that ensued:

'the boy's father, who at the time was sound sleeping, was called out, and fairly told what happened; without a minute dela he returned to the house, got hold of a rop hanging there, and griped his son by the arm in great passion, and addressed him in the following words: you damnd scoundrel this instant get these poor gentlemens money, which I am certain is all they have to depend upon, or, by the heavens, I'll hing you to that very tree you see this moment. The Boy shivering with fear went instantly for the money, which he had burried under ground about thyrty yards from his Fathers house.'

It was an uncharacteristic incident. No adult highlander on the mainland had attempted to rob the Prince or – a far more tempting proposition – to earn the £30,000 reward by betraying his whereabouts. But the embarrassing affair had a happy ending: indeed it diverted a disaster, because while Glenaladale and Macdonald were back at MacGrath's bothy an officer and two armed private soldiers from the government forces passed by the path they were on and 'if they had pursued their journey they would inevitably have fallen in with these persons' with fatal consequences. Once again, good fortune or the Almighty was on their side.

Having reassembled, the Prince's little party again travelled all night and came the following morning, 23 July, to a hillside above Strathclunie where the Prince 'suffered greatly by mitches'; despite being wrapped from head to foot in his plaid and being covered with heather, he still was to be heard sighing and groaning. Highland midges were more of a hardship to him than any amount of long nocturnal walks and narrow scrapes with the militia. By the early afternoon they could bear it no longer and decided to move on; hearing firing not far off (somebody else's father being shot perhaps?) they climbed to the top of Sgurr-nan-Conbhairean, between Glenmoriston and Strathglass. By this time they were wet through and spent a most uncomfortable night in an open cave where they could neither lean nor sleep. The Prince lit a pipe in a vain effort to warm himself up and – presumably – to keep the midges at bay.

In these circumstances, everyone was in favour of an early start the next day, 24 July: the guide set out at 3am and the Prince followed at 5am. At 7am they all met up again on a further hill top. It was somewhere here that they were approached by a highlander – who turned out to be also called John Macdonald – bringing them some milk. On approaching the party the newcomer recognised the Prince, despite the latter being well wrapped up with his head covered in a white nightcap and 'an old Bonet above'. On seeing the wretched condition the Prince was in – 'his shirt was the colour of saffron' we are told and he must have had very little sleep – the newcomer flushed 'as red as blood' and declared:

'I am sorry to see you in such a poor state, and hope, if I live, to see you in a better condition, as I have seen you before at the head of your armie . . . all I can doe is to continue faithful to you while I live, and am willing to leave my wife and children, and follow you wherever you incline goeing'.

The Prince was obviously moved by this affirmation of loyalty (which had to be translated to him from the Gaelic) and he in turn declared that he had always found Macdonalds loyal to his cause and that 'I shall admit you to my small party and trust myself to you'. He added his customary promise that when he 'came into his own' his new friend would not be forgotten.

In fact it was the newcomer who was about to admit the Prince to *his* small party. The Glenmoriston Men, of which he was one, lived in a much more commodious cave than those in which the Prince had lived so roughly in recent nights; it was at Corredhogha in the Braes of Glenmoriston. This cave resembled a grotto and was luxury indeed after what they had been through:

'He was refreshed with such cheer as the exigency of the time afforded; and making a bed for him, his royal highness was lulled asleep with the sweet murmurs of the finest purling stream that could be, running by his bedside, within the grotto, in which romantic habitation his royal highness pass'ed three days, at the end of which he was so well refreshed that he thought himself able to encounter any hardships.'

Indeed, John Macdonald was to add that they found themselves 'as comfortably lodged as we had been in a Royal palace'.

The Glenmoriston Men were a curious band of outlaws. There were eight of them – three Chisholms, two Macdonalds, a Macgregor, a Grant and a Macmillan – each with a price on his head. Since Culloden they had lived by raiding and plundering the government forces, stealing arms and food not only for themselves but for others in distressed circumstances in the surrounding glens. Had more of the Jacobite army taken to the hills in small groups such as this, let alone in larger units, they could have made the Highlands ungovernable. But, after Culloden, the will and the organisation were not there and, in any case, Cumberland's troops could have been relied upon to have taken savage reprisals from the civilian population if there had been any general guerrilla warfare. The Glenmoriston Men survived because they kept to their mountain fastnesses and befriended other Jacobites. They had hardly expected to find themselves playing host to His Royal Highness Prince Charles Edward Louis John Casimir Silvester Severino Stuart.

After the three days 'refreshment' they moved to another nearby cave for a further four days. At the end of this full week of rest and recuperation they heard news that suggested that another retreat was indicated: a certain Captain Campbell of the militia – known as Black Campbell – had encamped a bare four miles away. Accordingly, having left one of their number behind to watch what Captain Campbell might do, they set out northwards and by dawn the following day they had reached Strathglass. They were now in the country of Clan Chisholm, and – since they were told that Captain Campbell had not followed them – they slept in a shieling* without too much anxiety.

The Prince again sent scouts to Poolewe to bring him news of whether the expected French ship was now there, and meanwhile pressed on further northwards himself. He moved from one shieling to another, frequently passing the days in 'fast' woods, and eventually reached Glencannich. From there the Prince and his party climbed a peak to the north of the glen, which was almost certainly that now called Meallan Odhar (2300 feet) and which had earlier – according to eighteenth century maps – been called Binachen, hence its confusion with the present Beinn a'Chairein which lies to the south of Glencannich. This was in fact the furthest point north which the Prince reached in his travels (a point made in almost all the accounts and which would not have been the case had he climbed Beinn a'Chairein). It is not quite clear why he climbed this peak: possibly to try to spot the messengers returning from Poolewe.

When the messengers did catch up with him, it was once again with disappointing news. The only French ship had sailed away (it is uncertain whether this was the same one as had already been reported to have sailed away when they were at Glen Shiel) but a 'couple of gentlemen' had been landed to find the Prince and were

---

* These shielings were usually primitively constructed huts, sometimes of stone or turf, built by herdsmen in summer as temporary shelters from the weather. The Highlands were – and are – scattered with them and they were a god-send to the Prince on his travels.

making their way towards Badenoch, that is to the south-east. The Prince thought they must have despatches for him so he decided to go back on his tracks in the hope of making it easier for them to find him.

They crossed the Cannich water at Muchrachd, a Chisholm residence, and reached the forest of Fasnakyle, which runs along the south side of the water, where they hid up in thick woods for three days (9–11 August). They then heard that the government troops who had been searching for the Prince in Glenmoriston – presumably Captain Campbell's party – had gone back to Fort Augustus, so they felt it was safe to go back to Glenmoriston themselves.

The Prince was now anxious – as there was no point in going on to Poolewe – to rejoin his old friend and companion Cameron of Lochiel, whose 'skulking gound' was on the other side of Glengarry and Loch Arkaig. But when they got back to Glenmoriston they learnt that 'a strong party' was scouring the Braes of Glengarry still looking for the Prince. By 14 August it was reported that Glengarry was clear of troops and so the Prince and his party moved south again, along the line of the river Loyne and then along the south bank of Loch Loyne till they came to a place where they could ford the river Garry. This was none too easy:

'the rain came on so heavy that the water swell'd to a great height. Two of the company went first to try if they could wade the water, and they found it passable, even though it came up to their very middle'.

The Prince and the others then followed 'at the hasart of our lifes' (said John Macdonald), only to spend a most uncomfortable night a mile further on 'on the side of a hill, without any cover, though it rained exceedingly'.

The following morning the rain had not let up. But – still intent on finding Lochiel – they pressed on southwards across more wild country until they came to the north bank of Loch Arkaig at Achnasaul where they found another 'fast place' in the form of a cave in the wood of Torre Chrone, which must have been a considerable

improvement on the hut in which they had sheltered earlier in the
day and in which 'it rained as heavily within as without'.

By now the party was not only very damp but very hungry.
They had hoped to be joined by Cameron of Clunes – who knew this
strip of country well – with some food. But all they got was a
message from him suggesting another wood nearby in which they
could safely await his arrival the following day. Morale was low. But
when the advance party went ahead to reconnoitre Clune's wood,
they had a stroke of luck: they managed to shoot 'the finest deer (a
large hart) that could be, at the very place where the Prince
intended to pass the night'. Without more ado 'they most deliciously
feasted'.

The next day (16 August) Cameron of Clunes was as good as his
word and joined them and led them to yet another wood, this time at
the extreme eastern end of Loch Arkaig – a loch with which the
Prince was already familiar from his earlier journeyings. Becoming
impatient to join Lochiel, the Prince sent John MacPherson to sum-
mon him. Eventually, on 20 August, Lochiel's brother – Dr Cameron
– did arrive, accompanied by the Rev John Cameron, with Lochiel's
apologies for not coming himself. A further wait of several days was
necessary before it was deemed safe for the Prince to make the long
and arduous trek across to Badenoch to join Lochiel, and during that
time all the Glenmoriston Men (with the exception of Patrick Grant)
returned to Glenmoriston. Glenaladale too returned at around this
time to his own country: he had done right royal service to the
Prince and was now to continue this by looking out for French ships
on the west coast.

It was a tedious and uncomfortable wait, and at one stage there
was even an awkward scare when a party of Lord Loudon's government troops were thought to have discovered the hut at Torvault
where the Prince had recently been hiding, and he was consequently
obliged to retire to the top of Meall-an-Tagraidh and spend various
nights wrapped in his damp plaid on the summit or slopes of that
inhospitable peak. But eventually on 28 August he was able to set
out, accompanied by Dr Cameron, on the march south-eastwards
into Badenoch and towards his old friend Lochiel.

The whole chapter of events since he had broken through the

cordons around Moidart had been arduous and confused. The danger
of immediate capture – of stumbling unawares into a patrol or
ambush of redcoats or militia – had been less than formerly; but
the disappointments and discomforts had been as bad as ever.
The repeated reports of French ships having sailed off without
him had been disheartening in the extreme. The weather had broken
again and most of August had been as wet as only Scotland can
be; apart from the days in the Glenmoriston caves, the Prince had
been sorely exposed to this bad weather. He had also been lonely,
missing his old Irish companions – Sheridan, O'Sullivan, O'Neill –
and his faithful manservant Burke; although Glenaladale had been
with him throughout August and had proved a prudent and stout-
hearted guide, he was not as close to the Prince as his former
companions had been, and consequently towards the end of August
the Prince was increasingly obsessed with his desire to rejoin the
noble and civilized Lochiel who had been at his shoulder throughout the previous year's campaigning. But Lochiel had not been
able to come to him, at first no doubt because of his wounded
ankles and later apparently because it seemed more sensible for the
Prince to come to the comparative safety of Badenoch than for
Lochiel to meet him on less certain ground. It had been a frustrating
and debilitating period – with exhausting marches east, north and
south again – and by the end of the month the Prince had already
been on the run for nearly 140 days and nights. The government
troops might be flagging in their efforts to track him down, but
whatever comfort this provided was dulled by an uncomfortable
suspicion that the French were also faltering in their efforts to rescue
him.

* * *

Prince Charles Edward had broken through the cordon around
Moidart between the head of Loch Hourn and Loch Quoich. The
narrow unfenced road that runs along the north shore of Loch Garry
and Loch Quoich is now extended to Kinloch Hourn at the very head
of Loch Hourn. There was therefore a breaking point for our clamber
through Lochaber along the east of the Knoydart peninsula: we

could be collected by the Land Rover Discovery and taken to the
comfort of a bed in Invergarry before returning to Kinloch Hourn to
do the final gruelling passage up Allt Coire-Sgoiradail and down Allt
Mhalagain to Glen Shiel.

We were glad of a rest before this last part of the most arduous of
all the Prince's marches. The path that he took on that 'darkest night'
(after the false start in daylight when they had so nearly stumbled
into the redcoats rounding up 'muttons' for slaughter) is still a pronounced track. It starts beside a tiny lochan and climbs steeply
beneath steep crags till it joins the wider glen of Coire Sgoiradail.
The reason the track does not start at the foot of the main glen is
clear as soon as you reach it: the roar of a waterfall announces the
fact that the glen ends in a series of minor precipices which the track
has circumvented.

Coire Sgoiradail is a long slog. It climbs steadily into the fastness
of Kinlochhourn forest. Views of Loch Hourn are quickly left behind.
The going – as so often on a Scottish hillside – becomes soggier as
you go higher. The track must be used by sheep and presumably an
occasional shepherd, but any thought that one might meet another
human being here seems fanciful. It is a secret, enclosed landscape
that lies ahead with endless false summits and increasingly frequent
outcrops of rock and bare cliff faces. Even the deer seem to eschew
this barren landscape.

But one form of highland wild life was not absent. Looking up at
yet another horizon above us we saw the largest bird I have ever
seen in Britain: a golden eagle was systematically patrolling the sky,
quartering the ground beneath it in search of its prey.

Golden eagles are the most handsome and formidable of all indige-
nous British birds of prey, and the highlands of Scotland are still
their preferred habitat. It has been calculated* that one pair of
eagles might be expected in some parts of the highlands – such as
Wester Ross – to about every 16,000 acres of deer forest, and they
would normally hunt over an area of roughly this size. Their food is

---

* F. Fraser Darling and J. Morton Boyd give much fascinating information on the
life styles of the golden eagle, and on other Scottish wild life, in their *The Highlands
and Islands*.

varied: on the western seaboard, duck and other sea birds provide the main diet; inland and further east, grouse and blackcock, hares and rabbits, pheasant and ptarmigan, calves of red and roe deer, young lambs and carrion sustain the predator. A day's food for a golden eagle will vary from 8 oz to 2 lb of flesh, although they have been known to lift off prey or carrion weighing up to 11 lb. There is even a documented case of a golden eagle having been seen to lift a struggling wild cat 1,500 feet into the air and then drop it (over Mam Rattagan in Kintail) to its death.

Normally the golden eagle will prefer to make its eyrie on a craggy eminence, where its eggs are safe from interference by foxes, stoats or – worst menace of all – men. But in the Outer Hebrides they are often obliged to nest at almost level ground. Two eggs are normal, though frequently only one eaglet survives, and experts reckon that the fertility of eagles may be adversely affected by eating the carrion of sheep whose coats have been impregnated with the chemicals used in sheep-dips. At least the practice of shooting the rare golden eagle is now not only illegal but declining.

Having reached the top of the pass, among a litter of boulders around a tiny lochan, the view northwards looked deceptively reassuring. A long slope descended to a wide glen below with no trace of any human habitation but a faint path along the bottom of the valley. The path climbed out of view over a shoulder of hill to the north-west: this was Bealach Duibh Leac.

It was a further two hours till we had reached this point, and the final ascent had been an arduous scramble. Random boulders had given way to incipient cliffs. The way down the far side – by the Allt Mhalagain – was steeper and more alarming than anything we had encountered either that day or for some time. Loose rocks crashed ahead of us into the stream far below. How Prince Charles Edward had negotiated this terrain at night, even with expert guides, defeated our imagination. We knew he had had falls, but to fall here was to risk broken limbs as likely as twisted ankles.

Now we could see clearly in the evening light the wide Glen Shiel and the substantial river of the same name. This had been the route of an old military road long before the Prince had passed that way, and it was still marked as such on the ordnance map. To our right –

eastwards – patches of forestry lined the road that followed the course of the river and glen.

We reached the river near Achnangart. It was here that the Prince had arrived 'quite exhausted with fatigue' at three in the morning, and had then had to lie up all day within sound of the river and consumed with thirst. We were more fortunate, getting a lift to a hospitable B & B.

The next day we followed the Prince's route down the main glen – Glen Shiel – for about five miles until it merged into Loch Cluanie. Although he had probably avoided the most frequented track along the bottom of the glen, there was little point in our avoiding the road that now ran there as this was flanked with forestry. However it was possible and necessary to leave the road as it ran along the north shore of the loch if we were to emulate the Prince's ascent of Sgurr-nan-Conbhairean. We struggled up to the high ground where John Macdonald had accosted the Prince's party and had taken them under his protection.

There is no record of the route by which John Macdonald led the Prince from their meeting near Sgurr-nan-Conbhairean to the Glenmoriston men's cave; as the crow flies the distance is only a couple of miles, but both miles are made up of a succession of cliffs, so it seems likely that Macdonald would have made a detour to lead the party into his secret fastness up the only practicable approach – the glen carved out by the Allt Coire Sgreumh.

This was the route which Alasdair and I decided to take. It had the merit that we could get the Discovery well up a track following the River Doe (from the main Glenmoriston road) into the heart of the Ceannacroc forest. The Doe is a river as delightful as its name: although a peaty brown, the water flows fast and clear with occasional clumps of trees providing shade or shelter for the odd intrepid sheep.

But once one reaches the point where the Doe is formed by the confluence of its two component burns, the going gets much tougher. We crossed a final wooden bridge and then were climbing over open moorland. On the map, although there are no paths marked, the route looked clear enough; on the ground it proved all too easy to mistake one burn for another and one ridge for another.

As always, it was the compass that convinced us – as we walked due west – that we were in the right glen.

After two hours we could clearly see the cliff face at the head of the glen that, according to the ordnance survey map, contained 'Prince Charlie's cave'. As we got closer, it transpired that there were numerous clusters of big rocks, any one of which could have been the site of the famous grotto-like hideout of the Glenmoriston men. The burn petered out in a series of watery and treacherous ruts, waiting to reward a misplaced foot with a broken ankle.

'You take the rocks to the right and I'll take the ones to the left', said Alasdair.

I would have liked to have thought that he was offering his father the gentler terrain in deference to his advancing years, but I suspected that he thought the rocks to the left looked the more promising bunch. If so, he proved a good judge of country.

After forty-five minutes of clambering up to every likely redoubt, and wondering whether a succession of dubious caves could – with poetic licence – have been described as providing 'as comfortable lodging as a royal palace', and deciding they could not, there was a cry from Alasdair.

'This looks promising: come on over.'

I did, and we went round to the back of a clump of granite boulders that would not have looked out of place in the Khyber Pass. Sure enough, at the back there was a cleft between the rocks leading down into a wider passage off which could be discerned an inner chamber. Better still, a tiny burn trilled through the cave giving off the 'sweet murmurs of the finest purling stream'. Just as we decided we had certainly found our destination, we looked up and saw confirmation in the form of an inscription on the rock. This had been put up by a descendent of one of the Glenmoriston men and affirmed that we were in the cave where the Prince had so happily and safely recuperated from his exertions. Alasdair had found it.

We ate the last of our ginger-nut biscuits in celebration and walked, with a light step, the two and a half hours back to the River Doe and the waiting Discovery. Throughout the whole period since we left the road through Glenmoriston we had not seen another living soul. No wonder the Prince had been secure here.

The following day we had to pick a route at random through the hills between Glenmoriston and Glen Affric; there was no precise information on the line the Prince had taken. We decided to follow a logical route which coincided with a good walkers' track which ran from near Dundreggan Lodge, on the north bank of the River Moriston, due northwards for five miles to Loch na Beinne Bainne and then through more forestry to the hamlet of Tomich and from there by a narrow local road down to Loch Affric and the river of the same name at Fasnakyle House.

Alasdair had been commenting, as he often did, on the far greater density of wild life than human life in the Highlands and I thought it was appropriate to qualify his romantic views of Scottish chieftains by telling him something of the brutal story of the Highland Clearances of the last century which account for the present paucity of inhabitants. There seemed no better illustration of this than the history of the very region – Glen Affric – which we were entering. It was a long and sad tale.

When Prince Charles Edward reached Glen Affric and its continuation to the north-east – Strathglass – these glens were still well peopled with Chisholms and other clansmen. Had he come there seventy years later he would have found a very different scene, for this was one of the regions to be most affected by the Highland Clearances – the ruthless removal of residents to make way for the more profitable introduction of large-scale sheep farming.

John Prebble, in his moving account*, has told how the lowland graziers came to Strathglass and how Alexander, the 23rd chief of the Chisholms, listened to their tempting offers of a fortune in gold coin if only he would 'resettle' his clansmen and leave their broad glen open for 'improvement'. The old chief was tempted; but a thousand of his clansmen rallied outside Comar House while he was entertaining the graziers and represented to him – in fairly forceful terms – that the sheepmen were a worse menace to their traditional way of life than any marauding invader from the past. The graziers were chased off to the skirl of pipes.

But when the 23rd chief of the Chisholms died, his successor

* *The Highland Clearances* (London, 1963).

proved less attentive to the concerns of his clansmen. The Chis-holm's factor evicted almost half the residents of Strathglass – proba-bly about a thousand souls – in 1801; they joined the five thousand highlanders who emigrated in the first years of that decade from Fort William to Nova Scotia and other parts of Canada. Many perished of fever during the voyage on the packed emigrant ships. A few years later most of the rest of the Chisholms were moved out to make way for Cheviot and True Mountain Sheep. Some joined the newly formed Highland regiment of the British Army; others found tem-porary refuge over the hills to the north on the estate of Lord Lovat; but most ended up in lumber camps in the timberlands of Upper Canada.

Sheep farming had become big business in the Highlands, and it was incompatible with small croft holdings. The lairds, who had for so many centuries felt that the only possessions and status they needed were their castle or fortified house and the few thousand broadswords of their supporters at their back, now found they needed to gratify more expensive tastes if they were to maintain their prestige in the new world of the Regency.

For the period of the great clearances in the North – of the replacing of men by sheep – was to coincide with the period of the great highland revival in the South. While The Chisholm and the first Duke of Sutherland – like many other lairds – were burning crofts and implementing 'improvements' in their glens which obliged their tenantry to emigrate, the drawing rooms of London and Edinburgh were witnessing an unprecedented enthu-siasm for highland reels and tartan trews. The first decades of the nineteenth century saw the heyday of Sir Walter Scott's novels; they saw King George IV's corpulent Hanoverian figure decked in Royal Stuart kilt and plaid and painted by Sir David Wilkie; and they saw the Clanranald Macdonald of the day dancing reels such as Hamilton House with the King's mistress at Almack's Club in London.

All this high fashion led to high expense. The rents which had been paid by highland clansmen to their chiefs had traditionally been meagre or even nominal, because augmented by feudal services. Now the chiefs no longer wanted such services; the Forty

Five had put an end to the possibility of raising private levies; no longer was the fiery cross sent out across the hills and glens to muster loyal clansmen. What the chiefs wanted was a solid cash income from their estates to meet the expenses of phaetons on the Brighton road, of clothes to compete with Beau Brummell or of refinements for their elegant southern residences. All too often they also wanted capital sums to pay off their gaming debts. Thus estates which had once been seen as fiefs held in sacred trust came to be viewed as mere sources of income or capital, to be put down to sheep or sold off to graziers.

The first part of the process helped the recruitment of highland regiments: as the evictions attendant on clearances increased in frequency in the early years of the nineteenth century, so clansmen flocked to join their traditional regiments – from Ross and Inverness to the Seaforths, from Deeside to the Gordons, from Lochaber to the Camerons, from Argyll and Sutherland to the regiments of those names. In the battles of the Peninsular War and – above all – at the battle of Waterloo the presence of large numbers of highlanders was one of the great strengths of the British army. But as the clearances continued and intensified, men were not leaving the glens to join the army as there were no men left in the glens. The famous Highland Brigade under General Sir Colin Campbell which formed the thin red line at Balaclava in 1854 (after nearly half a century of further clearances) consisted of a single under-strength regiment of the 93rd (Sutherland) Highlanders. When the Duke of Sutherland himself went to Dunrobin Castle at the height of the Crimean War and held a public meeting, to explain the national threat represented by the Tzar of Russia and to offer inducements to fresh recruits to his regiment, he was given the same answer as his factor had received: 'Since you have preferred sheep to men, let sheep defend you!'

For Prince Charles Edward, the fact that Glen Affric and Strath-glass were still well populated in 1746 was a mixed blessing: it meant that the sight of men moving on the hill was not unusual, but it also meant that there were all the more eyes to spot him and – it must have been feared – all the more legs to run with news of him to the nearest garrison.

We thought of all these things as we strode past Fasnakyle House and were reunited with the Discovery. We drove through Cannich and headed towards mount Meallan Odhar.

Whatever reasons may or may not have prompted Prince Charles Edward to climb Meallan Odhar, our own motive in doing so was straightforward: he had done it, so we should too. The approach through the Fasnakyle forest and along the River Cannich revealed a sparsity of those thick woods in which the Prince had found shelter: here there were solid blocks of Forestry Commission conifers but otherwise only blue heather-clad hillside. The Sherwood-forest-type existence which the Prince had relished for his days here was possible no longer.

We passed Muchrachd, traditionally a Chisholm family property and the place where the Prince had forded the river and where there is now a bridge, and managed to get the Discovery along a good farm track on the north of the River Cannich as far as Liatre farmhouse. There a tumbling burn indicated the most direct line of approach to Meallan Odhar. Following the burn was not so easy: the bed of the stream was strewn with huge rocks and its banks were shoulders of deep heather and bell-heather. At times we were scrambling on all fours. After a mile of such slow progress, the burn and its banks flattened out into a little plateau filled with well-spaced old trees, mossy banks and lichen-covered rocks – as unlike the sinister blocks of serried pines on the other side of the river as could have been. Here we rested awhile before making the final assault on the summit; the gradient from there on was steady and steep rather than dramatic.

From the 2,300-foot hilltop the view was open and extensive. I speculated with Alasdair about the reason for the Prince having climbed Meallan Odhar. It was not impossible that he might have hoped to spy from here messengers coming from further north – from Poolewe, for instance, from whence there had been persistent rumours of French ships coming to search for the Prince.

'But why should they have taken so much bother?' Alasdair asked. 'After all, he wasn't a *French* prince was he.'

Why indeed. Alasdair had – as so often – put into words problems that had been nagging at the back of my own mind for some time. The French connection was a highly complex one: the Bourbons were at once the mainstay of the Jacobite cause and the source of all its greatest frustrations. As Alasdair and I tramped down the mountain, enduring that prolonged state of hardly-perceptible rain which is known locally as 'Scotch mist', I tried to put the French involvement into some sort of historical perspective for him, to help him understand the Prince's moods and movements.

Prince Charles Edward's relationship with France was a crucial theme throughout his months in the heather: his movements were directed by the expectation of French ships arriving to rescue him; his solvency was dependent on French gold, and his morale was sustained – or dampened as the case might be – by despatches reporting on the measure of sympathy for him and his cause currently prevailing at Versailles. But it was not only during the period of his flight that relations with the French court were a dominant consideration: they were of vital importance almost throughout his life and indeed also throughout the life of his father – the Old Pretender, or King James III as he was respectfully known at Versailles. To understand Prince Charles Edward's dependence on – and faith in – France, it is necessary to look back over the whole period of the Jacobite exile.

Among the staunchest supporters the Jacobites ever had was Louis XIV – the Sun King. He had befriended and sustained James II after the latter's flight from England in 1689, and awarded him an annual pension of 600,000 livres. He also made vigorous – if intermittent – efforts to restore him to his throne. The first of these was in 1692 when a French fleet was assembled on the Normandy coast, but was deterred by a combination of superior English seamanship and inclement weather (a powerful double which was to frustrate more than one attempt to restore the Jacobite monarchy). Louis XIV next turned to diplomacy but, although he gained some measure of international support for James II's son being accepted as heir to William and Mary as king of England as well as of Scotland, the Pope was unsympathetic and the diplomatic negotiations were still-born. Louis XIV turned back to the possibility of military solutions.

One of the basic problems about a French invasion of England was that the French expected to be supporting an uprising by the English Catholics and Jacobites, while the English opponents of William and Mary (and later of the Hanoverians) felt that they could only be expected to start an uprising in support of a French army already on English soil. Neither party felt confident or brave enough to act alone – or even first. While both sides hesitated, the moment passed and Louis XIV found himself committed by the Treaty of Ryswick in 1697 to desist from giving the Jacobites military aid against William III of England.

When four years later James II was dying in exile, Louis XIV's ministers advised him to take the opportunity to break with the Stuarts by declining to recognise his son – the Old Pretender – as James III. Louis XIV refused. For him, the doctrine of the divine right of kings was a compelling one. Far from declining to recognize 'James III', he went to the bedside of the dying James II and declared:

'I come to tell Your Majesty that, whenever it shall please God to take you from us, I will be to your son what I have been to you, and will acknowledge him as King of England, Scotland and Ireland.'

By 1702 England and France were at war again – on opposing sides in the War of Spanish Succession – and by 1708 6,000 troops were embarked at Dunkirk poised for an invasion of Scotland this time.

Once again the British navy – under command of Admiral Byng on this occasion – frustrated the invasion force. Once again also the English Jacobites were supine and – to add to the Stuarts' problems – James himself succumbed to measles. Another European peace treaty – that of Utrecht in 1713 – was signed and Louis XIV had to agree to James being required to leave France, ultimately for Italy.

The next chance of a Jacobite restoration with French help was to come about in 1714 with the death of Queen Anne. But James – staunch in his unpopular Catholic faith and feeble in most other respects – did not rise to the expectations of his Jacobite supporters. (Thackeray in his *History of Henry Esmond* gives a vivid fictional account of the opportunity for a Restoration that might have been his.) By the time of the abortive 1715 rising, Louis XIV was a dying man himself; he felt inhibited by the Treaty of Utrecht from giving

active support, but persuaded his grandson – King Philip V of Spain
– largely to finance the expedition. With Louis XIV's death James
lost 'the best friend he ever had', in Lord Bolingbroke's opinion.
Certainly the Stuart cause was to fare less well in France from then
on.

Louis XV was also to be a friend to the Stuarts, but a less consistent one and not an immediate one. Although he succeeded Louis
XIV – his great-grandfather – directly (his own father and grand-
father having predeceased Louis XIV) he was only five years old in
1715, and others less well-disposed towards the Stuarts were to rule
France during his minority. The first of these was the Duc d'Orleans,
the Regent; he had none of Louis XIV's sentimental attachment
either to the Stuarts or to the doctrine of the divine right of kings
(possibly because he was not one himself). He was a stickler for the
terms of the Treaty of Utrecht and obliged the Jacobites to disem-
bark the weapons they had loaded on to ships in French ports for an
invasion of Scotland.

Nor did things improve for the Stuarts with the death of Orleans
in 1723. Cardinal Fleury, who became the dominant influence in
French foreign policy for the next two decades, gave no succour to
the Jacobites. Indeed he would not even allow the Old Pretender to
re-enter France to use it as a springboard for a sudden reappearance
in Britain at the moment of George I's death in 1727.

Not until 1743, with Fleury's own death and the War of Austrian
Succession, did the tide turn again in France in favour of the Stuarts.
Louis XV was now a man of thirty-three (ten years older than Prince
Charles Edward) and at last felt himself in command of his own
destiny and – at the same time – increasingly vulnerable in the
European war in which he was engaged. An attack on England had a
strong appeal to him, and what better pretext than a restoration of
the Stuarts. An elaborate but secret plan was made: a Jacobite army
of 3,000 men would be landed in the Scottish highlands to draw
the Hanoverian troops north, while a much larger army of 10,000
French veterans of the continental wars – under the formidable
Marshal Saxe – would be landed in southern England and march on
London.

As always with plans to invade England, the problem was to

command the Channel for long enough to effect a safe crossing for
the invaders. This was to be achieved by Admiral de Roquefeuil
setting sail from Brest with a French squadron to lure the English
fleet westwards down the Channel and away from the short sea
crossing. The two traditional defenders of the English coast – superior British seamanship and bad weather – then again played their
part: Admiral Sir John Norris trounced Admiral de Roquefeuil, and a
series of storms off Dunkirk scattered and sank a large part of the
assembled invasion force. Louis XV reluctantly abandoned the whole
project.

But by then Prince Charles Edward had the bit between his teeth.
He had made a surreptitious return to France from his father's court
in Rome, slipping away from a hunting party before the English
spies – who continually kept the Jacobite court under surveillance –
realised he had gone. He had crossed Europe in disguise and in
haste. When he found that the 1744 project had been given up, he
tried in vain to kindle Louis XV's interest in reviving it with himself
– the Prince – at its head.

By this time – early 1745 – Prince Charles Edward was on the
Channel coast and raring to go. He was convinced that if an invasion
once got under way, then Louis XV would be obliged – indeed
delighted – to back it with a substantial army. The best course
seemed not to wait but to precipitate the action himself. By July
he had gathered a group of Franco-Irish supporters, chartered
two vessels, collected some arms and ammunition and embarked
– as we have seen – on the Forty Five rising. The whole strategy
depended on prompt and massive support from France. It is hard to
know to what extent the Prince genuinely felt confident of this, or to
what extent his protestations of confidence were whistling to keep up
the spirit of his supporters. Subsequent evidence showed that after
the Battle of Prestonpans, Louis XV did indeed try to revive the
invasion plan: another army, this time 15,000 men under the Duc de
Richelieu, started assembling at Dunkirk before moving to Boulogne
for a crossing to Rye. But it was not assembled fast enough: before
it was ready, the news had reached Versailles that the Prince was
in retreat from Derby. All that remained was for Admiral Vernon
to blockade Boulogne, and for the weather again to turn rough.

The Prince was left in retreat and unsupported to face Culloden alone.

The failure of French support might well have embittered the Prince towards Louis XV, but he chose to believe – rightly as it happens – that the King was on his side and that it was his ministers who were dragging their feet. 'A King and his Council', he had observed while talking to his companions in the Hebrides, 'are two very different things'. Some proportion of the money which Louis had sent had got through to him, and this meant that he could at least pay for the provisions and services he received during his long flight. He believed that Louis was encouraging the French ships that were trying to rescue him from the highlands after Culloden, and he knew how many such ships there had been. His hopes for the future, for another return to Scotland and another rising, rested on Louis; and he believed that he – Prince Charles Edward – and he alone could galvanize Louis into decisive action despite the cautious restraints of his ministers. Lastly he was confident – again rightly – of a warm welcome, indeed a hero's welcome, from Louis at Versailles could he but get safely away from Scotland. The breach between the two men, culminating in Louis's arrest of the Prince and forcible expulsion of him from France, lay in the future and far from the thoughts of the Prince as he waited hopefully and impatiently for despatches from his 'dear cousin' in France. The 'auld alliance' of France with Scotland was enjoying its final fling.

By the time I had tried to give Alasdair the gist of this we were back on the Cannoch river and ready to begin retracing our steps, as the Prince had done, through Fasnakyle forest again to Glenmoriston. Here the Prince had been held up on 13 August while he sent scouts ahead to see if the next stage of the journey – the Braes of Glengarry – was clear of government troops. Had he known it, it was the very day that Lord Albemarle (Cumberland's successor as Commander-in-Chief) had broken up his camp at Fort Augustus and marched his troops south, despairing of finding his quarry, and leaving behind only Lord Loudon with his one regiment and sixteen companies of militia.

We did not dawdle, but pressed on to Glen Garry. Where the Prince had forded the River Garry with difficulty we were able to take advantage of a bridge two miles beyond the western end of the loch. But while we avoided getting as wet as the Prince in crossing the river, we could not avoid getting as wet as him in the steady downpour of rain that greeted us on the southern side of Loch Garry. The six mile walk, first through forestry and then across open hillside, between Loch Garry and the east end of Loch Arkaig was completed in possibly the worst weather conditions of any part of our expedition.

As the mists came down, we consulted the compass ever more frequently to ensure that we were keeping to our correct bearing.

'So far, so good', said Alasdair, 'but what happens when we hit the next big patch of marsh and can't go straight ahead?'

'Then we have to go off to the side – eastwards – counting our paces as we go, until the marshy ground gets more solid in front and we can go ahead on our correct bearing. Then later, when the marsh is behind us, we have to count out the same number of paces back in the opposite direction – westwards – until we're on our original line again. In the jungle when I was in the army', I added, unable to resist telling my own campaign tales, 'we sometimes had to go off the route for miles to get round mangrove swamps or bamboo thickets, and it was jolly difficult to tell how far you'd gone, so when you next had to call up an airdrop of rations you were often guessing just where you were.'

'Did the rations sometimes not come?' asked Alasdair.

'Yes', I said 'and then all the men in one's platoon they knew were lost and one had lost them.'

There was a long silence and then Alasdair said softly through the mist:

'Daddy, I think we're lost now. The map shows we ought to be going downhill and we're climbing again.'

Alasdair was right. South was downwards according to the map, and our compass showed that we were trudging due south. But our feet and lungs told us we were going upwards. It was a bad moment, but happily not a very long one. We resisted the temptation to mistrust the compass (always a disastrous and – in my experience – unjustified mistrust) and were soon rewarded by finding that we were again on the downward path. Our short-lived upward gradient had been a spur too short to register on the inch-to-the-mile ordnance survey map.

Back on Loch Arkaig at Achnasaul the weather closed in on us as it had done on Prince Charles Edward when he was sheltering in the hut in which 'it rained as heavily within as without'. We knew that he had been forced to retreat to the summit of Meall-an-Tagraidh when a party of Lord Loudon's redcoats had got uncomfortably close to his hideout in Clunes Forest. So we decided that we must climb up the Gleann Ciaaig to reach the same summit.

The path started easily enough at a pretty waterfall by the road-side between Loch Lochy and Loch Arkaig; the ordnance map even marked an inviting 'forest walk'. The woods along the glen were a happy mixture of deciduous trees, rather than the monotonous pines of the Forestry Commission. The weather cleared. Rowan berries brightened the path and after three miles of gentle climbing we came to a primitive wooden bridge below a waterfall. Here the rowans were joined by the blue berries of the Bog Whortle, the pink of Sheep's Sorrel and the yellow of Field Milkthistle. The trees had given way to open rolling hills.

We followed the track below the ominously steep south face of Meall-an-Tagraidh in the hope that an easier way to the summit might open up. The path wound round the east side of the peak and ended in the forlorn ruins of Fedden – once a shepherd's bothie and sheep-pen but now a crumpled pile of stones at the foot of the mountain. Could the prince have sheltered here from the stormy weather and the advance of Loudon's troops? The contemporary accounts stated that he retired to the top of the peak, so we had no option but to climb it too.

We were rewarded for a 45 minute scramble to the 2,500-foot summit by a spectacular all-round view. To the east lay the high cliff faces of the Glengarry forest; to the south the wooded glen up which we and the Prince had walked; to the south-west some lesser peaks concealed most of Loch Arkaig, but to the north the land lay open over a wide and marshy valley descending to the solid blocks of forestry fringing Loch Garry. The summit formed a neat cone with no easy or hidden approach: it was not hard to see why Cameron of Clunes had insisted on this point as the safest retreat in the whole region.

It must also have been the windiest. We are told the Prince had to sleep wrapped only in his damp plaid. We felt no compulsion to do the same, and headed back to Achnasaul.

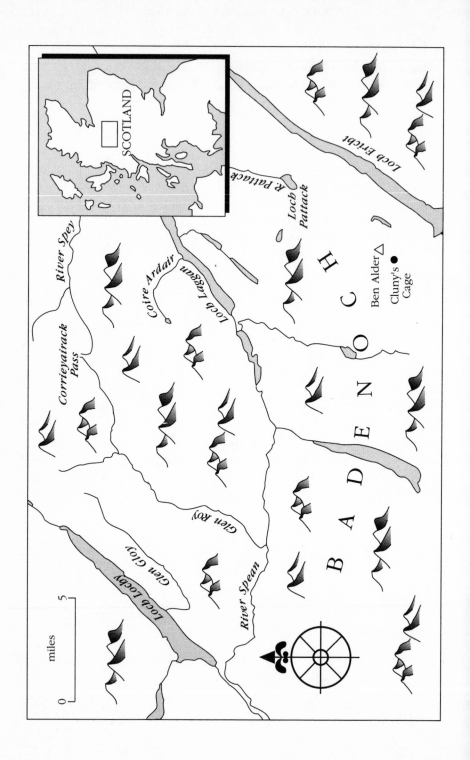

11

CLUNY'S CAGE

T HE march which Prince Charles Edward began on 28 August, to join Cameron of Lochiel in Badenoch, was one of the longest single stages of his journey. He was accompanied by Dr Archibald Cameron (Lochiel's brother), the Rev John Cameron, Macdonald of Lochgarry and Sandy MacPherson as well as three highland retainers. So impatient was the Prince to be off to meet Lochiel that he set out before keeping a planned rendezvous with Cluny MacPherson – into whose territory he was now going – at Achnacarry, and the luckless Cluny made the hazardous journey in vain, having to retrace his steps and meet the Prince later in Badenoch. They set out at night because, although Dr Cameron had reported that the Prince would now be safe in Badenoch, there was still a risk of being spotted on the march and the alarm again being sounded. Their destination lay due eastwards, but a straight line of march was impossible.

The little party first rounded the southern end of Loch Lochy and walked north-east up Glen Gloy, parallel with Loch Lochy, until they reached the river Tarff just short of Fort Augustus – where a Hanoverian garrison was still lodged. To have struck directly eastwards any earlier would have taken them over the high watershed between Glen Gloy and Glen Roy, but when they reached the Tarff they were able to follow the glen of that name south-eastwards until they came to the celebrated and bleak pass of Corrieyairack. They crossed over the pass (as indeed the Prince had done the previous year with his army on the way to his triumphs in

Perth and Edinburgh) but did not keep to the track, which would have led them on to the northern end of Loch Laggan, as they had done on the previous crossing; instead they turned south across a shoulder of Creag Meagaidh and came down Coire Ardair glen to the southern end of Loch Laggan. They rounded this in Glen Spean and set off across Ben Alder forest towards Loch Ericht. On such a long day's march, the Prince must have been relieved to have been met by Macdonell of Tullochrom who presented him with some fresh clothes and – even more vital – new shoes.

The following day – 29 August – the Prince reached the foothills of Ben Alder, and the day after that he was conducted to Mellanmuir (Meallan Odhar) where at 'a shieling of very narrow compass' he finally was reunited with his trusty friend and erstwhile lieutenant – Cameron of Lochiel.

Donald Cameron of Lochiel, whom the Prince had sought out for so long, was in every way one of the most engaging of his supporters. He has come down to history as 'Gentle' Lochiel, in part to distinguish him from his forebear – Sir Ewen Cameron, the 'Great Lochiel'. No one could have called Sir Ewen gentle: he was a fiercely loyal Jacobite who had held out for King Charles II longer than anyone else in the kingdom, and was renowned for having bitten out the throat of a Cromwellian officer with whom he was locked in close combat on the banks of Loch Arkaig. When not engaged in mortal combat, Sir Ewen was a passionate wolf hunter in the hills of his native Lochaber; local legend recalls that when he was caught out overnight on one occasion in a snow storm with his son, he kicked away a snowball on which the boy had planned to rest his head for the night, with a sharp remark about Camerons not needing pillows. A tartan plaid was all the comfort a Cameron of Lochiel needed for a winter's night on the hill.

'Gentle' his descendant Donald might be called in comparison, but his gentleness was far from softness. He shot a fellow clansman for stealing a sheep during the Forty Five campaign, and – as has already been recounted – he had been among the many chiefs to lead his clan into battle at Culloden, being shot through both ankles and carried off the field by his supporters, since when he had been recovering and 'skulking' simultaneously in Badenoch. His gentle-

ness had demonstrated itself by manly respect and compassion for
others: when the rebel army had been retreating past Glasgow earlier in 1746, he had personally intervened to prevent the sacking of
the city by the disgruntled highlanders – an act of clemency which is
recognised in perpetuity by the peeling of Glasgow's city bells when
any descendant of Gentle Lochiel pays an official visit to the city.

Prince Charles Edward had special reason to be grateful to
Lochiel. It will be recalled that it was his decision to bring out his
clan in support of the Prince – against his own original inclination to
await French military support before embarking on any general
rising – that had provided the general impetus for the standard
raising at Glenfinnan the previous August. He had been at the
Prince's side from that day onwards, until his wounds had prevented
him from accompanying the Prince and his Irish supporters in their
flight from the stricken field of Culloden. (Indeed, had Lochiel been
at the Prince's side in the days following the battle, things might
have been very different; at the least, there would have been less
criticism of the Prince for not going to Ruthven.) Now they were to
be reunited and not to be parted again. Lochiel would share the rest
of the Prince's hiding and hardships and go with him to France.

Even after his arrival in France in permanent exile, Lochiel
remained close to Prince Charles Edward, and the Prince for his part
– although not conspicuous for his consideration for his former supporters – remained staunch in his friendship for Lochiel. He invited
him to accompany him to his state entry into Versailles to call on
Louis XV. He also procured for him the colonelcy of the Regiment
d'Albanie in King Louis's service (although Lochiel said he would
prefer to return to the highlands of Scotland, to protect his own
people with French troops, than to command a lucrative regiment in
France) and he gave him generous presents.* But Lochiel did not
long survive the shattering of his ankles and – more tragically – of his
hopes. He died, grieving for his clansmen's fate, in France in 1748.
Sir Iain Moncreiffe of that Ilk has described him as 'perhaps the
finest highland chief there ever will have been'.

* One of his gifts is still extant: a magnificent silver globe engraved with a map
which opens to reveal a set of silver ink wells. It is illustrated in Sir Iain Moncreiffe's
The Highland Clans.

This was the man whom Prince Charles Edward met again on 30 August at Mellanmuir near Ben Alder. The circumstances of the meeting nearly went disastrously wrong: in fact, the royal party had as narrow an escape from being killed by their friends as any which they have from their enemies. Lochiel was hiding in 'a shieling of very narrow compass' when the Prince and his five companions approached. Donald Macpherson of Strathmashie, who was present, later recorded what happened:

'When Lochiel saw five men approaching under arms . . . taking the five to be of the army or militia who lay incampt not above five miles from them and probably in search of 'emselves, and as it was in vain to think of flying, tho' the number had been greater, Lochiel at the time being quite leam [lame] and not in any condition to travel, much less to fly, it was resolved, (which a message beforehand would have prevented) that the attackers, as they judged 'em to be, sho'd be received with a general discharge of all the firearms, in number twelve firelocks and some pistols, which they had in the small shiel house or bothie in which they at the time lodged. Whereupon all was made ready, pieces planted and levelled from within and they flattered 'emselves of geting the better of the searchers there being no more than their own number, and likewise considering the great advantage they had in firing at 'em without being at all observed and the conveniency of so many spare arms.'

But just as the Prince and his companions came into range, Lochiel recognised his own brother – Doctor Cameron* – as one of the party and realising what was afoot prevented the shooting. As MacPherson was quick to comment, 'the auspicious hand of Almighty God' had

* Doctor Cameron may have lived to wish he had died quickly by a bullet from his brother on that day. He continued to be caught up in Jacobite plots even after his escape to France, and was captured in Scotland again in 1753. The authorities did not want to reveal their knowledge of his current plots, so he was hung, drawn and quartered ostensibly for his part in the Forty Five. King George II was so irritated by Cameron's wife's pleas for clemency that he had her imprisoned, but he is thought to have relented towards Cameron himself to the extent of ordering that the more gruesome features of his execution were only to be carried out after he was already dead from hanging.

once again demonstrated that it was 'conspicuous in escorting His Royal Highness'. Lochiel, despite his lameness, rushed forward to greet his Prince and knelt at his feet. The Prince responded in a sensibly practical way to this touching display of loyalty, and said (again, according to MacPherson):

'Oh! no, my dear Lochiel . . . you don't know who may be looking from the tops of yonder hills, and if they see any such motions they'll immediately conclude that I am here, which may prove of bad consequence.'

The reunion was clearly the occasion for a celebration, and fortunately there was the wherewithal at hand to have what passed for a feast: 'plenty of mutton newly killed, and an anker of whiskie of twenty Scotch pints, with some good beef sassers . . . butter and cheese, and besides, a large well-cured ham'. All this good fare had been laid in previously for Lochiel's welfare. The Prince tucked in with a hearty appetite after his two days of hard walking and declared: 'Now, gentlemen, I leive like a Prince'. The Prince asked Lochiel if he always fared so well, and Lochiel confessed that Cluny had been looking after him royally.

Cluny himself reappeared on their third day at the shieling after his abortive attempt to rendezvous with the Prince at Achnacarry, and the Prince stopped him from kneeling too 'and kissed him, as if he had been an equal'. Prince Charles Edward was clearly impressed by Cluny's command of his surroundings and expressed his regret that Cluny and his regiment had not been with him at Culloden. 'I did not hear until very late that you were so near to come up with us that day', he said wistfully – obviously speculating in his mind that if he had had such competent reinforcements it might have influenced the issue of the battle in his favour.

The next day – 2 September – Cluny urged moving on to a shelter of greater security two miles further into the Ben Alder mountains, where they stayed in a bothie at Allt a Chaoil Reidhe which was 'superlatively bad and smockie'. But better lodging was to be available shortly. On 5 September they again removed, this time to the 'very romantic and comical' series of caves and caverns to be known as Cluny's Cage. This was probably the safest and one of the most comfortable (as well as being the last) of all the Prince's refuges during his five months' flight, and fortunately we have a very full description of it from Donald MacPherson:

'It was really a curiosity, and can scarcely be described to perfection. 'Twas situate in the face of a very rough high rockie mountain called Letternilickhk, which is still part of Benalder, full of great stones and crevices and some scattered wood interspersed. The habitation called the *Cage* in the face of that mountain was within a small thick bush of wood. There were some rows of trees laid down in order to level a floor for the habitation . . . There were betwixt the trees, growing naturally on their own roots, some stakes fixed in the earth, which with the trees were interwoven with ropes made of heath and birch twigs all to the top of the Cage, it being of a round or rather oval shape, and the whole thatched and covered over with foge [moss]. This whole fabrick hung as it were by a large tree, which reclined from the one end all along the roof to the other, and which gave it the name of the Cage; and by chance there happen'd to be two stones . . . in the side next the precipice resembling the pillars of a bosom chimney, and here was the fire placed. The smock had its vent out there, all along a very stonny plat of the rock, which and the smock were all together so much of a colour that any one could make no difference in the clearest day, the smock and the stones by and through which it pass'd being of such true and real resemblance. The Cage was no larger than to contain six or seven persons, four of which were frequently employed in playing at cards, one idle looking on, one becking, and another firing bread and cooking.'

Not only was the Cage secure and comfortable, but the company was good. Apart from Cluny MacPherson and Lochiel, there were Dr Cameron, Lochgarry, MacPherson of Breakachie (Cluny's brother), Allan Cameron and a number of MacPherson retainers to guard and look after them. They talked; they reminisced about what had gone wrong before and during Culloden; they regaled each other with tales of narrow escapes and daring escapades since the battle; they played cards and – of course, for by now the Prince was inordinately fond of a dram – they drank together. A week passed agreeably enough in this manner.

But while there was an air of leisure and relaxation of tension at the Cage, other activities were also going on. Cluny was taking elaborate precautions to ensure the Prince's continued safety. Although Donald MacPherson reckoned that the Prince had never been anywhere 'so private and secure', the fact was that Lord Loudon's camp of redcoats was only some six or seven miles away; this would have been a grave threat had it not been that Cluny 'kept good trustee spies of his friends in Loudon's camp so that no man could stir there without intelligence being brought to the Prince's quarters'. In fact, Cluny had decided that if an escape to the Continent were not to prove possible, he would extend the Cage and encourage the Prince to spend the winter there. With this longer stay in mind, Cluny was insistent that no-one but the Prince's immediate entourage should see him or know of his presence. Messengers were debriefed by Cluny or by one of his family and generally thought that he and Lochiel were the senior denizens of the Cage. The principle of 'need to know' was strictly observed.

But no-one wanted to over-winter at the Cage if it could be avoided. So, simultaneously with these precautions, it was arranged that Breakachie was to contact Colonel John Roy Stewart (an old campaigning comrade of the Prince's) and go with him to the east coast to try to charter a ship to take the Prince and his companions to France. Before Breakachie had time to accomplish this mission, the best possible news arrived at the Cage: French ships were waiting for them at Loch nan Uamh on the west coast.

That the French ships had managed to make contact with the Prince's supporters, and that they in turn had managed to get the news to the Prince – on the other side of Scotland in the remoteness of Cluny's Cage – was truly miraculous and (in Donald MacPherson's view) yet further proof that Prince Charles Edward was 'still the Almighty's particulare care'. The sequence of events had been fairly remarkable: two privateer vessels from St Malo – *L'Heureux* and *Le Prince de Conti* of thirty-four and thirty guns respectively – had sailed into Loch Boisdale in South Uist (that former haunt of the Prince) on 4 September, and had sent landing-parties ashore to seek news of the Prince's whereabouts. Among those with whom the landing-parties made contact was the Captain Macdonald of Clanranald's regiment who had previously crossed the Minch with the Prince; Macdonald now offered to pilot the privateers back to the mainland, which he did on 6 September. They made the passage under English colours and deceived the captain of a small Hanoverian ship which happened to be in Loch nan Uamh into thinking they were on his side; he was thus easily overwhelmed and held incommunicado. The English flags flying from their mast-heads and sterns also of course had the effect of deceiving the Jacobite supporters on the shore, who initially kept their distance. But eventually, when it became apparent to the commanders of the French ships that no other government forces were in the locality, they shed their disguise and let it be known that they were in fact French vessels seeking for the fugitive prince. Cameron of Clunes was the first responsible Jacobite contacted, and he quickly realised that this was a genuine chance for the Prince to make good his escape to France. He therefore in his turn contacted John MacPherson who set out to take the news to Cluny MacPherson at his Cage. By great good chance John MacPherson ran into Cluny himself 'on a very dark night' while the latter was away from the Cage on a mission for the Prince. Thus the news reached the Prince – at one o'clock in the morning on 13 September – with greater alacrity than anyone could have expected.

This nocturnal meeting between the two MacPhersons – John and Cluny – was only the last in a whole series of apparently coincidental encounters, frequently at night, that had occurred between the Prince's followers during the months of his flight. This is all the more remarkable as we know that the Prince's supporters avoided the main tracks and routes through the Highlands for obvious reasons of security: such tracks tended to go through inhabited glens where a sighting of the Prince could have been fatal. One is driven to the conclusion that each clan must have had a network of paths or trails of their own through the forests and glens of their own territory, and it was these which the Jacobite messengers habitually used. Thus a

Macdonald would meet a Macdonald or – as in this case – a Mac-
Pherson a MacPherson on their own private link-lines.

When the glad tidings of the French ships reached the Cage no
time was lost. So many rescue vessels already had come and gone
that the Prince was determined to grasp this last opportunity before
it too evaporated into the mists of the Irish sea. The middle of the
night was the time when the news arrived, but – as Donald Mac-
Pherson subsequently reported – 'on which minute his Royal Highness began his journey to the shipping'.

* * *

Prince Charles Edward had taken a week (28 August to 5 September) to travel from Clunes at the south west tip of Loch Lochy to
Ben Alder on Loch Ericht. This was largely because he had lingered
after his reunion with Lochiel until Cluny MacPherson could escort
him to the Cage. We had no intention of lingering and thought we
could do the same journey into Badenoch in three very long day's
walking, allowing ourselves to step aside from the route to sleep in
comfort on the way.

The precise route which Prince Charles Edward took from the
southern end of Loch Lochy to Badenoch has always been a subject
of some speculation: none of his companions described it in the
minute detail that was afforded to some of the other legs of the
journey. But – as we have seen – the best authorities indicate that he
followed Glen Gloy north-eastwards and parallel with Loch Lochy,
and then took the pass of Corrieyairack eastwards through the mountains. This would in any case have been sensible, since to have taken
a more direct route following Glen Spean would have taken him
through too many inhabited settlements, and to have taken a direct
easterly route not in the glen would have involved crossing numerous avoidable high ridges. His chosen route also had the advantage
that it was – at least in part – familiar ground: he had traversed the
Corrieyairack Pass the previous year with the nucleus of his army en
route for Perth and his further conquests. Now he had no army to
cheer him on, and no commissary to support him with rations and
supplies.

As we battled up Glen Gloy in the Prince's footsteps we made our first acquaintance with 'the Parallel Roads'. These are marked on the ordnance map as if they were 'an unfenced road, drive or track'. While planning our route we had envisaged that this would be good and easy walking – probably terrain for the Land Rover Discovery. But the parallel roads of Glen Gloy have nothing to do with real roads: they are the scars left behind on the landscape by the receding ice age. As the ice melted and froze again, so it left its mark – ribbons round the hillside – throughout Glen Gloy and Glen Roy. They are there today, traces of so many thousands of years ago that the brief passing of two and a half centuries since the Prince saw them signifies as nothing in their history.

The Prince passed on beyond the head of Glen Gloy to within two or three miles of Fort Augustus, where a garrison of English troops were stationed. We did the same, but pressed on into Fort Augustus to allow ourselves an unprecedented night's rest there. This little township still boasts the turreted stone fort built by General Wade in 1729 and named after William Augustus, the third son of George II and all too soon to enter the annals of Scottish history as Butcher Cumberland. For the rest, Fort Augustus is more distinguished by its situation than by its architecture. Once a strategic funnel through the Highlands, where a fortress could command military access to Glen Ness – 'the Great Glen' – its strategic value now is that it commands the route of the cars, caravans and charabancs that bring tourists to the highlands; mill shops have replaced crenellated towers, and the stranger is greeted not with a whiff of grape-shot but with a galaxy of tartan rugs and scarves, of woollen sweaters and clan souvenirs.

We went into one such mill shop, since Alasdair claimed that on our way through Fort Augustus en route for the west coast he had been too intrigued by the Caledonian canal to study the various tartans on offer there. Also in the shop was a soldier in the uniform of the Black Watch, possibly on his way to or from the regimental headquarters at Perth. Alasdair looked keenly at his kilt.

'That's one tartan you won't find here, Laddie. It's not any clan. It's "government tartan".'

Alasdair asked more about it, found books in Fort Augustus about the regiment (among them John Prebble's *Mutiny*), and finally ended up telling me a lot which I did not previously know about this regiment which had been founded – from the Militia companies raised by General Wade after the 1715 uprising – just four years before the Forty Five. It was always a very special regiment but one which had had to live down a chequered start before it began to accumulate its long roll of battle honours.

The rank and file of the Black Watch at the time of its establishment were soldiers of independent spirit who viewed themselves – unlike the common soldiery of England – as people of some social standing. It is recorded that when two of their number were invited to St James's Palace shortly after the formation of the regiment, so that George II might inspect their novel uniforms and watch their sword dancing, the King gave each of them a guinea at the conclusion of the ceremony. The soldiers thanked him politely, but as they left the palace tossed the coins to the porters. Highlanders did not accept tips.

A few years later, in 1743, the Black Watch was in trouble. Although originally they had been raised to garrison the Highlands, in that year they had been marched south into England, ostensibly to be reviewed by the King, but in reality to be sent overseas to fight in Flanders; however, rumour had it in the ranks that they were to be shipped to the dreaded West Indies where – according to the tales of old soldiers whom they encountered on the march south – they would be killed off like flies by the tropical fevers. All this they saw as a betrayal of the terms on which they had been recruited. Their morale was not helped by the fact that many of their own officers had been transferred elsewhere: the Earl of Crawford, for instance, had gone to the Life Guards. So in May 1743, while they were stationed at Finchley Common on the northern outskirts of London, about 120 of them decided to march home to Scotland; they determined to go peacefully and even resolved to pay for their food on the way. They set off at night, reaching St Albans by daybreak.

Inevitably this was seen as an act of mutiny. The Lords Regent (George II was in Hanover at the time, having failed to turn up to review the Black Watch after all) despatched orders and dragoons in all directions throughout the midlands: the mutineers must be found and either induced to surrender unconditionally, or attacked and slaughtered without compunction. Although the deserters (they did not see themselves as mutineers) kept away from roads and villages as far as possible and moved only at night, within three days they had been spotted – near Oundle in Northamptonshire. They had sought shelter in a thick wood running along a high ridge; it was a good position for a final stand. At one stage it looked as if it would indeed come to that: a squadron of dragoons surrounding them contemplated a charge and a massacre to end the whole affair. But in the end the dragoons decided it might be wiser to call up reinforcements and sit it out; and eventually the weary men of the Black Watch preferred to surrender and throw themselves on the mercy of the Crown. In small groups they slunk out of the woods and laid down their broadswords and muskets.

They were marched as captives back over the route they had taken, finishing their journey in the Tower of London. The inevitable court martial followed. George II indicated that his mercy could be extended to the majority of the mutineers but that 'an example of severity should be made on some of the most guilty'. In the end three mutineers were shot; the rest being transported to join other units in the Mediterranean, in Georgia and – in fulfilment of their worst fears – in the West Indies. It was a sad beginning to the glorious record of a great fighting regiment. (Their first battle honour was won in May 1745 – a few weeks before Prince Charles Edward's landing in Scotland – with their famous charge at the Battle of Fontenoy.) But it was hardly surprising that, when the Forty Five rebellion erupted so soon after the unhappy events at Finchley Common, the Black Watch was kept safely south of the Border, in fact as far south as they could be – in Kent.

I had tried, over our walks through the Highlands in the past weeks, to imbue Alasdair with a sense of Scottish history: I had ended by learning from him.

Two or three miles south of Fort Augustus lies the entrance to the Corrieyairack Pass, above Ardachy Lodge and with a good view over Loch Ness. Leaving civilisation and the twentieth century behind us, the next morning we began the long climb up to one of the most famous passes in all Scotland. Originally this – like so many highland tracks – had been a drove road for bringing the cattle down from Skye and the north-west to the markets of the lowlands. Its first military use was during the Covenanting Wars of the seventeenth century. Montrose has passed this way by forced marches in mid-winter before surprising the Campbells at the battle of Inverlochy. Then in the 1720s (a couple of decades before Prince Charles Edward had passed this way) a 'serious' road had been constructed. Its creator was of course the celebrated General Wade, builder of Fort Augustus, who had been sent to the Highlands by George I to ensure that there should be no repetition of the 1715 uprising. Wade realised that communications were the key to subjugating the Highlands; he constructed a network of trunk roads, the lines of many of which have been followed by his successors as road-builders (the A9 between Blair Atholl and Kingussie being a case in point). Wade's main objective was to link the garrisons in such far-flung outposts of the Hanoverian domains as Fort George, Fort Augustus and Fort William.

The Corrieyairack road was an important link in the chain. Its construction involved the use of 500 soldiers and cost £70 a mile; at 15 ft wide it must have appeared a positive motorway to the fugitive prince, who ironically had made the first military use of the new road (as distinct from Montrose's use of the old road) when he had led his rebel army this way the previous year. When we came to clamber up its rugged slopes it was more like five feet wide than fifteen; the loose rocks were so tough on our boots that we generally preferred to walk on the grass or heather verging the track than on the track itself; but at least it was a clear and unambiguous path. (If you do lose your way, local tradition has it that a ghostly highlander accompanied by two giant Baskerville-like hounds materialises out of the mist to direct you to safety.) For more than a hundred years after its construction, the Corrieyairack road could be passed by travellers in their horse-drawn carriages; by the end of the last century the carriages had given way to ponies, and by now the ponies have given way to an occasional courageous Land Rover (we passed one such on the day of our crossing) and a good many stoutly-shod walkers (we passed two during our seven hour crossing).

There is still plenty of evidence of General Wade's legendary

bridges. These span the various burns along the way; some are now
sadly tumbled down, but still providing enough masonry to give
evidence of their original elegance. The best preserved is the 150-ft-
long double-arched St George's bridge at Garvamore over the river
Spey at the extreme western end of the pass. (We saw and photo-
graphed this but it was not strictly on the Prince's route during his
second crossing of the pass.) General Wade did more than anyone to
achieve English domination of the Scottish highlands, and yet one
never hears a word against him: humane, imaginative and indus-
trious, he left behind him a legacy of sensible and useful roads, and
decorative and robust bridges. These are his permanent memorial,
but he deserved to be remembered too for other more strictly
military exploits. As a young officer he fought under Marlborough in
the Low Countries and with distinction in Spain in the War of the
Spanish Succession; after his highland command he was appointed a
Field Marshal and for a while during the Forty Five was commander-in-chief in England. By then he was an old man, but nonetheless it was perhaps fortunate for Prince Charles Edward that he
never had to confront Wade while south of the Border, as the old
warrior – even at 72 – might well have mauled Lord George Murray
and the youthful Prince.

Approaching the pass from the north – as we were – we climbed
slowly. Sometimes one was tempted to cut a corner, to take to the
heather and link two loops of the road. It was usually a mistake
which ended in scrambles and falls over peat hags: General Wade
had a surer eye for country than we had – his line was the optimum
line of advance. The summit of the pass at just over 2,500 feet was
windy and chilly, but in autumn it was hard to imagine it as quite so
severe as described by one winter traveller (Thomas Pennant) who in
1769 reported that 'people often perish on the summit of this hill'.
Having managed not to perish, we then began a much steeper
descent.

The eastern side of the Corrieyairack pass is a series of wide z-
bends – we counted seventeen – snaking down the mountainside.
The steep incline and rocky boulders make it a natural position for
defence: though no Khyber Pass, it could nonetheless be held by a
small body of determined men against a much larger force. After

Prince Charles Edward's passage of the Corrieyairack the previous year with his army, General Cope – his opponent – had to face a court of enquiry not only to account for his ignominious loss of the Battle of Prestonpans but also for his failure to defend the Corrieyairack Pass and prevent the Prince's advance on Perth. Cope answered the charges by explaining that his information had suggested that the Prince had reached the summit of the Corrieyairack before he could have done so; it would therefore have been Cope's redcoats who would have been on the attack and the Prince's highlanders who could have held the pass. Cope told the court:

'It was utterly impracticable to force a passage to Fort Augustus over the Corrieyairack whilst the rebels lay there to oppose us. To attack them on this strong ground . . . was to expose the troops to certain destruction'.

His explanation was accepted by the court, and also – having seen the ground – by us.

As we rounded one bend in the series of zig-zags that constituted the descent we were confronted with a scene that could have happened with equal probability to Prince Charles Edward. The road was blocked. Blocked by the travellers who most frequently used it: sheep. They progressed steadily, propelled forward by the shepherd who brought up the rear, and prevented from spilling out to right and left by two border Collies who snapped at the heels of any deviators from the path. We stood aside, recognising not only that sheep, like football supporters on their way to a stadium, have right of way by *force majeure*, but that they also had a historic right of way: they had been using this route for several centuries longer than recreational walkers.

Soon we had to leave General Wade's reassuringly clear road. The Prince had been nervous about staying on the established track as far as the Garvamore bridge; he had feared sentries, pickets or informers. So he and his tiny party had turned off the track southwards soon after the summit of the pass and, striking for seven miles through the hills, has passed between the White Falls on the Allt Chonnal and the ghostly Loch Spey – modest source of the mighty salmon river. Eventually he and we had emerged on the Allt Coire Ardair, a stream running steeply down from a mountain rescue point surrounded by cliffs to Aberarder on the north shore of Loch Laggan. The stream was flanked by a track, less unequivocal than General Wade's road but nonetheless clear to view. We were mightily relieved to see Loch Laggan.*

On the loch side there is a major road (the A86) and it was possible for us to rest for a night at a nearby B&B more comfortably than the Prince would have done in the heather. The following day, crossing the Spean at the west end of Loch Laggan presented no problem, and probably little in the eighteenth century: this is and was a natural site for a bridge. Once on the south side of the Spean however, the gradient soon increases again. The Prince had to cross Ardverikie forest before he came to Cluny MacPherson's clan heartland of Ben Alder forest.

A good track goes from the bridge near Moy Lodge along the south side of two small lochans that lie parallel with Loch Laggan, but then it is necessary to take a rougher track directly through Ardverikie forest, first climbing and then descending towards the River Pattack. There are two such tracks today each running up a burn, and we can be fairly sure that the Prince took the more northerly of them as that emerges on the Pattack close to the point where he met Cameron of Lochiel. We did the same.

The River Pattack ran across our front, trilling its way through clumps of alder trees and narrow gorges, past inviting rock pools and over sudden waterfalls, and looking for all the world like Burns's description of 'Ye banks and braes o' bonnie Doon'. As we came steeply down towards the Pattack we could see to the south of us the ruins of a stone bothie on the far side of the river and just north of Loch Pattack; it lay at the foot of the round hill of Meallan Odhar – the only trace of masonry in that area.

This, beyond reasonable doubt, must surely be the remains of that 'shieling of very narrow compass' where Lochiel was hiding and so nearly fatally ambushed the Prince's party. The setting was over-

* This section of the Prince's route is less well documented than the rest. There was a strong verbal tradition in the last century that he used the track described, but none of his companions confirmed this to Bishop Forbes.

looked by 'the tops of yonder hills' where the Prince thought that prying eyes might see if Lochiel knelt to him. The foundations of the old walls showed just how narrow the building had indeed been.

Lochiel and the Prince had feasted there on mutton and an anker of whisky with beef sausages, cheese and ham. We found it satisfactory – after the long morning's walk – to be able to do almost exactly the same. Our sandwiches, prepared by our hostess of the night before, had been made up from the same wholesome and sustaining ingredients as Lochiel's, and my flask of malt whisky seemed as appropriate a way of washing them down as had the anker of the same spirit two hundred and fifty odd years before. What made it even more satisfactory was that, on checking the date on my watch, I found it was the 30th of August – the very anniversary of the famous reunion.

We had no intention of prolonging the happy coincidence by staying in the ruins of the shieling for two days as the Prince had done. We knew that his next move had been to another scarcely more prepossessing bothie two miles 'further into Ben Alder' at Allt a Chaoil-Reidhe – the bothie described as 'superlatively bad and smockie'.

We could see the stream of this name flowing into Loch Pattack on the far side of the loch from where we sat and picnicked. A good track ran round the east and south sides of the loch for a mile, and then forked due south for another mile below the sharp rock screes of Coire Scon an Nid to join the stream at exactly the point where the only other building within a five mile radius was to be seen. A deserted lodge and bothie on the banks of the Allt a Chaoil-Reidhe seemed likely to be the spot where Cluny's bothie had been, at the junction of track and burn.

But although the Prince may have been further into Ben Alder here, there was still a risk of being overlooked by neighbouring summits. Indeed when we crossed the burn our attention was caught by a group of hinds moving across the ridge of the hills opposite: perhaps they had seen us and we had unsettled them. (No stalking was taking place that day and we had checked that there was no objection to our taking our proposed route.) Visibility was far too good for those seeking security in this part of the forest: safety – as the deer had illustrated – lay further into the mountains.

And it was further up Ben Alder itself that Cluny was to lead the Prince next, right into the very fastness of that labyrinth of 3,500 ft crags that lie around a sinister enclosed loch in the heart of the range. We turned our steps up a steep sheep-path that wound upwards in a series of twists; as so often, every crest looked like the final one until it was breasted and turned out to reveal another higher ridge above it. Big rocks and deep heather gave more cover from view here: we could see the whole valley below us, but were confident that – unless we imprudently silhouetted ourselves against a skyline – watchers from lesser hills would not have spotted us.

When we reached the hidden loch we started to look for the Prince's ultimate destination – Cluny's Cage. I had the description (given earlier in this chapter) firmly in my mind, and I lay in the long heather scanning the cliff faces opposite with my binoculars to see if any configuration of the ground seemed to match Donald MacPherson's account. Personally I was convinced for two reasons that it was here, in the heart of Ben Alder, that the Cage had been: first, it was only here among the high crags that the rock was the grey-blue colour of wood smoke and would have provided camouflage for their cooking fires which MacPherson describes; secondly, it was only here in the interior of the range that there were escape routes in a number of different directions if an enemy were seen approaching from one quarter.

We pressed on over the summit and down the far southern side of Ben Alder. Here, shortly before reaching the waters of the 15-mile-long Loch Ericht at Alder Bay, we stumbled on a cave marked on the ordnance survey map, like a number of others, as 'Prince Charlie's Cave'. Maybe this was the site of the famous Cage, but it seemed to me to be much less likely than some of the sites higher up. Here were fewer grey rock faces to conceal the rising smoke of the cooking fires; and here they could have been surprised much more easily with less chance of escape in different directions.

As we stumbled down the face of Ben Alder the clouds descended. Suddenly visibility was reduced to a few yards. We could hear a stag roaring above us and a waterfall somewhere below us. We felt very much alone in the heart of the highlands: if we tripped and fell, it might be long enough before someone found us here. The gentle, cheerful waters of the Pattack on the other side of the mountains felt very far away in space as well as in time.

We had come to the end of the road, the furthest point. From here we should be retracing our steps. We had walked a long way, over hill and moor, forest and marsh; we had sailed through some choppy waters; we had seen many familiar sights and a few – like the hidden tunnel at Corodale – that were quite unknown. We had not only got to know the story of Prince Charles Edward in intimate detail, but we had also got to know the Highlands and Islands as they are today with greater familiarity than would have been possible had we travelled in any other way. Alasdair and I had both learnt much about Scottish history and fable; and most important of all we had perhaps got to know each other a little better. We at least were grateful to the Prince.

12

FINALE

THE march back westwards across Scotland, to board the French ships which had finally materialised, was an altogether more light-hearted affair than the painfully slow and perilous march eastwards had been. It started with a practical joke of a rather robust variety.

Prince Charles Edward spent the first day of his return journey (they were still travelling for safety at night) in the smokey bothie at Uiskchilra where he had stayed before. On hearing that Colonel John Roy Stewart – a staunch supporter to whom the Prince had inexplicably given the nickname of The Body – was about to join them and had no idea that he was there, the Prince wrapped himself in a tartan plaid and popped out at Stewart so suddenly that the startled officer exclaimed 'Oh Lord, my master' and promptly dropped down fainting in a pool of water at the entrance to the bothie. This was considered excellent sport by one and all.

Stewart was accompanied by Macpherson of Breakachie who had managed to retrieve three of the Prince's personal pistols – valuable weapons mounted in gold and silver. The Prince was delighted and commented that it was truly remarkable that his enemies had not been able to lay their hands on his money, his clothing or his personal arms. The following day, when they were tired of resting and lying up at Moy after their night's march, the retrieved pistols were used for a boisterous shooting practice – bonnets being tossed up into the air as targets – amid general high spirits. The Prince, as always in shooting competitions, scored best.

On the evening of 14 September they set out again, marching most of the night round the southern end of Loch Laggan until they came to the edge of Glen Roy, where they again snatched some hours sleep and then, when daylight came, 'kept themselves private all day'.

The following night they aimed for Lochiel's seat – Achnacarry – but first had to cross the river Lochy with the aid of a full moon. This tricky operation was turned into a hilarious adventure in keeping with their current mood. Cameron of Clunes announced when they reached the river bank that he had managed to salvage a leaky old boat of Lochiel's which had been overlooked by the redcoats when they were burning the rest of Lochiel's boats; but Lochiel himself declared the vessel was quite unsound and unsafe. Clunes offered to make the first crossing, and then remembered that he had six bottles of brandy and that the whole party 'will be the better for a dram'. The Prince, who probably needed little persuading by this stage to have his share, was particularly pleased to hear that the brandy had been filched from the Hanoverian garrison at Fort Augustus. We are told that it was not long before three of the six bottles had been emptied. They then crossed the river in relays: Clunes leading the first boat-load, the Prince the second, and Lochiel bringing up the rear. By the final crossing the old tub was leaking like a sieve and, with so much water sloshing about in the bottom, the three remaining brandy bottles got broken. Nothing deterred, the boat-men lapped up the mixture of loch water and alcohol, declaring it 'as being good punch' and getting so merry that for the rest of the night 'they made great diversion to the company as they marched along'. The escape was fast becoming a party.

The dawn brought a certain sobering up, not least because Achnacarry when they arrived there presented a gloomy and inhospitable aspect having – as they already knew – been burnt to the ground by government troops on 28 May. Nonetheless they camped there during the day on 16 September, setting out in the evening for Glen Camgharaidh at the western end of Loch Arkaig. Here the Prince met Cluny MacPherson and Dr Cameron again and had an excellent feast of roast beef and bannocks.

This sustaining meal was only possible because of the foresight of

Cluny and others. They had realised some time before that there would be lot of coming and going across Scotland to keep the Prince posted with news, and they had therefore established caches of food at key points with trusty supporters. It was these provisions that were now being drawn upon: everyone was convinced that all the months of flight and eking out rations were soon to be at an end.

Indeed the end was come only two days later when they completed the last lap of the journey and 'arrived at the shipping'. They reached Borrodale to find the two French privateers – *L'Heureux* and the smaller *Prince de Conti* – anchored in Loch nan Uamh, the very place from which the Prince had set off for the Hebrides nearly five months before in the opening stages of his long flight, and very close to where he had originally landed on the mainland of Scotland.

They lost little time in going aboard *L'Heureux* (although some accounts relate that the Prince originally boarded the *Prince de Conti* and then transferred to the larger vessel). The Prince took with him – among others – Lochiel, Dr Cameron his brother, Lochgarry, Colonel 'the Body' Stewart and a total party amounting to 23 gentlemen and 107 'men of common rank'. Cluny MacPherson and MacPherson of Breakachie declined to embark, preferring to return to Cluny's cage and remain in Scotland.

L'Heureux was well manned and equipped with a crew of 300 and 34 guns. A favourable wind encouraged the two vessels to weigh anchor without delay, and they quickly made the open sea. It was little after midnight on 19/20 September 1746 and the Forty Five was over.

And much was over apart from the Forty Five. The clan system in Scotland was never to be the same again: the power of the chiefs was curtailed; the wearing of the tartan proscribed; the carrying of weapons prohibited. A sad and lengthy period of repression set in. The prison ships bore their cargo of Jacobite captives from Scotland to London where many succumbed to the inhuman conditions of their confinement. Large numbers were deported to the colonies as indentured labourers for life. Some of the captured chiefs were executed: the Lords Kilmarnock and Balmerino were beheaded on

Tower Hill on 18 August 1746; Lord Derwentwater met a similar fate in December, and finally the wily old Lord Lovat became the last man in England to face public beheading – doing so with that mixture of courage and effrontery which had characterized so much of his life. The officers of the Manchester Regiment, who had defected to the Jacobite cause, were less considerately treated: they were hung, drawn and quartered. There were many who must have rued the day when Prince Charles Edward set up his standard in the Highlands.

Also over was the Prince's own hour of glory. Although he was initially lionized in Paris society and received in state by Louis XV at Versailles, it was not long before that monarch found the embarrassment of harbouring this conspicuous Jacobite prince in Paris was too much for him. Prince Charles Edward was arrested on his way to the Opera and unceremoniously bundled out of France. Years of roaming Europe were to follow. Often under a false name and sometimes in disguise, the Prince wandered round the courts and cities of Italy and elsewhere. Sometimes philandering, never happily married and without a legitimate heir, always sensitive to his royal status, his most consistent activity was the hard drinking he had first taken up during his months of flight in the heather. He quarrelled with most of his old Scottish supporters and even with his family, being particularly incensed by the decision of his brother – Prince Henry – to accept a Cardinal's hat from the Pope, thus further identifying the Stuart cause with the Roman Church. Frequently pressed for money, he became mean and unreliable about remembering his debts: the debonair and open-handed Prince who shared his food and his purse was no longer recognisable in the sharp-faced, elderly alcoholic. By the time of his death, forty years after his departure from Loch nan Uamh, he was a threat to no-one but himself.

But desolated as was the Scotland he left behind him, and desultory as was the life that lay ahead of him, as Prince Charles Edward left Scotland that September night he could comfort himself with the reflection that 'some work of noble note' had been achieved. In his campaign through the Highlands and into England, the Prince had proved to be an indifferent strategist and a petulant commander; on the final battlefield of Culloden he had proved a defective tactician.

But in the five months flight that followed that defeat, he had for the first and last time in his life lived up to the ideals and aspirations of his romantic followers. When he had no option but to put his trust in others, he had done so fearlessly. When he had little to give, he had shared what he had. When those around him had been afraid of the perils of the sea, he had been calm. When all his companions were fearful for his safety, he alone was unconcerned and jocular. Those five months were to place him for all time in the national pantheon of Scottish heroes – as daring as Sir William Wallace, as patriotic as Robert the Bruce, and as tragic as Mary Queen of Scots. He may have left behind him little more than a name 'to point a moral or adorn a tale', but while posterity has proved uninterested in the moral it has been hypnotised by the tale for two and a half centuries.

SELECT BIBLIOGRAPHY

BINGHAM, CAROLINE *Beyond the Highland Line* (London 1991)

BLAIKIE, W.B. *Itinerary of Prince Charles Edward Stuart from landing in Scotland July 1745 to his departure in September 1746* (Edinburgh 1897)

DAICHES, DAVID *Charles Edward Stuart: The Life and Times of Bonnie Prince Charlie* (London 1973)

DARLING, F. FRASER and BOYD, J. MORTON *The Highlands and Islands* (London 1964)

EAMES, ANDREW *Four Scottish Journeys* (London 1991)

ENNEW, JUDITH *The Western Isles Today* (Cambridge 1980)

FORBES, BISHOP ROBERT *The Lyon in Mourning* (3 Vols.) (Edinburgh 1895)

GRANT, NEIL *Scottish Clans and Tartans* (London 1987)

KYBETT, SUSAN MACLEAN *Bonnie Prince Charlie* (London 1988)

LANG, ANDREW *Prince Charles Edward Stuart: The Young Chevalier* (London 1900)

LINKLATER, ERIC *The Prince in the Heather* (London 1965)

MACLEAN, ALASDAIR *A MacDonald for the Prince* (Stornoway 1982)

MACLEAN, SIR FITZROY *Bonnie Prince Charlie* (London 1988)

MCLYNN, FRANK *The Jacobites* (London 1985)

MONCREIFFE OF THAT ILK, SIR IAIN *The Highland Clans* (London 1967)

MORTON, H.V. *In Search of Scotland* (London 1929)

— *In Scotland Again* (London 1933)

POLNAY, PETER DE *Death of a Legend: The True Story of Bonnie Prince Charlie* (London 1952)

PREBBLE, JOHN *Culloden* (London 1966) *The Highland Clearances* (London 1963)

— *Mutiny: Highland Regiments in Revolt 1743–1804* (London 1975)

TAYLER, ALISTAIR and HENRIETTA *1745 and After* (London 1938)

TAYLER, HENRIETTA (editor) *The History of the Rebellion in the years 1745 and 1746: From a manuscript now in the possession of Lord James Stewart-Murray* (Oxford 1944)

YOUNGSON, A.J. *The Prince and the Pretender: A Study in the Writing of History* (London 1985)

INDEX

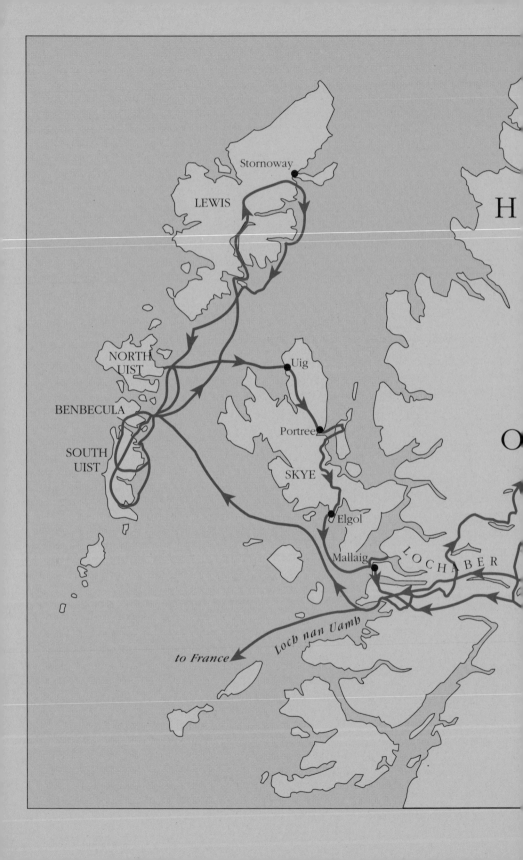

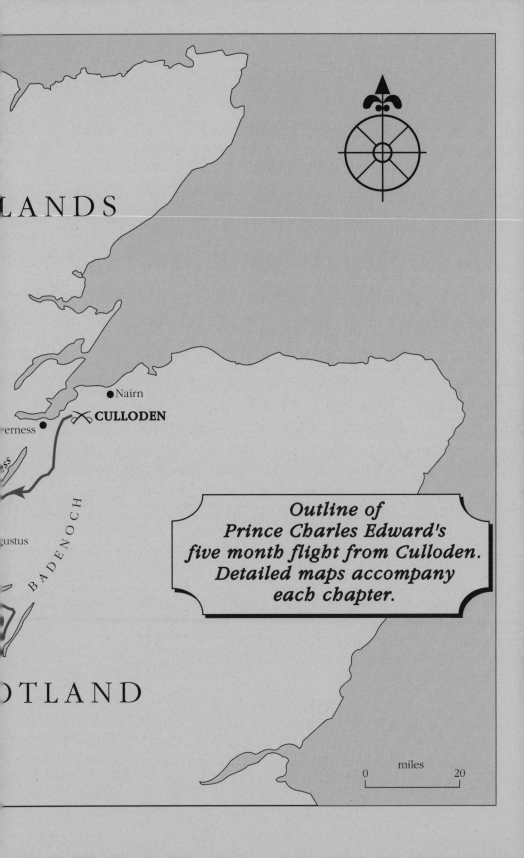

LANDS

●Nairn

✕ **CULLODEN**

●erness

ss

ustus

BADENOCH

OTLAND

Outline of
Prince Charles Edward's
five month flight from Culloden.
Detailed maps accompany
each chapter.

miles

0   20